What Was Neoliberalism?

WHAT WAS NEOLIBERALISM?

Studies in
the Most Recent Phase
of Capitalism:
1973–2008

NEIL DAVIDSON

Haymarket Books
Chicago, IL

Published in 2023 by
Haymarket Books
P.O. Box 180165
Chicago, IL 60618
773-583-7884
www.haymarketbooks.org
info@haymarketbooks.org

ISBN: 978-1-64259-915-2

Distributed to the trade in the US through Consortium Book Sales and Distribution (www.cbsd.com) and internationally through Ingram Publisher Services International (www.ingramcontent.com).

This book was published with the generous support of Lannan Foundation, Wallace Action Fund, and Marguerite Casey Foundation.

Special discounts are available for bulk purchases by organizations and institutions. Please email info@haymarketbooks.org for more information.

Cover design by Eric Kerl.

Library of Congress Cataloging-in-Publication data is available.

10 9 8 7 6 5 4 3 2 1

Contents

Preface

When the Scottish Marxist writer and activist Neil Davidson died at the tragically young age of sixty-two, he was working on a large number of manuscripts. Among them, this book on contemporary capitalism and ways of conceptualizing it was more or less complete. Some of Neil's friends and comrades are working to make available other books and edited collections that he was in the process of finalizing.

Undoubtedly, Neil would have made changes to the current manuscript if he had been able to do so, updating the examples—when he was forced to cease work on the book, Trump was still in office—and he would most likely have polished passages and nuanced some of his arguments; the reader may also notice occasional repetition across chapters, which Neil would doubtless have refined. Nevertheless, the book was sufficiently finished to justify publication. While predominately restricted to British examples, Neil's ambition was to illuminate the wider neoliberal era. *What Was Neoliberalism?* is a significant contribution to that debate; it is also a reminder of the intellectual power of a thinker who possessed immense historical and theoretical range and who retained an enduring passion for socialism.

Editing has been kept to a minimum to retain Neil's unique voice. In a few places, linking sentences have been added. A little more work was required to make the introduction publishable, but we resisted any urge to ventriloquize and have kept editorial interventions to those that are essential for clarity and coherence.

With the destabilizing of the market economy we begin to recognize the monuments of the bourgeoisie as ruins even before they have crumbled.

—**Walter Benjamin,**
"Paris, Capital of the Nineteenth Century"

It is asserted that economic activity belongs to civil society, and that the state must not intervene to regulate it. But . . . it must be made clear that *laissez-faire* too is a form of State "regulation," introduced and maintained by legislative and coercive means. It is a deliberate policy, conscious of its own ends, and not the spontaneous, automatic expression of economic facts.

—**Antonio Gramsci,** "The Modern Prince"

The End of Neoliberalism?

According to Hegel's most famous aphorism, "The owl of Minerva spreads its wings only with the coming of the dusk," by which he meant that we can only truly understand a historical period once it is over.[1] "A structural phase can be concretely studied and analyzed only after it has gone through its whole process of development, and not during the process itself, except hypothetically and with the explicit proviso that one is dealing with hypotheses."[2] The end of neoliberalism has been proclaimed several times before, often by the same people on different occasions. The late Eric Hobsbawm, for example, regularly produced obituaries throughout the eighties and nineties, lastly in his autobiography (2002), where he conceded that he had previously been wrong, before going on to make the same assessment again in response to the collapse of the dotcom boom.[3] Hobsbawm refrained from making a similar pronouncement in 2008, even though it would have had greater plausibility than its predecessors, but others were less cautious. "It is the end of the neoliberal era," wrote Scottish political journalist Iain Macwhirter in September, as the extent of the economic catastrophe became apparent. And within a month of Macwhirter proclaiming "the twilight of Thatcherism," his verdict appeared to be confirmed.[4] For states throughout the developed world—including those like Britain and the USA, which had been most committed to neoliberalism—bought massive and in some cases dominant stakes in failing banks, using levels of public spending we had previously been told were no longer available or which could not be used without distorting the market. One could therefore easily understand why the politicians, professors, and pundits who

1

assured us that the business cycle had been abolished, or that house prices would continue to rise indefinitely, or that nationalization was politically impossible might have invoked the Owl of Minerva Defense to explain their ignorance, stupidity, or deceit.

"And after dusk," David Blacker reminds us, "comes darkness."[5] Had neoliberalism genuinely been at an end, Thatcher's personal demise on April 8, 2013, might then have merely confirmed the sense of an ending. The rituals surrounding her funeral, although an obscene insult to her many victims, would have simply represented theatrical compensation for her admirers, who were otherwise left contemplating a world in which she is reduced to "a historic footnote in culture that had abolished history."[6] Unfortunately, as obituaries and commemorative pull-outs across the political spectrum, from the right-wing *The Daily Telegraph* to hard-left *Socialist Worker* attested, we still live in the world which she helped create. Insofar as responsibility has been allocated for the present debacle, it has been to the excesses of financial institutions like the Royal Bank of Scotland, or to the ineptitude of governments like those of Ireland, or even to the inadequacies of politicians like Gordon Brown—anything, it seems, other than the current organization of the capitalist system, still less the system itself. "What we are experiencing is not a crisis of capitalism," proclaimed an article in *Newsweek*. "It is a crisis of finance, of democracy, of globalization and ultimately of ethics."[7] Indeed, even the more astute supporters of the orthodoxy could declare that the entire debacle simply resulted from a collective failure to correctly understand the tenets of neoliberalism. For US economist Barry Eichengreen, "the problem lay not so much with the poverty of the underlying theory as with selective reading of it . . . shaped by the social milieu [that] encouraged financial decision makers to cherry-pick the theories that supported excessive risk taking."[8] The shameless recourse to state support by imperiled banks has not then been treated as an admission of error, nor does it even signify a particularly new development. Although neoliberalism began to replace Keynesianism, Stalinism, and other forms of state capitalism as the dominant form of capitalist organization from the mid-1970s, it continued to involve a highly interventionist role for the state, quite contrary to its official ideology; the state subventions which were rapidly forthcoming after the collapse of Lehman Brothers were merely a highly attenuated continuation of this relationship. Indeed, some commentators have quite plausibly described neoliberalism as a form of "privatised Keynesianism."[9]

We should be skeptical, then, when confronted with claims that "neoliberalism has self-destructed."[10] The current crisis has not led to a new period of "postneoliberalism."[11] Nor is it a crisis *of* neoliberalism, as is claimed by Duménil and Lévy.[12] In Alfredo Saad-Filho's terms, we are instead experiencing a crisis *in* neoliberalism, which, in the absence of successful resistance by the exploited and oppressed, will lead not to its extinction but to its further evolution.[13] Consequently, "the moment of truth never happened," as Richard Dienst writes. "There has been no transformative revelation, no collective coming-to-our-senses, no realignment with reality, no *Vergangenheitsbewalitgung* for the boomer generation." At best, there has been "an adjustment in rhetoric. . . . There might even be a new compromise within established opinion: the free market fundamentalists no longer need to claim infallibility in order to get what they want, while the idealists and sceptics can finally give up on the idea that there is any alternative to the present system."[14] The reasons for what Colin Crouch calls "the strange non-death of neoliberalism" are not hard to find. As he observes:

> It is necessary to start from acceptance that political and economic elites will do everything they can to maintain neoliberalism in general and the finance-driven form of it in particular. They have benefited so much from the inequalities of wealth and power that the system has produced, compared with the experience of strongly redistributive taxation, strong trade unions and government regulation that constituted the so-called social democratic period.[15]

There is, however, one fundamental difference between neoliberalism pre- and post-2008. The key figures in the former period were always more pragmatic and opportunistic than either their supporters or their opponents claimed. Nevertheless, they all shared a small but clear set of key objectives and strategies. Their successors in the current period no longer do so. Instead, they display an increasingly well-founded sense of panic and consequent incoherence. As Hobsbawm puts it: "None of the world's governments, central banks or international institutions know [how to overcome the present crisis]: they are all like a blind man trying to get out of a

maze by tapping the walls with different kinds of sticks in the hope of find-
ing the way out."[16] Yet in the midst of this chaos and uncertainty, the ruling
classes of the world have found one measure of agreement: that the cost of
the current crisis will be borne by the people over whom they rule, rather
than by themselves. Members of this class were unwilling to perform the
basic duty of citizenship by paying tax even when their fortunes were in the
ascendant. Journalist Robert Peston noted in a British context:

> Most of the super-wealthy would not have been able to accumulate
> or sustain their wealth without the stable infrastructure provided
> by the UK—and by "stable infrastructure" I mean an educated
> workforce, a National Health Service that sustains that workforce,
> roads, rail, police, a justice system safeguarding property rights, a
> fire service. None of that is provided by the tooth-fairy, though the
> super-wealthy often act as though they think it is.[17]

Peston clearly thought that the "super-wealthy" were even less likely to
volunteer themselves as a source of fiscal support to the state in conditions of
crisis, as has indeed turned out to be the case. It should come as no surprise,
then, to find out who will be required to pay instead. "Government spending
will have to be cut down to size," wrote another financial journalist, Martin
Wolf, in the *Financial Times* early in the crisis. "It is clear what this must mean":

> A sustained freeze on the pay bill; decentralized pay bargaining;
> employee contributions to public pensions; and a pruning of bene-
> fits. It is obvious, too, that this will mean massive and painful con-
> flict between governments and public workers. . . . The next prime
> minister is likely to end up quite as hated as Margaret Thatcher was.
> But, as she liked to say, there is no alternative. The unsustainable
> cannot endure. If UK policymakers do not take the needed deci-
> sions willingly, markets will force them upon them.[18]

Wolf may have subsequently balked at the attempt by the British coalition government to implement his program; but on the basis of his past
pronouncements, one suspects that this is a matter of timing and emphasis
rather than of fundamental disagreement.

We have, therefore, in many respects returned to our starting point in
the mid-1970s. After forty years of neoliberalism, the very same solutions

are still being offered to the same problems, with the same intended victims. But this is not an occasion in which "the great events and characters of world history" are repeated, "the first time as tragedy, the second as farce"; for if the ruling classes do achieve their goals, the repetition is unlikely to be cast in a comedic mode of emplotment. it will simply extend and deepen the original tragedy, in circumstances where the social welfare provision built up during the postwar era has in many countries already been significantly reduced.[19] "By the end of this decade," writes Aditya Chakrabortty, "that policy will have become a regime, Austeria."[20]

"Sovereign is he who decides on the exception," wrote the German legal theorist and future Nazi Carl Schmitt in 1922.[21] By this, Schmitt meant that sovereigns, which could be collective bodies, were defined by the ability to suspend established legal norms during moments which they deemed to be crises or emergencies. In effect, the decision to which Schmitt refers involves identifying those groups which are to be treated as outside the law. Walter Benjamin greatly admired Schmitt, despite the diametrically opposed nature of their political views, but, unsurprisingly, his notion of "the exception" was also the antithesis of Schmitt's, invoking not sovereignty, but catastrophe.[22] As he wrote in his last and greatest essay: "The tradition of the oppressed teaches us that the 'state of emergency' in which we live is not the exception but the rule."[23] In this passage, Benjamin was concerned not primarily to criticize Schmitt, but rather those social democratic and Stalinist conceptions of historical progress which treated fascism as either impossible or ephemeral under modern industrial conditions. For Benjamin, fascism was the latest form taken in the succession of emergencies to which the oppressed had been subjected throughout history.[24] He was not trying to minimize the singular horrors of fascism—the full extent of which were not apparent even in 1940—but was attempting to point out that it was different in degree rather than in kind from what the oppressed had previously suffered. The two men were not simply expressing different class perspectives, but discussing different conceptions of emergency or crisis. They are not, however, necessarily incompatible.

Resistance to the phase of neoliberalism has already begun, but the very fact that the outcome is as yet undecided means that the Owl of Minerva may not take flight for some time. We are not in a position to say whether the future of capitalism will involve a further mutation of neoliberalism, the replacement of neoliberalism by a new method of capitalist organiztion, or—however distant this may seem—the overthrow of the entire system; but we can say what neoliberalism was before 2008 and, equally importantly, what it was not. These are the issues I intend to address in what follows.

Up to this point, I have treated neoliberalism and contemporary capital-ism as if they were essentially synonymous, but this is of course precisely one of the major points at issue. The late Chris Harman was skeptical about the notion of neoliberalism as anything other than an ideology, or perhaps a set of policies.[25] In fact, the term neoliberalism can be sensibly used in three ways.

One use certainly is to describe the ideology which emerged in Central Europe during the 1930s in opposition to "socialism" (i.e., state planning and ownership) and which later migrated to the Economics Department at the University of Chicago. David Marquand argues against use of the term on the grounds that it is "confusing"—the term "liberal" having encompassed so many different positions since the early nineteenth century—and prefers "Chicagoan" in recognition of the Midwestern institutional base it acquired in the USA.[26] The adherents of this conception of neoliberalism—the only ones who have actually adopted the term as a self-description—were sup-porters of neoclassical economics but with an important difference: they did not believe that the market order was a spontaneous result of human activ-ity, but one which would have to be brought into being by the state. These positions were widely regarded as eccentric if not downright lunatic by both state managers and most professional economists from the Second World War until shortly before the crisis of the mid-1970s.

A second use is to describe the strategy used by regimes—in other words the alliances of state managers and politicians—which began to emerge from the mid to late 1970s, first in Chile, then the UK, then the USA, then New Zealand, then virtually everywhere.[27] This strategy was a response to the return of economic crisis which, stripped of all surrounding rhetoric, sought to shift the balance of forces between labor and capital, in the first instance by weakening the trade union movement. Any analysis of the way in which the strategy was successively applied would show that it emerged in a piecemeal fashion, involving many false starts ("monetarism"), impro-visations ("privatization"), and industrial struggles which could have gone either way (most of the major set-piece disputes down to 1985). It was not the implementation of a master plan derived from neoliberalism-as-an-ideology: capitalism was in crisis and ruling classes had a limited set of options, once Keynesianism and forms of state capitalism had been ruled out. It is therefore unsurprising that most arrived at the same responses: Hayek was not the anti-Marx to Thatcher's anti-Lenin.

The third use is to identify the entire period or—my preferred term— era of capitalism since the strategy began to be applied in the aftermath of the last-crisis-but-one. "Inevitably, '1973' is a metonym for changes too capacious for a single year to bear. . . . We might therefore date the cyclical ascent of finance back to this moment, though not because financial has 'pushed out' industrial capital—a conceptual model opening onto the catastrophic idea of good and bad capitalism, or healthy and unhealthy capitalism."[28] Ha-Joon Chang refers to the period between 1973 and 1979 as an interregnum between the Golden Age and that of neoliberalism proper.[29] It is important to understand, however, that it was not inevitable the post-1973 era would have this character. As I suggested elsewhere in relation to the British Miners' Strike, there were moments in most major countries when different outcomes were possible, but by the mid to late 1980s it should have begun to be clear that this was not a mere shift in the balance of class forces, which could be reversed by a victory or two, but a new settlement in favor of capital.

Other writers have identified different dimensions of neoliberalism. Manfred Steger and Ravi Roy, for example, also find three meanings in the term, one of which is similarly an ideology, but then we part company, as their others are "a mode of governance" and "a policy package."[30] In my view, however, both of these are simply aspects of what I call the strategic element of neoliberalism, since changes in the existing mode of governance was precisely one of the policy objectives which ruling class vanguards set themselves as a means of accomplishing the others.

What, then, is the relationship between the three dimensions of neoliberalism, as I understand them? First, the ideology was not, in most cases, what inspired the strategy: politicians arrived at some similar conclusions to those of neoliberal ideologues by a process of trial and error, in a situation where capitalist alternatives were extremely limited; but this was a convergence rather than inspiration. No one should imagine that, for example, Ronald Reagan's "military Keynesianism" gained the approval of the University of Chicago Department of Economics. Second, the relative success of the strategy ensured the nature of the era, but this was by no means decided until the mid-eighties: until that point it remained possible that the ruling-class offensive might be defeated. Once it emerged victorious in a sufficiently large number of key states, neoliberals were encouraged to press home their advantage in ways which helped to bring these societies closer to the original vision of the ideologues. "As time wore on and union power declined, as the initial crisis 'was solved,' a new ideology was born that saw marketization of every walk of life as a quasi-permanent political project: neoliberalism."[31]

Early in the neoliberal era, in what is probably the most rigorous presentation of essentially Stalinist categories, Ben Fine and Lawrence Harris divide the history of the capitalist mode of production into three stages: laissez-faire, monopoly capitalism, and state monopoly capitalism, the latter of which they regarded as being in place at the time of writing. Fine and Harris are clear that the history of the capitalist world economy and the social formations which operate within it do not follow this sequence. They do not regard imperialism, as defined by Lenin, as a stage in its own right, although they tend to associate it with the monopoly stage.[32] Fredric Jameson, following Ernest Mandel, also argues that there have been three stages ("fundamental moments") in capitalism: "These are market capitalism, the monopoly stage or the stage of imperialism, and our own, wrongly called postindustrial, but what might better be termed multinational, capital."[33]

All phases of capitalist development have hitherto both begun with the crisis of the previous phase, which usually continued as the system was restructured and the conditions for a new round of accumulation were prepared, and ended with their own crisis, requiring a new period of restructuring. But although crises may ultimately all have the same cause, in the tendency of the rate of profit to fall, and take the same form, in the overproduction of commodities, they are also always crises of the particular way in which capitalism is organized at that point in time. They are, in other words, *historical* events, the trajectories of which are determined by—among other factors—levels of working-class organization and resistance, the availability and strength of countervailing tendencies to that of the rate of profit to fall, and the capacity and ability of states to intervene.

It is true, however, that there are inadequate or misleading ways of periodizing capitalism. One is to treat aspects of capitalism which emerge during a particular historical period as if they were distinct stages in their own right, as Lenin did when he argued that imperialism was the latest (not "highest," as the English mistranslation has it) stage of capitalism. The features which Lenin and the other theorists of the Second International identified with imperialism—the export of capital, the fusion of financial and industrial capital and their fusion with the state, the division of the world into territorial spheres of geopolitical influence—have continued in the subsequent century, albeit in modified forms, but it would be implausible to argue that as a result we remain within a stage of capitalism which began in the last third of the nineteenth century. A second error is to follow Kondratieff in identifying shifts in technology as signaling the transition from one stage to another.[34] Technological innovation is obviously important but, as Michael Kidron once noted in a related context, "it is hardly autonomous."[35] Since there is no space here to argue a case at length, I will simply state what I think any adequate notion of the stages of capitalist development should involve.

First, stages should correspond to actual periods in the history of the capitalist system, with opening and closing dates, not to abstract characterizations of the unfolding of the capitalist mode of production. Provided that they are not actively misleading—such as "Keynesianism"—the descriptive terms which we use to identify historical stages are less important than recognizing the ways in which they are distinct from each other. To quote R. H. Tawney in a related context, "Verbal controversies are profitless; if an author discovers a more suitable term by all means let him use it."[36] The issue is one of content, not nomenclature.

Second, stages have to be understood at a global level. Unlike the other periodizations given above, mine include the Stalinist states as an integral part of the capitalist system.

Third, the stages are not hermetically sealed off from each other. All are characterized by features which are constitutive of the capitalist mode of production; some retain characteristics which overlap from the previous stage; and even the new characteristics occur with different intensities within different nation-states.

Fourth, the stages themselves have to be broken down into substages.

Fifth, the driver for the opening of a new stage is a crisis of the capitalist system. The world economy has experienced four systemic crises since the emergence of capitalism as a global system; the years 1873, 1929, and 1973 marked the commencement of the first three. As Gérard Duménil and Dominique Lévy write: "Each of these earthquakes introduced the establishment of a new social order and deeply altered international relations." The period which opened in 1973 with one great crisis of capitalism closed with another still greater crisis in 2008; it is less clear, however, as Duménil and Lévy also claim, that "the contemporary crisis marks the beginning of a similar process of transition."[37] Like the era which immediately preceded it (1929–1973), this one included periods of both slump (1973–1981) and boom (1982–2007). The real question, therefore, is whether neoliberalism is a useful way of characterizing the entire historical period from 1973 to 2008 and possibly beyond. "Crisis is a process," writes Alex Law, "not a fixed condition." But, as he then notes, this is not how it is currently understood: "Instead of a moment of exception precipitating a turning point, crisis becomes a normalised, semi-permanent condition."[38] Therefore "[i]t may be ruled out that immediate economic crises of themselves produce fundamental historical events; they can simply create a terrain more favorable to the dissemination of certain modes of thought, and certain ways of posing and resolving questions involving the entire subsequent development of national life."[39]

There are of course many inadequate or misleading theories of neoliberalism—I criticize several of them in the pages that follow—but of which concept is this not the case? There are many inadequate and misleading theories of imperialism, but the thing does, alas, still exist. The notion of state capitalism is an interesting case in point. First used by German social democrats opposed to revisionism in the 1890s, it existed in various anarchist, ultra-left, and social democratic versions at least before the First World War; it was applied to the Soviet Union almost from when the October Revolution took place. Marxist thinker and activist Tony Cliff gave the concept a properly scientific content for the first time, although this did not of course prevent orthodox Trotskyists from accusing him of Menshevism, anarchism, and ultra-leftism.[40] There are unscientific theories of neoliberalism, just as there were unscientific theories of state capitalism.

Of course no single term can encapsulate every aspect of a historical period, and some of these changes are the result of processes, like the substitution of dead for living labor in manufacturing, which have been intrinsic to capitalism since its origins; others, like the shift from extraction or manufacturing to services are more recent, but nevertheless represent long-term developments. But even these take place in the *context* of neoliberalism. The unionization of new industries was never automatic or easy at any point in the history of capitalism, but when, for example, call centers emerged during the 1980s, it was in circumstances where it was more difficult both because of the neoliberal victories and because the revolutionary left showed no serious interest in organizing them. Some changes were, however, quite specific to neoliberalism: privatization, including that of housing stock; the conscious destruction of particular industries like mining; debt as a substitute for wage increases; the "new managerialism" and the rise of assessment regimes in the workplace; and so on.

There seem to be two reasons for our suspicion of the term "neoliberalism" to denote a historical period, one valid, the other not. The valid reason is a response to some of the ways in which certain characteristics of neoliberalism, especially financialization and debt, have been used to explain the present crisis. Writers unwilling to abandon core tenets of Marxist crisis theory have argued instead that its origins have to be found in the systemic long-term problem of profitability experienced by the system since the late 1960s.[41] I agree with these authors, but reasserting the inescapability of the law of the tendency of the rate of profit to fall (TRPTF) is a necessary but insufficient approach and can produce its own problems. The school of Political Marxism associated with Robert Brenner, for example, tends to focus on the underlying exploitative and competitive relationships constitutive of the system, rejecting attempts at periodization as being focused on mere epiphenomena.[42] But capitalism has never existed in a pure form, operating according to the model established by Marx in *Capital*, and this is precisely why we attempt to identify successive stages of capitalist development. Indeed, one way of characterizing these periods is precisely by identifying the shifting nature of the main countervailing tendencies to TRPTF. There have been three main periods in the history of capitalism. First, the period of "classical capitalism"—that is, the one most closely approximating that described by

Marx—which entered crisis in 1873. This led to the second period, involving the simultaneous formation of monopolies within the heartlands of the system and expansion of colonialism without, ultimately leading to the fusion of both these processes in a new phase of capitalist development variously known as "finance capitalism," "monopoly capitalism," or "imperialism." The crisis of monopoly capitalism in 1929 in turn led to a third stage, consisting of the consolidation of state capitalism and underpinned from the start of the Cold War by the permanent arms economy, most completely in the Stalinist states, with social or liberal democratic variants in the advanced West and hybrid forms emergent in non-Stalinist areas of the former colonial world.[43]

This brings me to the invalid reason for rejecting the concept of neoliberalism: our reluctance to accept, at least until very recently, that a new stage or period did in fact open in 1973. Faced with changes to capitalism, it is possible to adopt one of three main positions. One is to claim that there has been a fundamental transformation requiring the abandonment of preexisting positions. "New, new, new. Everything is new," as Tony Blair exclaimed to no doubt bemused representatives of the Socialist International shortly after Labour's election victory in 1997.[44] But even among actual socialists there are of course right- and left-wing responses to allegedly novel situations. The defunct journal *Marxism Today*, associated with the Eurocommunist wing of the former Communist Party of Great Britain, adhered to a right-wing version, in which changes to capitalism since the Second World War had supposedly so weakened the working class and its organizations that only alliances with sections of the middle class could deliver "progressive" outcomes.[45] Italian "autonomism" is a left—indeed ultra-left—response to an earlier set of changes, the emergence of the so-called "mass worker" during the Italian postwar miracle; only in this case the prospects for the working class are apparently excellent, not least because, in the late version associated with Michael Hardt and Antonio Negri at least, the working class has grown to engross everyone who is exploited or oppressed by capital in any way, in the form of a "multitude" which constitutes the new "dangerous class."[46] The latter claim shows that even individual concepts can have both optimistic and pessimistic versions. Guy Standing, for example, argues that what he calls "the precariat" is also the new dangerous class, but not, as in the case of Hardt and Negri, because of their potential to overthrow capital, but because of their potential susceptibility to far-right demagoguery.[47] In the face of this type of theoretical impressionism and the political indeterminacy to which it gives rise, a sense of the continuities involved in capitalism is an indispensable barrier to the adoption of fashionable stupidities.

But there is a second position that, far from exaggerating changes to capitalism, refuses to acknowledge that it has undergone—or in some versions, can undergo—*any* significant changes. Continuity is all. More commonly, this "fundamentalist" approach is encountered in the politics of the most dogmatic sections of the revolutionary left, where the assertion of eternal truths such as "capitalism is still capitalism, the working class is still the working class" substitute for any real analysis. The most famous example of this is of course the position adopted by the mainstream Trotskyist movement in 1948, who adhered, not to general claims about the nature of capitalism, in this case, but to specific claims made by Trotsky in 1938 that then became the measure of orthodoxy. Whatever their original merits, history had overtaken and rendered invalid Trotsky's views on the nature of Stalinist Russia, the prospects for the world economy, and the range of revolutionary outcomes in the Third World.

A series of groundbreaking works by Tony Cliff between 1948 and 1963, particularly "The Nature of Stalinist Russia" and "Permanent Revolution," exemplify a third possible response to change, starting from the understanding that capitalism both involves underlying continuities, without which it would cease to exist, but also undergoes periodic changes in form, which are the expressions of its historical development. Revolutionaries have to recognize and respond to the latter, rather than denying their existence just because they threaten to disrupt venerable organizational forms or established interventionist strategies. They should instead look for what new possibilities these changes offer, however unfamiliar or unsettling they may be.

Writing in 1979, Cliff used the metaphor of "the downturn" to encapsulate the situation of retreat and demoralization that the British working class were beginning to undergo in the late 1970s, although the term was rapidly extended to encompass the global decline in the class struggle from the postwar high point between 1968 and 1975. Cliff "was concerned with a shift in the balance of class forces, not with a change in the nature of society."[48] It is obvious that no one could have predicted what was to come from the van-tage point of the late 1970s, not least because—as is always the case at deci-sive turning points—the future direction was undetermined, dependent as it was on the outcome of the global class struggle. But by the beginning of the 1990s, the outline should have been clear: the mid-1970s had seen the beginning of a new period in the development of capitalism. We were deal-ing with a change in society, not just a change in the balance of class forces. But compared to our analysis of the period between 1948 and 1973, clarity failed to emerge from our discussion of the subsequent decades. Why?

The theory of the permanent arms economy was never as complete an explanation for the postwar boom as was sometimes assumed. In retrospect, it appears as an exceptional interlude in the history of capitalism, after which unresolvable crisis and the "stagnation of the productive forces" proclaimed by Trotsky on the eve of the Second World War would resume, inevitably leading to a revival of the class struggle, regardless of temporary setbacks: "Capitalism in the advanced countries is no longer expanding and so the words of the 1938 Transitional Programme that 'there can be no discus-sion of systematic social reforms and the raising of the masses' living stan-dards' fits again."[49] There would be no more countervailing tendencies to the TRPTF, at least of any significance. The concluding passage to Chris Har-man's *Explaining the Crisis*, first published in 1982—the year the neoliberal boom began—expresses the perspective:

> This does not mean that the world economy is doomed simply to decline. An overall tendency towards stagnation can still be ac-companied by minor booms, with small but temporary increases in employment. . . . The present phase of crisis is likely to go on and on—until it is resolved either by plunging much of the world into barbarism or by a succession of workers' revolutions.[50]

Harman later noted that the notion of "permanent crisis" was wrong: "It was a mistake on my part to use such a formulation—although I think excusable as we faced only the second real recession my generation had ex-perienced and did so a mere four years after the end of the first." But this concession was less significant than it at first appeared: "It may not be in permanent crisis, but it is in a phase of repeated crises from which it cannot escape, and these will necessarily be political and social as well as economic."[51] I am not clear whether there is any substantive difference between undergoing a permanent crisis and merely experiencing an endless series of repeated crises: both formulations involve the same reluctance to admit that capitalism might be capable of recovering from the recession which opened in 1973.

Of course, there were immensely challenging implications for revolutionaries in a situation where it might not be enough to simply retrench while intervening as best they could until the balance of forces was once more in their favor. It was as if reaching an understanding of a new period, one in which both labor and capital were being profoundly restructured, and then developing a perspective and a strategy based on that understanding was simply too massive, too much of a distraction from our immediate tasks to undertake. Without that understanding, however, our ability to accomplish even these immediate tasks will remain in doubt. "But history has shown us too to have been wrong, has revealed our point of view at that time as an illusion," wrote Engels in 1895, reflecting on the German Revolution of 1848: "It has done even more; it has not merely dispelled the erroneous notions we then held; it has also completely transformed the conditions under which the proletariat has to fight."[52] Comparable reassessments of both the "erroneous notions" which we have held since the 1970s and of "the transformed conditions under which we have to fight" are now in order. Of course, preparation of such an assessment involves knowledge already acquired from ongoing practical intervention as much as from theoretical study, but even direct experience of the struggle has to be interpreted.

My aim is to treat the neoliberal era as a totality. Whatever my other disagreements with Harman on this issue, he was certainly right to say that crises cannot be understood simply in economic terms and, as Loïc Wacquant has written, "the prevalent conception of neoliberalism is economic."[53] At best, discussions of it as a historical phenomenon focus on the terrain where the economic and the political intersect. But to consider neoliberalism as a totality, which any Marxist account is surely bound to do, we must pay at least as much attention to the social domain, which overlaps with and mediates between the economic and the political. The central question here concerns the social basis of neoliberalism. Every variety of capitalism has to draw support from classes below the bourgeoisie; but each variety of capitalism draws support from different classes—or different class fractions—below the bourgeoisie. What were these in the case of neoliberalism? In disciplinary terms, then, we need a historical sociology, in addition to a political economy of our subject.

As Bob Jessop has pointed out, neoliberalism has always been characterized by spatial differentiation in which several varieties operated simultaneously. His typology involves four geographically demarcated moments, each reflecting the structured inequality of the global capitalist system.[54] Two of these forms can be found in the developed capitalisms of the West. The first involves *neoliberal regime shifts*, above all in the English-speaking world, where the institutional characteristics of the Great Boom—social or liberal democracy in politics, Keynesianism in economic management, and Fordism in industrial organization—were replaced during the dominance of parties belonging to the New Right. The second involve *neoliberal policy adjustments*, for example in the Scandinavian and Rhenish countries, where partial adaptations to neoliberalism were made while retaining some elements from the former period. The third involve *neoliberal system transformation* in the former Stalinist states of Russia and Eastern Europe, and to a lesser extent in Southeast Asia, where the existing state capitalist economies were transformed with varying degrees of abruptness into particularly extreme versions of the Western multinational capitalist model. The fourth involves *neoliberal structural adjustment programs* in the Global South, which are essentially an aspect of contemporary imperialism as exercised by Western-dominated transnational institutions like the International Monetary Fund (IMF) and the World Bank.[55]

In what follows I am primarily concerned with the first moment of "neoliberal regime shift" and therefore draw mainly on the experience of Britain and, to a lesser extent, the US, although other examples such as New Zealand could also be added. This is not because events in any of these states have chronological priority, although the components of the neoliberal order were first assembled into a coherent package in Britain, in both vanguard neoliberal form during the premiership of Margaret Thatcher and social neoliberal form during that of Tony Blair.[56] Many began to be introduced elsewhere before Thatcher had taken office, across all of the areas covered by Jessop's typology of forms, from New York City in the First World (1975), to China in what was then the Second (1978), and to Chile (1973) and Jamaica (1976) in the Third. The reason why any overview of the neoliberal experiment has to focus on the twin metropolitan heartlands is rather that understanding neoliberalism, like understanding any significant social phenomenon, can best be achieved by focusing on its most developed forms: "Human anatomy contains a key to the anatomy of the ape," as Marx put it.[57] These forms are not necessarily the most typical of the phenomenon, nor in the case of neoliberalism do they necessarily reveal the future pattern of development elsewhere in the world, since it has reinforced rather than undermined the inherent unevenness of capitalism; but subjecting them to scrutiny can perhaps reveal the essence of what we wish to understand and thereby more effectively oppose.

CHAPTER 1

False Intellectual Antecedents
and True Material Origins

The Innocence of Mr. Adam Smith

According to Margaret Thatcher, her policies simply recapitulated those first advocated in Scotland two hundred years previously. How accurate is this claim? Or, to put it another way: how fair is this accusation? In his biography of Thatcher, Hugo Young quotes her as saying, "The Scots invented Thatcherism, long before I was thought of," dryly adding that this "was believed to be a reference to Adam Smith, the economist, and possibly the philosopher David Hume."[1] In her autobiography, Thatcher noted with bemusement the failure of her "revolution" to win hearts and minds in Scotland, "home of the very same Scottish Enlightenment which produced Adam Smith, the greatest exponent of free enterprise economics till Hayek and Friedman."[2] Friedman himself pointed to the supposed contemporary relevance of Smith in a speech to the Mont Pelerin Society conference in Saint Andrews, on the bicentenary of *The Wealth of Nations*:

> Adam Smith was a revolutionary. He was attacking an entrenched system of governmental planning, control and intervention. His attack, reinforced by social and economic changes, ultimately succeeded, but not for some seventy years. By today we have come full

circle back to the kind of arrangements that Adam Smith was attacking in 1776. His book was about as pertinent an attack on our present structure of governmental control and intervention as it was on the structure of his time.[3]

The more openly pro-market figures in Smith's homeland, like Scottish National Party member Michael Russell, have a similar view: "Adam Smith was the father of modern capitalism and it is high time that his own people rediscovered his genius, particularly as, in his own land, that genius is currently tarnished by the half-baked economic models espoused by most of our political parties."[4] Many on the left accept these nostrums at face value and merely reverse their value judgements. For Elmar Altvater: "Some of the most striking ingredients of neoliberal intellectual approaches can be traced back to the origins of liberal thinking in the early 18th century," among whose proponents he includes Smith and Hume.[5] One Scottish historian, the late James Young, claimed that "Adam Smith was a pioneer of the vicious anti-humanist economics of capitalism" and linked him, somewhat implausibly, "with all the other advocates of anti-gay entrepreneurship; aggressive immoral and naked capitalism; and post-modernism."[6] These comments confirm an observation by two of Smith's more acute recent interpreters: "It is no longer thought necessary to examine how and why Smith argued in favour of the market, nor indeed how he qualified his case."[7]

Anachronistic misconceptions concerning Smith could of course be corrected by the radical expedient of actually reading *The Wealth of Nations* and *The Theory of Moral Sentiments*, preferably after situating them in their historical context, namely Scotland's emergence from feudalism. When Smith attacks unproductive labor, he is not making some timeless critique of state employees but thinking quite specifically about Highland clan retainers. When he opposes monopolies, he was not issuing a prophetic warning against the nationalization of industries in the twentieth century but criticizing those companies which relied for their market position on the possession of exclusive royal charters in the eighteenth. Above all, unlike his modern epigones, he did not see the market as a quasi-mystical institution that should be made to penetrate every aspect of social life but rather as a limited mechanism for liberating humanity's economic potential from feudal and absolutist stagnation.

Even so, the advocacy of Smith and his colleagues for what they called "commercial society" was very conditional indeed, Smith himself being famously suspicious of businessmen and their conspiracies against the public.[8] This was understood as late as the final decades of the nineteenth century. Carl Menger was only exaggerating slightly when he wrote in 1891: "Smith placed himself in all cases of conflict of interest between the strong and the weak, *without exception* on the side of the latter."[9] More importantly, perhaps, Smith intuited, long before capitalist industrialization began in earnest, that it would lead to massive deterioration in the condition of laborers and their reduction to mere "hands." Understood in the context of the Scottish Enlightenment conception of human potential, the description of pin manufacture at the beginning of *The Wealth of Nations* not only celebrates the efficiency of the division of labor, but also shows the soul-destroying repetition that awaited the new class of wage laborers.[10] It was uneasy anticipations such as these, which Smith shared with Sir James Steuart and Adam Ferguson, that later informed Hegel's conception of alienation and, through him, that of Karl Marx.[11]

What is political about political economy? Stanley Aronowitz notes of its Enlightenment proponents that:

> When they spoke of "political economy" these founders did not refer exclusively—or even principally—to the relationship of labor and commodity markets to the state. By "political" they meant the terms under which the production, distribution, and consumption of goods and services takes place and, more specifically, the share of the social product that accrues respectively to labor, capital, and agricultural interests. . . . The economy is only one aspect of a social totality that consists of economic, social, political, sociocultural, and ideological relationships that are closely connected.[12]

A far more plausible theoretical source of neoliberalism is neoclassical economics, above all the marginalist reaction against both the classical political economy associated with Smith and the Marxist critique which sought to build on what he and his contemporaries had accomplished. In economic, theory marginalism represented the final retreat from scientific inquiry, however imperfect, into ideological justification. It was signaled by the abandonment of the law of value, with its dangerous claim that the socially necessary labor required to produce commodities was also the objective measure of their value. The tenets of marginalism were first set out by Leon Walras in his *Elements of Pure Economics* (1874) and ultimately codified by Alfred Marshall in his *Principles of Economics* (1890), although they have a long prehistory dating back at least to the 1830s.[13] In relation to neoliberalism, the most important thinkers have been those of the Austrian school, above all, Menger, Ludwig von Mises, and Friedrich von Hayek. Their attitude to Smith is instructive.

Within a decade of his death in 1790, Smith's work began to be presented in a way that minimized its more radical elements, as part of the reaction to the French Revolution.[14] Even in this form, Smith presented a problem for the neoclassical school: Walras saw his work as being tainted by "unscientific" social and moral considerations; Menger regarded it as flawed because of Smith's insistence that the national economy was not simply an abstraction—a view incompatible with the "atomism" or methodological individualism of the marginalists.[15] Nevertheless, the marginalists needed, for reasons of ideological continuity, to claim Smith as a forerunner whose work they had completed, above all in relation to his advocacy of the market, which they removed from any historical context. "It was only the 'marginal revolution' of the 1870s," wrote Hayek, "that produced a satisfactory explanation of the market processes that Adam Smith had long before described with his metaphor of the 'hidden hand.'"[16] The source of this misidentification lies in Hayek's belief that there are two types of rationalism: constructivist and evolutionary. According to Andrew Gamble, adherents of constructivist rationalism "believe that human societies can be mastered by human beings and remodelled according to rational criteria." Adherents of evolutionary rationalism—among whom Hayek numbered himself, Smith, and other Scottish Enlightenment figures like Ferguson and Hume—show "a distrust of the powers of human reason, a recognition of the extent of human ignorance about the social and natural worlds, and therefore a stress upon the unexpected, unintended consequences of social action."[17] Hayek's ignorance of both the theory of the Scottish Enlightenment and the history of capitalist development in Scotland leads him to treat *The Wealth of Nations* as a description of how "commercial society" works rather than as a program for bringing it about; but considered in the latter way, Smith was as much of a constructivist rationalist as Marx—which was, of course, precisely why Hayek's predecessors regarded him with such caution.[18]

The neoclassical school claimed that capitalism, defined as a system of competitive markets, was the only rational means of organizing economic activity. Providing these markets are subject to minimal interference, their operation will result in the effective allocation of productive resources between different branches of the economy and provide the impetus for innovation to take place within competing enterprises. The veneration of markets in neoclassical theory was accompanied by an extreme hostility to any institutions which impede or distort their operation. These included those components of civil society said to act as monopolies, which invariably turned out to be effective trade unions rather than, for example, multinational companies; but the most important anti-market institutions were, potentially at least, states. I write "potentially" because, contrary to a common misunderstanding, neither neoclassical economists nor their neoliberal descendants were necessarily opposed to states as such. Both knew that the very emergence of large-scale capitalist markets in the first place was not a natural, organic process but a highly artificial one incubated by state power. "Historically, markets are generally either a side effect of government operations, especially military operations, or were directly created by government policy," writes David Graeber, with only the faintest hint of exaggeration.[19] Karl Polanyi noted that economic liberals during the nineteenth century "without any inconsistency call upon the state to use the force of law [and] ... even appeal to the violent forces of civil war to set up the preconditions of a self-regulating market."[20] State power has been used to impose and reimpose market relations, and this is perfectly compatible with both neoclassical and neoliberal theory. States so conceived should not be considered in any sense as minimalist, except in relation to market intervention. Indeed, the first economists to take the name of "neoliberals" were German members of the neoclassical school during the 1930s, like Alexander Rüstow, whose response to the Great Depression was the slogan, "free economy, strong state."[21]

For members of the neoclassical school, problems occurred when the state acted as a rival means of economic organization that could threaten the existence of private capital, although they tended to oscillate between two explanations for this. In one, the state is an autonomous institution whose leading personnel ("state managers," in the current terminology) pursue their own parasitic interests at the expense of productive capitalists. In the other, which tended to predominate in neoclassical discussions, the state is an instrumental institution directed by the politicians who might be opponents of capitalism, or—if subject to election—at least liable to make decisions detrimental to capitalism in order to meet the uncomprehending demands of the electorate. The latter might involve the persistence of pre-bourgeois social forms, as in Joseph Schumpeter's attempt to explain imperialism as an effect of aristocratic influence on international politics, or of "socialist" attempts to impose collectivist controls over productive resources, as in Hayek's attempt to define Nazi Germany in these terms on the grounds that the state was responsible for directing aspects of economic activity.[22]

One problem with this doctrine was that it could only with the greatest difficulty be reconciled with reality. While it was obviously true that the bureaucratic state was increasing both its power over and penetration of society, this was not only a function of what the neoclassical school regarded as socialism, but rather of non-market requirements of capitalism itself: internally, to simultaneously manage an increasingly complex division of labor and maintain a social order riven by class conflicts; externally, to acquire markets, raw materials, and opportunities for capital investment, and to prevent national rivals from doing likewise—imperialism, in other words.[23] The growth of the state was most marked in those countries which experienced a rapid increase in the size of the working class, created both through industrialization at home and the territories controlled through colonial expansion abroad. In those with more stable social structures, already replete with imperial possessions, the state had less of a presence, as A. J. P. Taylor recounts in a classic passage describing Britain ("England") on the eve of the First World War:

> Until August 1914 a sensible, law-abiding Englishman could pass through life and hardly notice the existence of the state, beyond the post office and the policeman. He could live where he liked and as he liked. He had no official number or identity card. He could travel abroad or leave his country for ever without a passport or any sort of official permission. He could exchange his money for any other currency without restriction or limit. He could buy goods from any

country in the world on the same terms as he bought goods at home.
For that matter, a foreigner could spend his life in this country without permit and without informing the police. Unlike the countries
of the European continent, the state did not require its citizens to
perform military service. . . . Substantial householders were occasionally called on for jury service. Otherwise, only those helped the
state who wished to do so. The Englishman paid taxes on a modest
scale . . . . The state intervened to prevent the citizen from eating
adulterated food or contracting certain infectious diseases. It imposed safety rules in factories, and prevented women, and adult
males in some industries, from working excessive hours. The state
saw to it that children received education up to the age of 13. Since
1 January 1909, it provided a meagre pension for the needy over the
age of seventy. Since 1911, it helped ensure certain classes of workers against sickness and unemployment. This tendency towards
more state action was increasing. Expenditure on the social services
had roughly doubled since the Liberals took office in 1905. Still,
broadly speaking, the state acted only to help those who could not
help themselves. It left the adult citizen alone. All this was changed
by the impact of the Great War.[24]

But even Britain, the society most admired by neoclassical economists
for the supposedly minimal role played by the state, was not untouched by its
expansion. As arch-bureaucrat Sidney Webb reported in the last decade of the
nineteenth century, those who claimed to reject the state were often simply
oblivious to how much they actually relied upon it, at least at the local level:

The Individualist Town Councillor will walk along the municipal
pavement, lit by municipal gas and cleansed by municipal brooms
with municipal water, and seeing by the municipal clock in the
municipal market, that he is too early to meet his children coming
from the municipal school, hard by the county lunatic asylum and
municipal hospital, will use the national telegraph system to tell
them not to walk through the municipal park but to come by the
municipal tramway, to meet him in the municipal reading room,
by the municipal art gallery, museum and library, where he intends

to consult some of the national publications in order to prepare his next speech in the municipal town-hall, in favour of the nationalization of canals and the increase of the government control over the railway system.[25]

The creation of these state-owned institutions was at any rate the result of conscious policy choices; but there was another respect in which capitalist markets created bureaucracies: "English liberalism . . . did not lead to a reduction of state bureaucracy, but the exact opposite: an endlessly ballooning array of legal clerks, registrars, inspectors, notaries, and police officials who made the liberal dream of a world of free contract between autonomous individuals possible."[26]

However, it was not London, England, but Vienna, capital of the Austro-Hungarian Empire and the home of many key neoclassical economists, which was perhaps the leading European example of extended state organization at a municipal level. Typically, Hayek ascribed these departures from liberalism to the influence of German ideas which were contrary to "liberty."[27] But, as I have suggested above, it is possible to explain these developments without recourse to his idealist delirium. Keith Tribe notes: "It was not 'German ideas' that undermined classical liberalism, but the internal and external dynamics of industrialization and democracy—what in another language used to be called progress."[28] Although Max Weber shared the methodological individualist assumptions of his Austrian colleagues, he was far more realistic than them in this respect. Bureaucratization was the fate of modern societies and, while it was subject to countervailing tendencies, would ultimately prevail.[29] In his view, socialism would greatly extend the process of bureaucratization by removing the countervailing power of private ownership, but it would retain capitalist specialization: "The modern economy cannot be managed in any other way."[30]

However, in Germany after unification—and especially after the Socialist electoral gains in 1878, Bismarck attempted a two-pronged strategy, on the one hand banning the SPD, but, on the other, setting up:

a top-down alternative to the free schools, workers' associations, friendly societies, and the larger process of building socialism from below. This took the form of a program of social insurance (for unemployment, health, and disability, etc.), free education, pensions, and so forth—much of it watered-down versions of policies that had been part of the Socialist platform, but in every case, carefully purged of any democratic, participatory elements.[31]

The Great Crash of 1929 plunged the world economy into a prolonged crisis, for which neoclassical orthodoxy had no solutions and from which it was only lifted by preparation for war and ultimately by war itself. It was this practical failure of the neoclassical school, rather than its intellectual incoherence, which ultimately consigned it to the margins of intellectual influence after 1939. Nicholas Wapshott writes of Marriner Eccles, the multimillionaire Mormon banker: "He was a hard-nosed former Republican who owned First Security Corporation, which ran twenty-six banks, as well as one of the largest beet sugar producers in America, a vast dairy chain, and lumber companies, among other businesses":

> "There is not cause or reason for the unemployment with its resultant destitution and suffering of fully one-third of our entire population," he told a Senate committee hearing in 1933. A return to full employment could be brought about, he said, only "by providing purchasing power sufficiently adequate to enable the people to obtain the consumption goods which we, as a nation, are able to produce." He went on, "The nineteenth century economics will no longer serve our purpose—an economic age 150 years old has come to an end. The orthodox capitalist system of uncontrolled individualism, with its free competition, will no longer serve our purpose."[32]

But when Keynesianism subsequently became the dominant ideological tendency within bourgeois economic thought, it by no means abandoned all the macroeconomic assumptions of neoclassicism. What it questioned was rather the realism of those assumptions in relation to the operation of markets. In particular, Keynesianism rejected claims that aggregate demand always equaled aggregate supply, that prices were determined by the quantity of money in circulation, and that the future expectations of economic actors were always rational.[33] A far more fundamental critique, which focused in on the central role allotted to markets in neoclassical theory, was launched by Karl Polanyi during the Second World War. In a striking passage, much quoted in recent years, Polanyi identified the likely outcome of allowing markets unlimited sway:

> To allow the market mechanism to be sole director of the fate of human beings and their natural environment, indeed, even of the amount and use of purchasing power, would result in the demolition of society. . . . In disposing of a man's labor power the system would, incidentally, dispose of the physical, psychological, and moral entity "man" attached to the tag. Robbed of the protective covering of cultural institutions, human beings would perish from the effects of social exposure; they would die as the victims of acute social dislocation through vice, perversion, crime, and starvation. Nature would be reduced to its elements, neighborhoods and landscapes defiled, rivers polluted, military safety jeopardized, the power to produce food and raw materials destroyed. Finally, the market administration of purchasing power would periodically liquidate business enterprise, for shortages and surfeits of money would prove as disastrous to business as floods and droughts in primitive society.[34]

This vision demonstrates that Polanyi had a far greater grasp of the implications of uncontrolled ("free") market capitalism than Keynes or any of his followers. We need not assume that the capitalist class would consciously seek to implement a program which had these catastrophic results, only that an anarchic system in which the need for individual capitals to successfully compete overrides any collective responsibility to society or nature. It would take thirty years from the publication of *The Great Transformation* in 1944 for the devastation envisaged by Polanyi to once again become a threateningly plausible scenario.

Myths and realities of the Great Boom

The neoclassical theoretical tradition was kept alive, in all its extremism, by small bands of adherents like the Mont Pelerin Society, founded in 1947, or the Institute of Economic Affairs (IEA), founded 1955, which built up intellectual capital for themselves in journals and pamphlets throughout the Keynesian era. Few members of the bourgeoisie, let alone the wider population, took seriously the arguments produced by these institutions at the time. Ralph Harris, the first director of the IEA, unsuccessfully stood as a Conservative candidate in Scotland during the 1951 and 1955 general elections, despite the latter being the only occasion when that or any other party has won an absolute majority of votes anywhere in Britain since the attainment of universal suffrage. "The atmosphere was wholly hostile to the right-wing position," he recalled.[35] This was unsurprising, since the postwar boom (1948–1973) was the greatest period of economic expansion in the history of capitalism. The system had grown "twice as fast between 1950 and 1964 as between 1913 and 1950, and nearly half as fast again as during the generation before that."[36] And growth was largely uninterrupted by cyclical business fluctuations, let alone recession.[37] The ascendancy of the neoliberals began after the onset of the crisis, not before. David Hare later reflected on his play *Knuckle* (1974) as a prediction of Thatcherism:

> In the history books, it is Margaret Thatcher who is credited or blamed with adjusting the country to a new more ruthless kind of capitalism where no-one has any responsibility except to look after themselves and their own families.... But if this version of history is correct, it is very hard to see how by 1974, five years before Thatcher's election to power, a casual dramatist has already written a play which turns on the very argument which would transform conservatism. Thatcher may indeed have overseen the triumph of the unsparing new philosophy, but she was not its author. It had been simmering away among renegades for a long time.[38]

The assumption is sometimes made that, because Hayek was awarded the Nobel Prize for Economics in 1974, this reflected a more widespread recognition of his ideas. Not so. It appears that the prize was awarded to Hayek jointly with Gunnar Myrdal, a Keynesian social democrat, to forestall any allegations that the committee was politically biased. If anything, this signaled the beginning of the swift process which, by 1980, saw the neoliberals replace Keynesians as the dominant tendency in university economics departments.[39]

These achievements are often thought to have been the result of a general adoption of Keynesian policies, but if they were indeed responsible for the boom, why were they unable to prevent the return to slump in 1973–74? Some writers have recognized that this does represent a problem and have argued instead that there was no Keynesian revolution: "Keynesianism when it was tried was not needed and when it was needed was not tried."[40] But this goes too far. Policies which would eventually be described as "Keynesian" were introduced, for example during the American New Deal, before the publication of *The General Theory of Employment, Interest, and Money* (1936) and independently of Keynes's influence. Keynes himself recognized the affinity of these policies to his own ideas in a letter to Roosevelt of 1933 in which he urged the president to be cautious.[41] His stance here was characteristic of the way he tended to vacillate between recognizing the radicalism inherent in some aspects of his theory ("the declining marginal efficiency of capital") and shrinking from the implications of what this might mean in practice.[42] The fate of the New Deal is, however, indicative of the failure of direct state intervention and expenditure to restore economic growth in conditions which were not already propitious. The American economy achieved a partial recovery from 1933, but collapsed back into recession by 1937; sustained recovery was only achieved with rearmament prior to US entry into the Second World War. The role of Keynesianism after the war was similarly limited. Many of the reforms for which the period is best remembered, such as the creation of the National Health Service, were not Keynesian in inspiration, while others with which he was associated, such as deficit spending, were only deployed during the early 1970s when growth began to falter amid rising inflation.

A return to recession after the Second World War was averted by an unintended consequence of the permanent arms economy that accompanied the Cold War, namely the absorption of capital that would otherwise have reentered the circuit of productive capital into what was—in strictly economic terms—waste. This led to important constraints on the growth of the organic composition of capital and consequently counteracted the tendency of the rate of profit to fall.[43] Other mechanisms had performed the same function earlier in the history of the system, notably investment in colonial possessions outwith the reproductive circuits of capital and luxury spending by the ruling class, but none of these involved expenditure on a comparably massive scale. Nevertheless, preventing a slump is not the same as causing a boom, although high levels of arms spending did contribute towards it by feeding through to other sectors of the economy through the so-called "multiplier effect." Leaving aside the short-term effects of postwar reconstruction, two other processes were required. One was the generalization of "Fordist" high-productivity, mass-consumption regimes across the core of the system, above all in the production of cars and electrical household goods.[44] The other was the industrialization of those areas of Europe and North America which had previously been based on small-scale, family-based agriculture or petty commodity production, effectively bringing millions of new productive workers into the labor process and consumers into the market for mass-produced commodities.[45] In the Stalinist regimes of Eastern Europe, very similar processes were at work as in the West, including industrialization, economic growth, and, less often noticed, the increased availability of consumer goods.[46]

A failure to understand the way in which the Great Boom was in many respects the most successful era in capitalist history has given rise to several popular misconceptions about the neoliberal period which followed. These are set out most clearly in two of the most widely read books about neoliberalism, David Harvey's *A Brief History of Neoliberalism* (2005) and Naomi Klein's *The Shock Doctrine* (2007), both of which have, in other respects, greatly contributed to our understanding of it. Harvey argues that neoliberalism is concerned—at least in part—with "restoring, or in some instances (as in Russia and China) creating, the power of an economic elite."[47] There are, however, two problems with this aspect of Harvey's position.

One is the notion of "restoration." Western levels of state ownership and control characteristic of the postwar period did not constitute socialism, and so it is difficult to see how the capitalist ruling class in the West can be said to have ever lost power. Some of Harvey's supporters recognize the difficulties here, and tend to shift ground arguing instead that neoliberalism has "undermined the potential of 'bourgeois democracy' to return critics of the market [to office]" and has involved "taking back most of the gains made by the trade union movement and the forces of popular democracy, minimal though they might be argued to be."[48] But this is a different and more defensible position, concerned with the balance of power between the main social classes during the Great Boom. To claim that a "restoration" took place is inadvertently to perpetuate the neoliberal myth that developments during this time were ultimately detrimental to capital, when in fact this was the period when it enjoyed the highest levels of growth in the history of the system.

It is certainly true that a number of concessions were won by or granted to the working class, and it is for this reason that the reputation of what Eric Hobsbawm calls "the Golden Age" remains high, particularly in contrast to what he calls "the Landslide" that followed.[49] It rests on two main factors. One was high, indeed for practical purposes full, employment. The other was the expansion of the "social wage," meaning not only transfer payments in the form of unemployment benefits and pensions, but also subsidized housing and health, and social service provision free at the point of use. Both of these factors were necessary to capital: on the one hand to gain the support of the labor force, thus helping to ensure social stability; on the other to aid increases in productivity, thus contributing to international competitiveness. Consequently, these measures were not necessarily dependent for their introduction on social or even liberal democratic governments. In most of Western Europe outside Scandinavia, it was Christian Democrat governments who were instrumental in establishing welfare states. Even in Britain, where postwar social welfare was at least partly initiated by the local representatives of social democracy, the process began under the Conservative-dominated wartime coalition and was inspired by liberals like William Beveridge.[50] For some writers this does not represent a particular problem, since they regard all political parties at the time as sharing the same essentially benign attitude to the working class. Here Harvey's position dovetails with those of writers very far indeed from his own historical and geographical materialism. For Francis Beckett, both New Left and New Right are equally responsible for neoliberalism: "So the dull settlement that had given the baby boomers all their chances in life, created by the Attlee government and maintained by Macmillan, Wilson, Heath and Callaghan, had few defenders among the children of the sixties, being too radical for some and not radical enough for others."[51] Beckett is here employing precisely the same idiotic notion that power and influence can be ascribed to an entire generational cohort that was first popularized by the subjects of his complaint ("the generation gap"). More importantly, it ignores a number of important facts.

British levels of social provision were by no means the most generous in the West. Writing in 1968, Michael Kidron pointed out that welfare payments form "a smaller proportion of gross national product, . . . a smaller part of the average worker's take home pay, . . . and a smaller relative charge on capital" than in most other Western European countries, with consequently worse specific conditions in relation to paid holidays, severance pay, inflation-proof pensions, and family allowances.[52] Nor were these economic considerations the only ones which cast some doubt over the extent to which capitalist power was in retreat. "Far from introducing a 'social revolution' the overwhelming Labour victory [in 1945] brought about the greatest restoration of social values since 1660," runs Anthony Howard's famous assessment.[53] Yet it is one which recent research, for example into the relentless repression of gays under both Labour and Conservative postwar governments, tends to support.[54] As Elizabeth Wilson notes, "in the fifties Britain was a conservative society described in the rhetoric of a radical ideology."[55] It is regrettable that some writers continue to describe it in these terms.

In the USA, social welfare was even less generous, tended to exclude larger numbers of workers, and, where it did exist, was not provided by the state as a right, but by capital as deferred wages on the basis of collective bargaining with unionized workforces.[56] Although some reforms were directly introduced during the New Deal of the 1930s, above all Social Security, their expansion, let alone the introduction of more general social welfare provisions such as Medicaid and Medicare, were the result of the movements of the 1960s, above all that for Black civil rights. However, these were implemented not by the Democrats but by the Republicans during Richard Nixon's first term between 1968 and 1972. On August 15, 1971, Nixon claimed "I am now a Keynesian in economics" after freezing wages, prices, and rents.[57] Carl Freedman points out that it was only under Nixon that federal spending on domestic social programs was greater than military spending and, by the time he left office, the former was, at 40 percent of the federal budget, 12 percent higher than it had been under Johnson. This included massive expansion of medical research, particularly into cancer, the passing of the Clean Air Act and creation of the Environment Protection Agency, and the introduction of automatic cost-of-living adjustments to Social Security. Freedman further points out that Nixon also supported school desegregation and affirmative action programs, although this was more Machiavellian in intent, in that Nixon hoped to stimulate a white backlash which would be directed not at him or his party, but at the institutions and groups most associated with supporting the Black population—the federal government and white liberal "establishment"—which were in turn associated overwhelmingly with the Democratic Party.[58] In any event, these policies proved quite compatible with the saturation bombing of Cambodia and the targeted assassination of leading members of the Black Panthers. More to the point, however, Nixon was also responsible for mainstreaming what Jeremy Engels calls "the politics of resentment," which had been incubated by Barry Goldwater and George Wallace earlier in the 1960s:

> Nixon radically altered American definitions and practices of democracy by redefining the conflict at the heart of democracy. It was no longer the rich versus the poor or the few versus the many. Instead he divided "the people" into "the great silent majority" versus the tyrannizing minorities seeking to oppress it.[59]

The coexistence of welfare provision with imperial expansion and domestic repression can be traced back to the immediate postwar period. It is for this reason that notions of a postwar "compromise" or "deal" between labor and capital are deeply misleading, even if considered as metaphors.[60] In the most important case, the USA, the left was decisively defeated and the trade unions depoliticized for a generation. But the fundamental point about all reforms associated with the welfare state in Britain, the New Deal and Great Society programs in the USA, or their analogues elsewhere, is therefore that they were not just compatible with capitalism but organized in line with its requirements. And this is the case even where the reforms in question were originally demanded and subsequently defended by the labor movement. In a book published in 1957, the very heart of the postwar boom, Richard Hoggart wrote: "It is often said that there are no working-classes in England now, that a 'bloodless revolution' has taken place, which has so reduced social differences that already most of us inhabit an almost flat plain, the flat plain of the lower-middle- to middle-classes."[61] Hoggart did not in fact believe this, and the remainder of the book is an attempt to demonstrate the continuing existence of the working class. Writing nearly fifty years later, in a book which is consciously modeled on Hoggart's, Lynsey Hanley noted that "the revolution, it turned out, was bloodless because it never actually happened."[62] Edward Thompson made the point powerfully in relation to Britain as the Keynesian era was coming to an end:

> The reforms of 1945 were assimilated and re-ordered within the system of economic activities, and also within the characteristic concepts, of the capitalist process. This entailed a translation of socialist meanings into capitalist ones. Socialised pits and railways became "utilities" providing subsidised coal and transport to private industry. Private practice, private beds in hospital, private nursing-homes and private insurance impoverished the public health service. Equality of opportunity in education was, in part, transformed into an adaptive mechanism through which skilled labour was trained for private industry: the opportunity was not *for* the working class but for the scholarship boy to escape *from* this class. . . . In short, what was defeated was not each "reform" . . . but the very meaning of reform as an alternative logic to that of private enterprise, profit and the uncontrolled self-reproduction of money.[63]

In other words, as Hilde Nafstad and her colleagues write, "welfare states should not be understood simply as a protective reaction against modern capitalism, but as varieties of modern capitalism."[64] "The welfare state, I believe, began the destruction of the independent life of the British working class . . . making the populace a supplicant citizenry dependent on the state rather than themselves."[65] "The historical logic embedded in the great victory of civilized over barbaric capitalism corroded away precisely those social and political instincts responsible for the triumph in the first place."[66]

The other problem with Harvey's account is that it also endorses the Stalinist myth that the USSR and its satellites and imitators were "post-capitalist" societies, which consequently required an entirely new capitalist class ("economic elite") to be created after their demise. However, rather than view these societies as being fundamentally different from those of the West, as was endlessly declared in the Cold War propaganda of both sides, it is better to see them as existing on a continuum of state intervention, with two extremes, the USA and the USSR, at opposite ends of the scale. In Eastern Europe, the state itself assumed the role of a "collective capitalist." As Paul Mattick writes: "Arising at the same time as the mixed economy, the state-capitalist system may be regarded as Keynesianism in its most developed and consistent form."[67] Between the two extremes lay many states which combined elements of both, most in the post-colonial world, particularly those which were to be classified as the Newly Industrializing Countries. Nigel Harris noted that South Korean development "was as state capitalist as any East European economy and as Keynesian as any West European social democracy" and, although a major contributor to the growth of world trade, "as regards the role of the state," it was "as 'socialist' as most of the countries that applied that term to themselves."[68]

This raises the question of why the two camps were in such potentially lethal opposition if both were fundamentally capitalist, but the answer is less obscure than is sometimes supposed. Capitalist nation-states, after all, had been known to go to war with each other for reasons of geopolitical rivalry before the onset of the Cold War, notably in 1914 and 1939. Here, however, there was an additional reason. Mattick observed that the displacement of "the market system by the planned system" or the complete supersession of private capital by state capital, would be experienced by individual capitalists as "their death warrant," and would not be accepted by them without opposition or even, as he suggested, "civil war."[69] The same is also true on the other side, as any attempt to reintroduce private capital into wholly state capitalist economies would mean that some sections of the bureaucratic ruling class would lose their privileged positions in a situation of market competition—as many did after 1991, particularly in former East Germany, although in Russia perhaps as much as 80 percent still managed to transform themselves into private capitalists or managers.[70]

Like Harvey, Klein treats the postwar period as one hostile to capitalism.[71] For her, neoliberalism is the application of a doctrine, lovingly preserved by ideologues like Milton Friedman, for which capitalists have been awaiting their opportunity to apply since the introduction of the American New Deal or the creation of the European welfare states. Klein, therefore, sees neoliberalism as the manifestation of the inner logic of corporate capitalism (although perhaps not of capitalism itself) and "shock" as the means by which it can be realized. She quotes Friedman's statement that "only a crisis—actual or perceived—produces real change" and argues that neoliberalism is a "shock doctrine" that takes advantage of disaster (a "crisis") in order to impose the idea of the new market order.[72] As a result of this perspective, Klein has a tendency to treat every geopolitical event since 1973 as one either consciously undertaken or opportunistically manipulated to impose neoliberalism, a fixation which imbues neoliberal policies with a strategic coherence they never possessed in practice. For even if we accept that neoliberals have opportunistically intervened to take advantage of disaster situations in recent decades, why was it only at a certain stage in postwar history that crises were manipulated to produce these outcomes? Two examples will serve to illustrate the point.

One is from the core of the world system. At the end of the Second World War, it quickly became apparent that Britain had massive unresolved economic problems, the immediate expression of which were in a balance-of-payments deficit and declining reserves of sterling. These were not helped by a massive rearmament program, the costs of which began to erode the welfare state within a few years of it being initiated. When the Conservative Party was returned to office in 1951, some members of the new administration, led by the unlikely figure of Rab Butler, drafted a proposal ("Operation ROBOT") to simultaneously float the pound and make it convertible against other currencies, which would have immediately led to sterling falling in value against the dollar. The central intention here was to put an end to balance of payments difficulties that were already characteristic of the British economy. Exports would be given a massive boost, while at the same time imports would fall; domestic prices would be high, but wages would have to be held down to avoid inflationary pressures, not least by allowing unemployment to rise. In effect, the government would be forced to cut funding of the welfare state, especially the housing program, as well as its overseas military commitments. The plan was dropped, largely as a result of the nervousness of Churchill and his closest allies over the likely electoral consequences of a policy which was so redolent of those followed during the depression years of the 1930s.[73]

Historians have tended to treat this episode as a typical example of the consensual thinking which supposedly prevented deep-seated problems from being tackled before the election of Margaret Thatcher in 1979.[74] Neoliberal politicians who served in her cabinets, like Nigel Lawson, have similarly argued that many of the problems they were forced to deal with might have been avoided had a stand against interventionism been taken at this time.[75] The point, however, is that an experiment of this sort would have been, in capitalist terms, both destructive and unnecessary. Destructive, because it was contrary to the type of economic structures being put in place in the advanced capitalist West; most obviously, it would have destroyed the Bretton Woods agreement, the only components of which to have been put in place were precisely the fixed exchange rates that British actions would have undone. Unnecessary, because from the end of the Korean War in 1953 the British economy began to experience boom conditions, which meant that any attempt to limit trade union power or redefine the limits of the welfare state could be postponed. British capitalism did indeed have serious underlying problems, but in conditions of generalized expansion, very few members of the British ruling class felt it was necessary to take the course of action later initiated by the Thatcher governments. Those who did argue for proto-Thatcherite solutions in the 1950s, like Enoch Powell or Ralph Harris, were marginal to political and intellectual life and remained so until the 1970s.

The other example is from the Global South. The Indonesian coup of 1965 was a successful attempt by a section of the local ruling class, backed by the US and Britain, to destroy the power of the Communist Party and the left more generally, in what was at that point the most extreme use of counterrevolutionary violence since the Second World War. But neither internal nor external forces sought to impose what we would now call a neoliberal economic program on the country, even though this was the perfect opportunity to do so. Klein draws parallels between the group of Indonesian economists trained at the University of California, the so-called "Berkeley Mafia," who advised the military both before and after the coup, and the "Chicago Boys," who played a similar post-coup role for the Chilean Junta ten years later. She elides, however, the nature of the economic policies followed in the former case, which were quite different from the latter.[76] Indonesia under Suharto was regarded as a reliable ally of the West in the Cold War, but continued the strategy of state-led economic development initiated by the pre-coup regime. This was similar to those of the other Newly Industrializing Countries of East Asia, particularly Taiwan, Singapore, and South Korea, although it was accompanied with even greater levels of corruption. Indeed, so far was Indonesia from what became regarded as neoliberal

norms that the financial crisis of 1997 and the overthrow of Suharto the following year in a political revolution saw much comment on the necessity of
dispensing with so-called "crony capitalism." No less a neoliberal luminary
than Alan Greenspan described Suharto's Indonesia as being a "particularly
appalling" example of this "in the last third of the twentieth century"—in
other words, during the very period in which Suharto enjoyed US support
following the US-backed coup which brought him to power.[77]

Klein is of course right to say that, in the later case of Chile, it was only
in the aftermath of a violent seizure of power by the military that the neoliberal regime could have been put in place; but this was no more the motiva-
tion for the coup than it was in Indonesia. It was rather carried out to crush
the political aspirations of the working-class movement which had looked
to Allende and the Popular Unity government, and which by 1973 was beginning to organize on its own behalf. In fact, the generals initially had little
idea what economic policies to introduce and, in an earlier period, might
well have looked to the Catholic corporatist model introduced by Franco to
Spain after 1939—it had, after all, been followed more or less faithfully by
almost every previous Latin American dictatorship. As Karin Fischer points
out, "it took about two years before the neoliberal faction ascended to positions of authority, which enabled technocrats to advance their far-reaching
organizational program." Far from there being "a prior decision to establish
a new type of institutional order," as has been retrospectively assumed, "the
insurrection only determined that the future of the country would be decided by some combination of different forces represented in the junta."[78]
Something had happened to make neoliberal solutions necessary as well as
possible to implement. In retrospect, the arrival of the Chicago Boys to over-
see the implementation of Pinochet's program of privatization and deregulation has a wider significance, but initially it appeared to have no resonance
elsewhere and even subsequent coups to that in Chile did not immediately
adopt neoliberalism. Klein herself notes that the Argentinean dictatorship
which came to power in 1976 did not immediately follow its Chilean predecessor in privatizing social security or natural resources, which were only
achieved decades later by the successor civilian governments.[79] Indeed, as
far as Latin America is concerned, the general pattern of neoliberal implementation has been closer to that of Argentina than that of Chile.[80]

In other words, if Klein's thesis was correct, the policies we now associate with neoliberalism would have been introduced much earlier in the twentieth century than they in fact were. Instead, even the most ferociously counterrevolutionary regimes followed the dominant economic model of state intervention. In fact, the only area to even approximate to what would later become the neoliberal ideal was the British colony of Hong Kong, one of the Asian Tigers, but unlike Taiwan, Singapore, or South Korea, with minimal state intervention: no business regulation, no welfare provision, no (or flat-rate) taxation, and a steady supply of labor fleeing from repression in Maoist China.[81] It is certainly the case that, in the Global South, the military repression of regimes reflecting the reformist aspirations of the working class and the oppressed opened up opportunities for multinational corporations to play a greater role, but the latter have not themselves always pursued neoliberal policies, nor have they always demanded them from the states with which they have had to deal.

It is also true that major new capitalist organizations were established during this period to lobby governments for greater support, notably the Business Roundtable in the US, founded in 1972. These are often assimilated to ideological think tanks like the Mont Pelerin Society and the IEA.[82] But the CEOs of the Business Roundtable were not initially lobbying for what we now think of as neoliberal measures. Klein is wrong to say: "Friedman's vision coincided with the interests of the large multinationals, which by nature hunger for vast new unregulated markets."[83] Multinational corporations have wanted different policies at different times. As Richard Vinen recounts for postwar Europe:

> Economic policy did not spring from the imposition of state authority over industry but rather a convergence of the two. This convergence came partly from changes in the state: new departments were set up to deal with economic matters, and were often staffed by businessmen. The private sector also changed. Small companies run by an owner whose own capital was at risk might feel very alienated from the state. Large companies, however, were run by managers whose own capital was not at risk, and who could afford to take a relatively detached view of many issues.[84]

Hostility to the state was more general across the capitalist class as a whole in the US than anywhere else in the world, an attitude which David Vogel ascribed on the eve of the neoliberal era to a failure by American capitalists to understand not their individual business interests, but the collective interests of their class (hence their opposition to the New Deal); to the relative absence of the state in the initial process of industrial development; and to the sheer dominance of US capital: *"In this sense, an anti-state ideology is a luxury that can only be enjoyed by a relatively powerful and successful bourgeoisie."*[85] Even in the US, however, these suspicions of the state had largely been overcome by the 1960s, for similar reasons to those in Europe. "It may seem the height of grandiloquence to say so," opined business journalist Theodore Levitt in 1967, "but there is abundant evidence that the American business community has finally and with unexpected suddenness actively embraced the idea of the interventionist state."[86] The example of the Business Roundtable is a case in point. As Sidney Blumenthal writes:

> They want big government to be the marketing agency and brokerage firm to big business. The CEOs appreciate the methods of big government, when they serve their interest, because they seem so similar to those of big business. What they want from big government is faster service and preferential treatment. They believe government should be run like a subsidiary. So they think of reforming government, not eliminating it.[87]

Nor did this acceptance only extend to measures directly supportive of business. As late as 1975, one leading corporate chairman, Stanley Marcus of Neiman Marcus, thought it implausible that a significant number of his contemporaries would ever again oppose reformist social legislation:

> Who amongst the business community today would seriously propose that congress repeal our child-labor laws—or the Sherman Antitrust Act? The Federal Reserve Act, the Securities Exchange Act? Or workmen's compensation? Or Social Security? Or minimum wage? Or Medicare? Or civil rights legislation? All of us today recognize that such legislation is part of our system; that it has made us stronger.[88]

In many respects, the trajectory of the two openly right-wing governments which immediately preceded the neoliberal era, that of Heath in Britain (1970–74) and of Nixon in the US (1968–74) demonstrate how far even they were from introducing it.

There is a neoliberal myth, assiduously promulgated by Thatcher and her inner circle, which holds that the Heath government of 1970–74 had intended to introduce the radical policies later implemented by the Thatcher governments after 1979, but failed to do so because of its shameful and unnecessary retreat in the face of labor-movement resistance. In other words, neoliberalism could indeed have been introduced earlier than it actually was, if not for a failure of will on the part of those espousing it. As Anthony Seldon points out, this assessment is "ahistorical." In particular, it exaggerates the extent to which Heath had broken from traditional one-nation conservatism: "Heath was never a believer in Laissez-faire, but was a traditional Tory who saw the state as an essential deliverer of economic and social policy." Insofar as some positions of the government did indicate a serious move to the right, on tax and spending cuts, for example, "the motives for policies were instrumentalist and opportunistic, not ideology." From the point of the working class, this scarcely made Heath an attractive proposition, as the immense struggles during this period, above all against the Industrial Relations Act, bear testament. Seldon is right, however, to identify the absence of any of the preconditions for what was to follow:

> There was no alternative and acceptable philosophy available which would have provided the intellectual underpinning for an assault on the prevailing orthodoxy of Keynesianism. . . . [T]here was no popular intellectual and media backing for a full frontal assault on Keynesian consensus-type policies, even if he had wanted to do so. . . . Finally, and most tellingly, the three main architects of the Thatcher revolution were all present in the Heath Cabinet. . . . To criticise the Heath Government for failing to persist with new right policies during 1970–1974 when Thatcher, Joseph and to a lesser extent Howe were in key positions and failed to argue strongly for such policies, is a plain absurdity.[89]

Similar arguments could be made for the Republican Party in the US at the time of Nixon's election in 1968. Judith Stein comments that it is necessary to "distinguish social from economic liberalism":

Nixon and most of the nation concluded that growth had become self-generating. The consumer demand created by the economy, supplemented when necessary by deficit spending, would be sufficient incentive for industrial modernization. In 1969, as in the Democratic 1960s, there appeared to be no conflict between consumption and investment, labor and capital, equity and growth. Business did not need subsidies to produce, and government needed revenue to regulate and compensate. Thus Nixon was for tax reform, not reduction.

Nixon was scarcely unaware that the US had entered a social crisis by the late 1960s, however:

> The answer was not to contract out government functions to private institutions, but "to make government more effective." A young Donald Rumsfeld did just that with the poverty program. Rumsfeld called himself a "modern Republican," meaning one who accepted the mixed economy plus elements of the welfare state. It was not an accident that Nixon approved laws expanding Social Security and Medicare. He set up the Environmental Protection Agency (EPA) and signed the Occupational Safety and Health Administration (OSHA) Act, a Clean Air Act, and numerous other pieces of environmental legislation. All these reforms were evidence that liberal hegemony had not ended in 1968.[90]

Only in postwar West Germany did the ideas which began to be dominant in the mid-1970s have any serious influence beforehand. These were heavily promoted by the original neoliberals of the 1930s and led to the Federal Republic of Germany being virtually the only area of Europe where policies of deregulation, the abolition of wage and price controls, and of lowering taxes were introduced. Yet even this was only possible for two reasons. One was the way in which these constraints on private capital were associated with the Nazi regime.[91] The other was of longer standing: "The state played a limited role in Germany partly because industrialists had traditions of organization that allowed them to dispense with the discipline imposed by the state elsewhere [in Western Europe]."[92] By the late 1950s, however, West Germany had adopted the type of corporate interventionism that would through the 1980s be held to distinguish Rhenish capitalism from the neoliberal Anglo-Saxon variant, even while claiming to retain what was actually referred to as neoliberal economic policy.[93] Wolfgang Streeck recalls interviewing West German industrial managers of the postwar period who were nostalgic for the "allocation economy" which prevailed through most of the Great Boom: "I even heard managers suggest that the differences between the organized capitalism of the West and the state socialism of the East were not as dramatic as one might have believed at the time: only that delivery periods were even longer in the East."[94]

How not to explain neoliberalism (1): blaming the 1960s

Ironically, critics of neoliberalism have also claimed that the social liberalism of the 1960s gave rise to the cult of individual self-gratification which, in turn, is supposed to have contributed to the rise of empty consumerism.[95] This accusation was originally made from the left on the tenth anniversary of the French May by Regis Debray, for whom the events were functional for capitalism: "What first appeared as constraints on individual existence turned out to be constraints on turning the entire social field into commodities." In a supposed example of Hegel's Cunning of Reason, "the May revolutionaries were the entrepreneurs needed by the bourgeoisie." In a famous image, Debray describes the revolutionaries as being like Columbus: they set sail for China, only to make landfall in the Americas, in their case, California.[96]

> While the philosophy of the sixties seemed progressive at the time, it was really symbolised by the television picture from 1968 of a flower child in a flowing skirt, dancing in a circle and singing, "Down with police, down with income tax." It was the direct intellectual predecessor of the Thatcherite view that there is no such thing as society. The children of the sixties were the parents of Thatcherism.[97]

"Unglamorous, unhip Harold Wilson with pipe, Gannex, and compromises," writes Polly Toynbee, "emerges as the unlikely 60s hero," presiding with Home Secretary Roy Jenkins over the "abolition of capital punishment, divorce reform, abortion reform, an end to theater censorship, the Race Relations Act, the gay rights Sexual Offences Act, and the Equal Pay Act." Yet "out of all this revolution against 'the system' came a 'me' individualism that grew into neoliberalism. Early hippy ideals of Silicon Valley soon morphed into each-for-yourself, pay no taxes, screw all governments. Antiestablishment 'freedom' has many dark sides."[98]

> By emphasizing permissiveness, humor, and fun, the spirit of May was largely molded by the very thing whose damaging effects it denounced in politics. That was the paradox of the movement: it depended on euphoria of the consumer age. . . . May '68 gave only the impression of opposing the capitalist creation of needs. In reality it was the dynamic of capitalism that multiplies cravings for independence and the emergence of the hedonistic utopia, a cultural revolt demanding "everything right now."[99]

Howker and Malik have a similar position, although they trace the origins of what they call "individualism" back to the emergence of youth culture in the 1950s. Their clinching argument is that "in 1979 Margaret Thatcher received a 16 percent swing in support from young people aged 18–35—the baby boomers—significantly more than any other group, and they made up more than one third of the electorate." The reason for this group supporting Thatcher apparently was because she promised to reduce taxes, thus providing them with more disposable money to spend on the commodities through which they defined their personalities.[100] The point is now almost a cliché: "The middle-class campus radicals of the 1960s and 1970s imagined that they were dismantling capitalism; actually, they were themselves products of a consumerist society, and their narcissistic 'alternative' culture further stimulated consumer demand."[101]

> The counter-culture leant toward extreme libertarianism, "do your own thing" being the closest to a political manifesto it ever produced, and such libertarianism was an uneasy partner to any sort of socialism or social democracy. Ironically, in its demands for total freedom from policing, and for economic self-sufficiency, the counter culture had more in common than most would now care to admit with old traditions of right-wing American frontier individualism—a strain of individualism that now survives mostly among the militias of Montana who despise hippy morality as the root of America's decline.[102]

For these authors, such libertarianism led easily to support for Reaganism and Thatcherism a decade later, but their main inheritors are not the militia movement but the yuppies, whose representatives "were trying to smash the state, but this time it was the Welfare State."[103]

Eric Hobsbawm once argued that, during the sixties, the cultural libertarianism of the youthful revolt was not an accompaniment to the struggle against capitalism or even for political reform (the "big things"), but an alternative to it:

> But what if the "big things" were not the overthrow of capitalism, or even of some oppressive or corrupt political regimes, but precisely the destruction of traditional patterns of relations between people and personal behaviour *within existing society*? What if we were wrong in seeing the rebels of the 1960s as another phase or variant of the left? In that case it was not a botched attempt at one kind of revolution, but the effective ratification of another: the one that abolished traditional politics, and in the end, the politics of the traditional left, the slogan, "the personal is political."[104]

In more general terms, Hobsbawm referred to the "unlimited autonomy of individual desire" and "a world of self-regarding individualism pushed to the limit":

> Paradoxically the rebels against the conventions and restrictions shared the assumptions on which mass consumer society was built, or at least the psychological motivations which those who sold consumer goods and services found most effective in selling them. The world was now tacitly assumed to consist of several billion human beings defined by their pursuit of individual desire, including desires hitherto prohibited or frowned upon, but now permitted—not because they had now become morally acceptable but because so many egos had them.[105]

As Tony Judt writes, "the individualism of the new Left had respected neither collective purpose nor traditional authority. ... What remained to it was the subjectivism of private—and privately measured—interest and desire."[106]

The attacks on social democracy by the 1960s generation that benefited from it most—as statist, or even "totalitarian"—now seem hysterical, devoid of any real sense of historical perspective. For them, the "welfare state" was normal, familiar, and rather boring, a perspective it is hard not to find outright offensive today. Their politics were based on the assumption that affluence, social peace, and equality were permanent rather than the brief historical aberration that they were.[107]

"The very success of the mixed-economy welfare states—in providing the social stability and ideological demobilization which made possible the prosperity of the past half-century—has led a younger generation to take that same stability and ideological quiescence for granted and demand the elimination of the 'impediment' of the taxing, regulating, and generally interfering state."[108]

> The paradox of the welfare state, and indeed of all the social democratic (and Christian Democratic) states of Europe, was quite simply that their success would over time undermine their appeal. The generation that remembered the 1930s was understandably the most committed to preserving institutions and systems of taxation, social service, and public provision that they saw as bulwarks against a return to the horrors of the past. But their successors— even in Sweden—began to forget why they had sought such security in the first place.[109]

Recent memoirs of the sixties by those who participated in the sexual experimentation and consciousness-raising of the time contain self-criticisms of their inability to distinguish between liberation and libertarianism, a distinction which only became apparent as countercultural slogans about collective freedom were recycled in defense of the individual acquisitiveness and instant gratification characteristic of neoliberalism.[110] In some cases, this was not a distortion of, but an extrapolation from what was already present in aspects of the counterculture. As Charles Shaar Murray notes:

> The line from hippie to yuppie is not nearly so convoluted as people like to believe and a lot of old hippie rhetoric could well be co-opted now by the pseudo-libertarian Right—which has in fact happened. Get the government off our backs, let individuals do what they want—that translates very smoothly into laissez-faire yuppyism, and that's the legacy of the era.[111]

Murray is thinking here of the subsequent career of Richard Neville, although that of Richard Branson would illustrate the point equally well. Arthur Marwick writes that "most of the movements, subcultures, and new institutions which are at the heart of sixties change were thoroughly imbued with the entrepreneurial, profit-making ethic," by which he means "boutiques, experimental theatres, art galleries, discotheques, nightclubs, 'light shows,' 'head shops,' photographic and model agencies, underground films [and] pornographic magazines."[112]

> The sixties was a time of entrepreneurialism and private enterprise, a time of the creation and satisfaction of new consumer needs, a time of expansion in the service and entertainment industries. Such developments anticipated aspects of Thatcherism (an international phenomenon), rather than being antithetical to them. More critically, those elements of sixties lifestyles which Reagan and Thatcher detested continued to be present during the seventies and were very evident throughout the eighties.[113]

"The 1960s were an exciting decade that I watched on television," wrote J. G. Ballard, one of the great surrealists of twentieth-century British literature.[114] Tom Wolfe called the 1970s the "Me Decade," a third "great awakening" after the first two religious movements of the eighteenth and nineteenth centuries: "Whatever the Third Great Awakening amounts to, for better or worse, will have to do with this unprecedented post–World War II American luxury: the luxury of so many millions of middling folk, of dwelling upon the self."[115] As Ian MacDonald noted, "The individualism of the Me Decade, as Tom Wolfe dubbed the Seventies, was a creation of the Sixties' mass mainstream, not of the peripheral groups which challenged it." Nor is this the only paradox; in his view the hostility of vanguard neoliberalism to the Sixties is quite undeserved:

> The irony of modern right-wing antipathy to the Sixties is that this much-misunderstood decade was, in all but the most superficial senses, the creation of the very people who voted for Thatcher and Reagan in the Eighties. It is, to put it mildly, curious to hear the Thatcherites condemn a decade in which ordinary folk for the first time aspired to individual self-determination and a life of material

security within an economy of high unemployment and low inflation. The social fragmentation of the Nineties which rightly alarms
conservatives was created neither by the hippies (who wanted us to
be "together") nor by the New Left radicals (all of whom were socialists of some description). So far as anything in the Sixties can be
blamed for the demise of compound entity of society it was the natural desire of the "masses" to lead easier, pleasanter lives, own their
own homes, follow their own fancies and, as far as possible, move
out of the communal collective completely. The truth is that, once
the obsolete Christian compact of the Fifties had broken down,
there was nothing—apart from, in the last resort, money—holding Western civilization together. Indeed the very labour-saving
domestic appliances launched onto the market by the Sixties' consumer boom speeded the melt-down of communality by allowing
people to function in a private world, segregated from each other
by TVs, telephones, hi-fi systems, washing-machines, and home
cookers. . . . What mass society unconsciously began in the sixties,
Thatcher and Reagan raised to the level of ideology in the Eighties:
the complete materialistic individualisation—and total fragmentation—of Western society.[116]

The US rock critic Richard Goldstein remembers at least part of the
crowd at the Monterey Festival in 1967 as "members of a new aristocracy,
courtly and enlightened" and notes "the perfect lack of edge, the casual in-
sularity, that these people displayed":

I was witnessing the birth of a new class pretending to be classless,
and it was imperial to the core. The descendants of this bangled illu-
minati now dine on free-range meat and artisanal cheese. They col-
onize neighborhoods, driving out the poor and turning slums into
Potemkin works of art. You know these hipsters by the tilt of their
fedoras, but their ancestors flashed peace signs.[117]

Mark Lilla describes contemporary young Americans at the turn of
twenty-first century, "holding down day jobs in the unfettered global economy while spending weekends immersed in a moral and cultural universe
shaped by the sixties."[118]

Corporatism, according to David Graeber, was also subject to this critique:

> From the perspective of sixties radicals, who regularly watched anti-war demonstrations attacked by nationalist teamsters and construction workers, the reactionary implications of corporatism appeared self-evident. The corporate suits and the well-paid, Archie Bunker elements of the industrial proletariat were clearly on the same side. Unsurprising then that the left-wing critique of bureaucracy at the time focused on the ways that social democracy had more in common with fascism than its proponents cared to admit. Unsurprising too, that this criticism seems utterly irrelevant today.[119]

As Ron Jacobs writes:

> The two personas of the counterculture could be generally classified as the political and spiritual elements. In part because it did not challenge the status quo politically, the latter was able to mutate and survive. It was also co-opted. The political elements disintegrated partially because the nature of the counterculture could not sustain a Marxist analysis and also most political organizations that organized among the youth became considerably more doctrinaire in their analyses beginning in late 1968, choosing already defined theories to analyze the situation and trying to force the moment to fit those theories. This was only possible to a certain degree, no matter how creative one's attempts. Of course, the vast majority of youth remained in the 1970s, like their predecessors in the 1960s, pretty apathetic about politics of any kind. Also, they were seeing themselves less and less as part of a counter-culture and conversely also seeing the counter-culture as just another form of consumerism. This trend continued as the 1970s wore on and the most consciously oppositional elements of the counter-culture diminished in numbers and influence.[120]

According to David Hepworth:

> 1971 was the year the loose alliance of groups and individuals who had rallied under the banner of the alternative society de-merged into different factions, ranging from people who wished to bring

about the violent overthrow of the state through those who considered themselves in permanent opposition of bourgeois values to
those who simply wanted the right to pursue their lives free from
post-war strictures.[121]

Selina Todd writes about one London feminist group which met in the
flat of Judy Walker, a working-class activist. She notes that it "was one in
which working-class and middle-class women were able to find common
ground for campaigning":

> But the relationship between class and feminism was never without
> tension. Many working-class women disagreed with middle-class
> feminists' belief that male behaviour was primarily to blame for wom-
> en's exploitation. . . . Other women felt that feminism didn't deal with
> the underlying injustices that shaped working-class women's lives.

Walker herself did cleaning work for several members of the group
when she was short of money. Todd comments: "As the end of the 1970s
approached, some middle-class women's fight for liberation continued to be
eased by the labour of less privileged women."[122]

> [Michel-Antoine Burnier] developed this attack on the Marxist
> conception of revolution by means of a magazine called *Actuel*,
> launched in 1970 with an American flavour and at the cutting edge
> of cultural happenings: . . . "We said to ourselves that we had to un-
> dertake a revolution in spirit, which was present in 1968 but which
> had been stifled by Trotskyism, Maoism, the October Revolution,
> the Paris Commune, which was all terribly archaic. The real message
> was that everybody can speak to each other, it's a free democracy,
> at last people can have sex. . . . We secretly said to ourselves, "this
> paper will be a machine to kill off the *groupuscules*, the little political
> factions, we will get them through the revolution in spirit, sexual
> liberation, music and happenings," and we got them. We killed the
> revolution . . . . I was very happy with the ways things turned out.[123]

As David Hare writes:

> Critics, both of left and right, like to look back on the social revo-
> lutions of the 1960s and claim that such revolutions were nothing

more than surface changes in lifestyle. What, they ask, did a more progressive approach to personal morality, to music, to dress and to youth actually achieve? I knew the answer, because I had experienced at first hand the price of life in a repressed and moralising suburbia. If lifestyle could kill, why on earth was it not worthwhile to change it?[124]

As Stephen Eric Bronner notes, "it simply never occurred to many that radical cultural tastes need not imply radical politics or vice versa. . . . In this way, the principle problem arose with conflating cultural and political radicalism."[125]

"Of the many potent myths associated with the sixties, the most wrongheaded is a widespread tendency to equate and conflate the decade's youth culture with its left-wing counterculture," writes Susan Jacoby:

> The youth culture derived its immense power precisely from its capacity to transcend social and ideological boundaries that Americans had long taken for granted, and that transcendence was made possible by a huge young demographic and a completely apolitical marketing machine eager to meet every desire of those under the magical mark of thirty.[126]

For Jacoby:

> The year 1969 represented the last moment when the "cultural revolution," as distinct from the other strands of political struggle, might have crystallised as an autonomous cultural force. The precipitation did not occur. Had it *coincided* with the forms of struggle to come, in the 1970s, its subsumption into a wider trajectory might have had revolutionary consequences. It did not. The history of radical politics in this period is the history of missed conjunctures.[127]

As Guy Standing says, "the tirade against the previous generation presents a false picture; it neglects class":

> Many in the older generation suffered the ravages of de-industrialisation, as miners, steelworkers, dock workers, printers and so on were shunted into history. And most women had the added burden

of economic marginality. The inter-generational interpretation could almost be a diversionary tactic, since it accords with a conservative view that carefully leaves out the role of globalisation.[128]

One of the most celebrated figures of the decade–John Lennon himself–provided a more acute class analysis. In an interview with *Rolling Stone* he noted that "[t]he people who are in control and in power and the class system and the whole bullshit bourgeois scene is exactly the same except that there is a lot of middle class kids with long hair walking around London in trendy clothes and Kenneth Tynan's making a fortune out of the word "fuck." But apart from that, nothing happened except that we all dressed up. The same bastards are in control, the same people are runnin' everything, it's exactly the same. They hyped the kids and the generation. We've grown up a little, all of us, and there has been a change and we are a bit freer and all that, but it's the same game, nothing's really changed. They're still doing the same things, selling arms to South Africa, killing blacks on the street, people are living in fucking poverty with rats crawling over them, it's the same. It just makes you want to puke. And I woke up to that, too. The dream is over. It's just the same only I'm thirty and a lot of people have got long hair, that's all."[129]

David Hare writes of going, late in 1974, to the Broome Street Bar in the SoHo district of New York, for the first time since 1965, and noting that the clientele "had moved from hippy to yuppie without passing through action":

> In such bars, the talk had once been of civil rights, of Vietnam and of revolution. These days, to judge from what I was overhearing, it seemed to be exclusively about yourself. . . . At no time did anyone in the bar seem to discuss anything which was happening in the non-relationship world. . . . The point was no longer to make the finest possible society. It was to gild the finest possible cage.[130]

As the music critic Greil Marcus wrote in the mid-1970s over the failures of the previous decade, "dreams can be imprisoned inside those who once held them":

> Those dreams are worn down and dissolved as the world mocks them by its own versions of reality; they are dissolved because the

one who once felt alive because of them must live in that world. He or she does not conform to it, necessarily, but adjusts to it in a hundred ways every day: with every thought he turns away from, with every word she does not speak, with every fantasy of violence, liberation or death that fades into the nightly dreams one does not understand and does not want to.

And, in an especially prescient passage, Marcus imagines the type of culture which this retreat will produce: "Within such a culture there are many choices: cynicism, which is a smug, fraudulent sort of pessimism; the sort of camp sensibility that puts all feeling at a distance; or culture that reassures, counterfeits excitement and adventure, and is safe."[131] In his 1976 song "The Pretender," Jackson Browne captured something of the tragedy involved in these individual acts of capitulation. "I want to know what became of the changes we waited for love to bring," his character asks. "Were they only the fitful dreams of some greater awakening?" He then recounts the world into which the sleepers have awakened, dominated by the routines of work, for which the only consolations are consumption and empty sex, before concluding:

> I'm going to be a happy idiot
> And struggle for the legal tender
> Where ads take aim and lay their claim
> To the heart and the soul of the spender
> And believe in whatever may lie
> In those things that money can buy
> Though true love could have been a contender
> Are you there?
> Say a prayer for the pretender
> Who started out so young and strong
> Only to surrender[132]

The former Black Panther turned musician and producer Nile Rodgers wrote of the New York disco scene in the late 1970s:

A new way of living, with a new kind of activism, had emerged, and my new crew... embodied it. As founding members of this fledgling counterculture lifestyle, we held our meetings and demonstrations on the dance floor.... All revolutionary movements are fueled by a desire for change to an unsustainable status quo. This revolution's warriors were engaged in a battle for recognition. "Sex, drugs, and disco" was the new battle cry. The underground, now ethnic and more empowered than ever before, was becoming mainstream.[133]

In Jeremy Gilbert's words: "It's surely no accident that *Thriller* becomes the most successful album of all time at precisely the historical moment when the Left is on the brink of its greatest defeat. Somehow that album and its success constitute both a moment of massive collective desire, and of that desire's full capture by the individualized, commodified logic of post-Fordist consumer capitalism."[134]

In most cases, however, it might be fairer to say that the failure of the revolutionary aspirations of May led to many demands for liberation being satisfied only in capitalist forms, through the consumption of commodities. Dominique Lecourt has written that the fate of the movements of 1968 "represents a major recuperation, in which such original forms of struggle as the women's movement, the ecological movement, and the gay movement are pressed into the service of an apologia for the underlying kernel of the dominant bourgeois ideology against which these struggles are engaged." This outcome was not inevitable, but understanding it involves, as Lecourt points out, "the limits which these struggles continue to come up against, and which for the most part relate to the inability of the worker's movement to date to reappropriate their positive content."[135] It is of course true that, in the absence of an overall victory, capital will always find ways of making partial achievements for social liberation compatible with, or indeed into examples of, commodified relations. The cliché that the left "won" in terms of the social and the cultural while it "lost" in terms of the political and the economic—indeed the idea that such a division is possible under a system as totalizing as capitalism—is a kind of wishful thinking typical of economically secure ex-radicals who can now openly engage in "lifestyle choices" impossible before the sixties.[136]

How not to explain neoliberalism (2):
the power of free-market ideas

The first false assumption about neoliberalism is to imply that politicians became convinced of the correctness of neoclassical ideas, which are assumed
to be congruent with the interests of multinational capital. Interestingly,
the standard-bearers of both social democratic and neoliberal economics
both emphasized the overwhelming importance of ideas. "I am sure that the
power of vested interests is vastly exaggerated compared with the gradual
encroachment of ideas," wrote Keynes, "soon or late, it is ideas, not vested interests, which are dangerous for good or evil."[137] While Hayek declared: "If
in the long run we are the makers of our own fate, in the short run we are the
captives of the ideas we have created."[138] The transmission belts by which the
neoclassical tradition gradually returned to a position of intellectual dominance were the free-market think tanks.[139] "Although the role of national
institutions is indispensable in explaining the advance (or retardation) of
specific doctrines across countries," writes Philip Mirowski, "the origins
and the advance of neoliberalism cannot be explained without careful consideration of the transnational discourse community created by the found-
ers of the Mont Pelerin Society."[140] The lineage has been traced most directly
by Neal Lawson: "Without von Mises there would have been no von Hayek,
without von Hayek no Fisher, without Fisher no IEA and without the IEA
no Joseph or Thatcher. And without Thatcher, no turbo-consumerism."[141]

In 1974, *The Economist*, at that time still advocating a more-or-less Keynesian approach, accused Sir Keith Joseph of being a "follower" of Friedman. Joseph responded by saying "the evolution of my views owes little to him":

> On the contrary, it stems primarily ... from critical re-examination
> of local orthodoxies in the light of our own bitter experience in the
> early 1970s. . . . By early this year [1974], we had a historically high
> rate of inflation, an enfeebled economy, the worst relations with
> the trade union movement in decades, and a lost election with the
> greatest fall in our share of the vote since 1929. Surely this was suffi-
> cient incentive to rethink—we are practical people who judge ideas
> and policies by results.[142]

Ten years later, another of Margaret Thatcher's intellectual mentors,

Alfred Sherman, wrote a piece for *The Guardian* which similarly emphasized how crisis conditions encouraged a greater receptivity to the ideas of
what was then called the New Right: "Ideas from Hayek and Friedman . . .
were assimilated precisely because experience had already created a place
for them by convincing people that neo-Keynesian economics, trade-union
hegemony and the permissive society had failed."[143]

More recently, Norman Lamont recalled in an interview with Daniel Stedman Jones: "You know, if one's being honest, all this happened gradually.
All credit to Mrs. Thatcher but it is quite, sort of, self-deceiving if people like
myself pretend that we saw how all this would happen. We didn't."[144]

The shifts did not of course begin with the election of Thatcher or Reagan. Stuart Hall rightly noted that neoliberalism (or the "Thatcherite project" as he was calling it at this point) did not begin in 1979 but in 1975, with
the adoption of proto-neoliberal policies by the governing Labour Party. Yet
how does Hall explain how this came about? It is through the influence of
neoliberal ideas on the then prime minister, James Callaghan:

> One of the siren voices, singing the new song in his ear, is his son-
> in-law, Peter Jay, one of the architects of monetarism, in his mis-
> sionary role as economic editor at *The Times*. He first saw the new
> market forces, the new sovereign consumer, coming over the hill
> like the marines. And, harkening to these intimations of the future,
> the old man opens his mouth; and what does he say? . . . Social de-
> mocracy is finished.[145]

But as Michael Howard and John King write, a historical materialist explanation for neoliberalism involves "multiple causes," and these "form a hierarchy of importance" in which "the weakest explanations of neoliberalism
are those concentrating on the role of ideas." The reason for this is quite simply because there is one common feature uniting all the intellectual progen-
itors of neoliberalism: "they were all wrong."[146] By this they mean that the
writers concerned did not foresee the triumph of neoliberalism, but rather
that of the state. This does not seem to me to be an entirely adequate argument since the whole point made by supporters of the ideological basis of
neoliberalism claim that the warnings and alternatives of the proto-neoliberals were precisely what laid the basis for its ultimate success. More to the

point is the argument that actually existing neoliberalism is not the system which was imagined by Hayek or Friedman. William Davies writes:

> What Stigler, Friedman, Director and their colleagues really admired was not the market as such, but the competitive psychology that was manifest in the entrepreneurs and corporations which sought to vanquish their rivals. They didn't want the market to be a place of fairness, where everyone had an equal chance; they wanted it to be a space for victors to achieve ever-greater glory and exploit the spoils. . . . Chicago-style competition wasn't about co-existing with rivals, it was about destroying them. Inequality was not some mortal injustice, but an accurate representation of differences in desire and power.[147]

Here is Friedman, recalling his address to the fiftieth anniversary meeting of the Mont Pelerin Society in 1997:

> To judge from the climate of opinion, we have won the battle of ideas. Everyone—left or right—talks about the virtues of markets, private property, competition, and limited government. No doubt the Mont Pelerin Society and its many associates around the world deserve some credit for that change in the climate of opinion, but it derives much more from the sheer force of reality: the fall of the Berlin Wall; the tremendous success of the Far Eastern Tigers— Hong King, Taiwan, Singapore, and Korea—and, more recently, Chile. However, I went on, appearances are deceptive. In the realm of practice, our economies are less free than they were when the Society was founded. . . . We have gained on the level of rhetoric, lost on the level of practice.[148]

There is certainly a discrepancy between neoliberal theory and practice; but let us concede that some of these ideas were eventually adopted, in however modulated a form. In a detailed study of the influence of Australian neoliberal think tanks over the 1996–2007 Howard government, Damien Cahill concluded that they mainly "furnished the Howard government and its sympathisers with discursive frames for legitimising neoliberal policy agendas and delegitimising opponents."[149] In other words, rather than inspiring policy positions, they gave ideological support to those which the government were already intent on adopting. "But one gets the sense that they are taking this ideological *doxa* a little too seriously, getting too intimate with its assumptions and thus missing the protean miscarriages and false starts that animate neo-capitalist governance structures." Indeed, as Peter Fleming notes, "neoliberal apologists . . . probably relish the idea of left-wing debunkers spending years reading Hayek."[150]

But to the extent that capitalists, state managers, and politicians did become predisposed to listen to neoliberal arguments in the 1970s, why did they do so at that point in time when they had not done so for the previous thirty years? The dominant explanation of the emergence of neoliberalism involves a narrative which can be summarized as follows. Throughout the Great Boom, the multinational corporations were unable to impose their program because of what J. K. Galbraith termed the "countervailing power" of labor movements and reformist governments.[151] When the opportunity to achieve their real aims eventually presented itself, however, the former restraints on corporate activity were quickly overcome. The conditions for the business agenda to be advanced in such an uncompromising way were established with the acceptance of recharged neoclassical doctrines by politicians and state managers who had previously rejected them. What led to this change of mind?

The long-term effects of capitalist globalization

During the period of unparalleled growth associated with the Great Boom, three developments took place in the world economy which established the framework for what followed by rendering obsolete the largely national assumptions within which economic policy had been conducted since the Great Crash of 1929. The first was the unprecedented threefold expansion of international trade, growing twice as fast as actual output across the period, with the biggest increase taking place in the decade immediately prior to the crash of 1973–74. But as the economies of the major states became more dependent on imports and exports than internal transactions, the relative differences between production costs across borders became far more significant than when the bulk of trade had been territorially self-contained.

The second development was the advent of cross-border production, utilizing world forces of production rather than only those of one territorial state—a process driven, above all, by the need to achieve economies of scale which were only possible within a multinational market. We need to be careful of exaggerating the impact of this change: the spread of production across several states, and the consequent partial detachment from the control of any one, tended to be a regional rather than a truly global phenomenon, and it remained more difficult for capital to simply close production in one area and move it to another than multinational corporations would have workforces and governments believe. Nevertheless it did strengthen the position of multinational corporations and weaken that of states in relation to each other.

The third development was another example of internationalization, but in this case of finance rather than production. It had two aspects. One was the increase in large-scale foreign direct investment (FDI). The scale of FDI in particular needs to be understood: it grew twice as fast as goods and services in the 1960s, four times as fast in the 1980s, while in the 1990s: "FDI soared by 314 per cent, utterly eclipsing the 65 per cent increase in world trade and the 40 per cent increase in world gross domestic product."[152] The other aspect was the creation of "offshore" banking and flows of money capital unlimited by national boundaries: unlike factories, money can be moved with ease and is not dependent on protection of a territorial state or states. More than any other development, this made government policies vulnerable to attack when they were seen to be acting against the interest of capital.

None of these developments rendered states completely powerless in the face of markets—that is the myth of globalization assiduously cultivated by politicians seeking to evade responsibility for their actions. As Jacques Rancière notes: "The same states that surrender their privileges to the exigencies of freely circulating capital discover them straight away in order to close their borders to the freely circulating poor in search of work."[153] Neoliberalism represented a choice, but it was a choice increasingly difficult to avoid so long as the goal was the preservation and expansion of capitalism at all costs. When Nixon devalued the US dollar and detached it from the gold standard in August 1971, this first of all neoliberal policy decision was therefore, as Morris Berman points out, "the *result* of globalization," of the cumulative changes brought about by the resumption of the internationalization of capital after 1945.[154]

The point is of some importance, since it is widely accepted on the left that neoliberalism and globalization are synonymous. The confusion here is understandable. Neoconservatives chose their own name and are consequently willing to be described as such; neoliberals had their name fixed on them by opponents and are consequently reluctant to embrace it, preferring instead to present themselves simply as supporters of globalization, an apparently benign process unfairly associated with a nonexistent ideology by an unscrupulous left. It is indicative that one of the very few commentators to have claimed the label "neoliberal" is the arch-buffoon Thomas Friedman, here advising the US presidential candidates in 2003: "You win the presidency by connecting with the American people's gut insecurities and aspirations. You win with a concept. The concept I'd argue for is 'neoliberalism.'"[155] Virtually the only person with any credibility I can identify who has used it in a positive sense is Peter Oborne. Reviewing David Whyte's edited collection on the extent of corruption in Britain, Oborne writes that while "Whyte is correct to argue that [his] examples point to a contemporary malaise . . . it is by no means clear that the problems he identifies are linked to neoliberalism." Whyte quite correctly notes, for example, that "police corruption dates well before the neoliberal revolution."[156] More typical are the comments of Financial Times journalist Martin Wolf, who complains: "With prefixes 'neo-liberal' or 'corporate,' globalization is condemned as a malign force that impoverishes the masses, destroys cultures, undermines democracy, imposes Americanization, lays waste the welfare state, ruins the environment and enthrones greed."[157] The term "globalization" began to be used by pro-marketeers like Wolf in the early 1990s, just as neoliberalism was identified as the currently dominant form of capitalist organization by the radical left.[158] The temptation, to which many socialists have succumbed, is therefore to treat globalization merely as a neutral-sounding disguise behind which lie the dogmas of market fundamentalism.[159] In fact, globalization was implicit in human social development from the moment trade, migration, and conquest led different societies to experience exchange, interpenetration, or assimilation.

As Marx and Engels noted in 1848, rather earlier than anyone else, capitalism greatly increased the speed and extent of these processes.[160] The demands for an "alternative globalization" or "globalization from below" make clear, however, that the character of globalization need not be forever determined by capitalism. Indeed, it is not wholly determined by capitalism even now. As Robert Holton explains, globalization has three aspects. First: "The intensified movement of goods, money, technology, information, people, ideas and cultural practices across political and cultural boundaries." Second: "The inter-dependence of social processes across the globe, such that all social activity is profoundly interconnected rather than separated off into different national and cultural spaces." Third: "Consciousness of and identification with the world as a single place, as in forms of cosmopolitanism, religion or earth-focussed environmentalism."[161] The establishment of a genuine socialist society would bring to fruition the most positive aspects of globalization, not least the dismantling of borders for the benefit of people rather than the movement of money or commodities. Globalization can take, and currently has taken, a capitalist form, and capitalism can take, and currently has taken, a neoliberal form; but neither process was or is inevitable. Leslie Sklair, for example, argues that "generic globalisation" has four main dimensions: new electronic communications media, post-colonialism, transnational social spaces, and cosmopolitanism. Although these are currently deployed in ways which embody "capitalist globalization," they can also play a critical function which points towards an alternative "socialist globalization."[162] Insofar as there is a relationship between capitalist globalization and neoliberalism, it was that the former set the conditions for the latter: a highly internationalized economy which had now returned to crisis conditions.

During the Great Boom there was general support for state intervention among the larger businesses and corporations, while small business retained their traditional hostility to it. These differences expressed the relative security of their positions within the market: corporations were protected from the worst exigencies of price competition and were able to plan for longer-term investment growth, often in alliance with the state; small businesses were much more vulnerable and, to them, the state simply represented a source of predatory taxation and bureaucratic regulation. Increased global competition changed the relative position of the corporations, so that all but the largest transnational corporations were placed in a similar position to the small businesses of the postwar period, in terms of their relative size within the market: "The process of globalisation has sharply increased the degree of competitive pressure faced by large corporations and banks, as competition has become a worldwide relationship." Corporations still needed a home state to act as a base, but they increasingly required it to behave differently. Neoliberal globalization "pushes them towards support for any means to reduce their tax burden and lift regulatory constraints, to free them to compete more effectively with their global rivals."[163] Corporations therefore began to demand some of the policies long advocated by Hayek and Friedman, and politicians and state managers began to implement them, not as Klein claims because individual opportunities to do so which previously had been missing finally presented themselves, but because changed conditions of accumulation required changed strategies. Given the limited number of these available (assuming them to be in interests of capital), it is unsurprising that the new practices now demanded began to overlap with existing theories.

Wolfgang Streeck notes that a legitimation crisis does not simply involve two players, namely the state and the population over which it rules, but three: the state, the working class, and capital, represented by "profit-dependent owners and managers.... Contrary to neo-Marxist theories, a legitimation crisis may therefore grow out of discontent on the part of 'capital' with democracy and its associated obligations."[164]

The short-term effects of capitalist crisis

The second, more dramatic development was the resumption of economic crisis in 1973/4. "It was not a global crisis, as is often asserted, for East Asia was actually booming—and so were the oil producers."[165] As Ashley Lavelle writes, globalization is a "proximate" explanation for the rise of neoliberalism, the end of the postwar boom an "ultimate" one:

> Thus, the rapprochement [of social democracy] with neo-liberalism is best understood as a response to changed economic conditions, which in turn shaped the ideological and political climates to put pressures on governments to open up their economies to cross-border flows of investment and trade, in the process creating the "globalisation" many mistakenly credit with undermining traditional social democratic politics.[166]

The precise causes of the return to crisis after 1973 have been widely debated, but some key features are highlighted by most analysts. Increased price competition from West Germany and Japan within the advanced world was made possible by intensive investment in technology and relatively low wages. This forced their hitherto dominant rivals—above all the USA—to lower their own prices in a situation where production costs remained unchanged. American corporations were initially prepared to accept a reduced rate of profit in order to maintain market share but, ultimately, they too undertook a round of new investments, thus raising the capital-labor ratio and increasing the organic composition of capital, leading to consequent further pressure on the rate of profit.[167] As Al Campbell writes, neoliberalism was therefore a solution to "a structural crisis of capitalism" in which "policies, practices and institutions" which had hitherto served capital accumulation no longer did so: "More narrowly, one can say that capitalism abandoned the Keynesian compromise in the face of a falling rate of profit, under the belief that neoliberalism could improve its profit rate and accumulation performance."[168] But, as I have suggested above, the inadequacy of Keynesian policies was itself the result of changes to the nature of the world economy that had taken place during the long boom, and which made these policies increasingly difficult to apply with any possibility of success.

The emergence of neoliberalism as a conscious ruling class strategy, rather than an esoteric ideological doctrine, therefore took place in response to the end of the postwar boom, but in changed conditions created by that boom. The failure of Keynesianism and other forms of state capitalism predisposed many capitalists, state managers, and politicians not just to accept, but to wholeheartedly embrace theories which they would earlier have rejected as eccentric, or even dangerously destabilizing; but even then, the policy shifts which followed were as often pragmatic adaptations as they were born of ideological conviction. Robert Reich is therefore right to argue that existing neoclassical theories "offered a convenient justification for the shift already under way. . . . They did not cause the shift; at most, they legitimised it."[169] Because of this, the more credible advocates of capitalist globalization, like Martin Wolf, have been able to emphasize the way in which neoliberalism (although he refuses the term) has been an adjustment to capitalist reality rather than an adoption of theoretical dogma: "To many critics, the last two decades of the twentieth century were the age of a manic 'neo-liberalism' imposed by ideological fanatics on a reluctant world. This picture is false. The change in politics was, with very few exceptions, introduced by pragmatic politicians in response to experience."[170]

Wolf wants to defend the neoliberal order, without conceding the term; but the essential point is correct. As Andrew Gamble writes, neoliberalism as "a global ideology" was less significant than "the competitive pressures of capital accumulation in forcing the convergence of all capitalist models and all national economies towards neo-liberal institutions and policies."[171] But the theories did have a function. As G. A. Cohen wrote:

> Considered as practical proposals, the theories of Friedman, Hayek and Nozick were crazy, crazy in the strict sense that you would have to be crazy to think that such proposals (e.g., abolition of *all* regulation of professional standards and of safety at work, abolition of state money, abolition of *all* welfare provision) might be implemented in the near, medium, or long term. The theories are in that sense crazy precisely because they are uncompromisingly fundamental: they were not devised with one eye on electoral possibility. And, just for that reason, their serviceability in electoral and other political contests is very great. *Politicians and activists can press not-so-crazy right-wing proposals with conviction because they have the strength of conviction that depends upon depth of conviction, and depth comes from theory that is too fundamental to be practicable in a direct sense.*[172]

In public pronouncements, neoliberals initially tended to focus less on restoring profitability and more on reducing the amount of state expenditure and the size of the state itself (although usually treated as synonymous these are of course very different goals) and controlling inflation, since these could be presented as beneficial to citizens as taxpayers and consumers. But regardless of the way in which neoliberal goals were expressed, the major obstacle to the reorganization of capital required by the crisis lay elsewhere. The Argentinean military junta of the 1970s had originally regarded their main opponent as the Peronist movement, but as one member later admitted, "by 1976 we already knew that the problem was the working class."[173] I have already argued that the imminent threat of revolution was no longer a threat by the mid-1970s, so in what sense was the working class "the problem"?

In 1972, when the crisis was gathering but had not yet broken, Andrew Glyn and Bob Sutcliffe claimed that the decline in profit share going to British capital was caused by increases in money wages forced by working-class strength and the inability of capital to pass these on as price increases because of the rising level of international competition. They also saw this as a general explanation for the declining profit margins across the advanced capitalist world.[174] But this could not have been the case. On the one hand, there was no crisis during the 1950s, when real wages were rising much more quickly than in the late 1960s and early 1970s. On the other, during the latter decades, all of the major economies went into recession simultaneously, even though levels of labor organization and militancy were massively different.[175] In effect, this argument simply ascribes a different and positive value to the ideological claims of the bourgeoisie concerning union power. In a British context, for example, Anthony Burgess expressed this attitude well in an attempt to rewrite Orwell's *Nineteen Eighty Four*, where the trade unions have taken the role of Big Brother. His hero complains: "Whoever's running the government, the workers can reduce it to impotence. Do what we say or we strike. 'And,' his voice grew deep and harsh, 'there's a day or two of token resistance in the name of holding back inflation or keeping our exports competitive. Then more money printed with nothing to back it.'"[176]

In fact, rather than wage pressure being the problem which caused the crisis, it was the crisis which made wage pressure into a problem, or at least one which could no longer be tolerated. During the Second World War, the Polish economist Michal Kałecki predicted that although "a regime of permanent full employment" would actually increase profits, employers would nevertheless oppose such a development because it would build working-class self-confidence, encourage industrial action for improved wages, and "create political tension." In the end, Kałecki wrote, "'discipline in the factories' and 'political stability' are more appreciated than profits by business leaders."[177] The Golden Age did of course see many intense industrial struggles, but no concerted attempts to roll back the position of trade unions until the very end. Kałecki underestimated the extent to which employers would be prepared to accept pressure on wages, however unwillingly, provided the rate of profit was maintained at a sufficiently high level. Once it began to fall, as it did from the late 1960s, this situation was no longer sustainable for capital, meaning not only attacks on workplace terms and conditions, but also on those aspects of the welfare state—the "social wage"—which were beneficial to the working class. The main source of funding for welfare provision came from redistribution within the working class itself; but to the extent that it was also a cost to capital, a drain on investment, it was one which capitalists had reluctantly been prepared to pay so long as the system was expanding. When it began to contract, as it did after 1973, these costs to capital, like wages, had to be reduced, by directly attacking provisions directly in the hands of employers (pensions, health insurance) and shifting the burden of taxation even more decisively onto the working class. "Some people will obviously have to do with less," announced an editorial in *Businessweek* in 1974 with unusual candor, then adding: "Yet it will be a hard pill for many Americans to swallow—the idea of doing with less so that big business can have more."[178] How was this to be achieved—and who was to achieve it?

> Well Papa go to bed now, it's getting late
> Nothing we can say can change anything now
> Because there's just different people coming down here now and they see things in different ways
> And soon everything we've known will just be swept away.[179]

CHAPTER 2

Vanguard Neoliberalism

Regimes of Reorientation, 1974–1991

T he unevenness of the global spread of neoliberalism indicates not only the relative strength and determination of national labor movements but also the presence of these qualities among the politicians who were intent on making neoliberalism a reality. Throughout the Golden Age, the capitalist class had called to order social democratic politicians like Harold Wilson in Britain or François Mitterrand in France when their policies were perceived, however unreasonably, as being too concerned with defending the interests of their supporters. Their normal methods for disciplining disobedient politicians involved currency speculation, withholding investment, and moving production—or at least threatening to do so, which was often sufficient to achieve the desired effect. These police actions by capital were often aided by state managers who tended to be more conscious of what capital would find acceptable or permissible than mere elected representatives of the people. Within weeks of coming to office in 1964, Wilson was informed by the governor of the Bank of England that he could not implement the program on which the Labour Party had been elected because of business hostility and the consequent weakness of sterling in the face of market speculation.[1] In 1976, the next Labour government was presented with Treasury figures on the likely public sector borrowing requirement for 1977–78, which officials had deliberately inflated by almost

100 percent in order to force the government to approach the IMF for an unnecessary loan. The loan was then granted on the condition that spending cuts which the Treasury regarded as necessary were made.[2]

But economic or bureaucratic resistance to government agendas is a blunt instrument, capable of blocking or reversing one set of policies and making others more likely, not of bringing about a complete reorientation in policy terms. Capitalist states are sets of permanent institutions run by unelected officials who act in the interests of capital more or less effectively; parliamentary government is a temporary regime consisting of elected politicians who act in the interests of capital more or less willingly.[3] But in times of crisis, capital requires politicians who will decide on a particular strategy and fight for it with absolute conviction, if necessary against individual members of the capitalist class themselves. During the 1930s, Antonio Gramsci discussed this type of ruling class response to crisis as "an organic and normal phenomenon. . . . It represents the fusion of an entire social class under a single leadership, which alone is held to be capable of solving an overriding problem of its existence and of fending off a mortal danger."[4] By autumn 1976, leading figures on the right and center of the Labour Party had essentially accepted the monetarist case for reducing public spending and indeed a number of other New Right positions besides, including those on immigration and education—in some cases from intellectual conversion, but in most from temporary expediency, at least at this stage. As the financial journalist and early neoliberal Samuel Brittan recalls:

> Whenever I spoke to international or British gatherings on "Thatcherism" in the first few years after 1979, the audiences were prepared for an attack or a defence. But they were taken aback by the contention that however much they were denounced by Labour in opposition, the most characteristic features of financial Thatcherism were also pursued by the last Labour Government from 1976 to 1979, with only modest backsliding in the period approaching the 1979 election.[5]

The result, however, was to both give credibility to the arguments of those who advocated these solutions from principle and to expose Labour's own inability to deliver them in the face of opposition from a still-powerful trade union movement and its own left wing.[6] The British Labour Party is by no means a typical example of global social democracy, but the inhibitions it still experienced during this period were typical: only in the exceptional case of New Zealand after 1984 did an incumbent social democratic party transform itself into the agent of neoliberalism before it became the dominant form of contemporary capitalist organization.

We need to be clear that it is not the nature of capitalist states themselves that required to be changed: they still need to perform the core functions described at the beginning of this chapter. There is no "neoliberal state," but there are "neoliberal regimes," as Paul du Gay and Alan Scott explain:

> By taking the so-called Keynesian state as its base-line model, both neo-Marxist state theory and some broadly Weberian approaches . . . have incorporated non-essential aspects of the state's activities into its identity or definition. Thus, the shedding or out-sourcing of those activities is read as evidence of an absolute decline or a change in the nature of the state itself. . . . We need to disaggregate the state into instruments ("means" in Weber's sense) and regimes. A change in the latter does not entail a transformation of the former. States outlive regimes. While the notion of changes of the state not in terms of its *form* but of its *modality* implicitly or explicitly acknowledges this, this shift of emphasis alone remains too weak to fully capture the longer-term historical continuities in the state as a historically particular form of political association. The state/regime distinction encourages us to interpret recent and contemporary developments differently. With respect to the former, rather than read the policy shifts of the last thirty years or so as a transformation of "the state," we have interpreted them as adjustments to changes in the environment within which states have had to operate, and in particular to the dominant regime in the sense of a coalition of social groups and confluence of ideas (even the term "environment" here is somewhat misleading as these shifts have often themselves been state led, or by-products of state action).[7]

The establishment of neoliberal hegemony in the late 1970s usually required an entirely new political regime, one which did not reluctantly acquiesce in policies it would rather have avoided, but which was fully committed to their implementation. Initially, this meant the established parties of the right. During the General Election campaign of 1979, in what turned out to be his final days as senior policy adviser to James Callaghan, Bernard Donoughue recalls him rejecting the possibility of a Labour victory on the grounds that a once-in-thirty-years "sea-change" was occurring in British politics which would make their campaigning irrelevant: "There is a shift in what the public wants and what it approves of . . . and it is for Mrs. Thatcher."[8] Callaghan was being unfair to the public by ascribing to it a change in attitude which had actually occurred among sections of the bourgeoisie and the middle classes, but his sense of an ending was nevertheless accurate.

In a British context, the role of Margaret Thatcher was therefore crucial to what followed. Her government directly represented capital insofar as it was opposed to the working-class movement ("vertically"), but could not represent every component of capital ("horizontally") because there was no general agreement on capitalist strategy during the late 1970s, not least because individual capitals could and did suffer from the one eventually adopted from 1979 onwards.[9] In the transition from capitalism to socialism, the working class requires two types of organization: revolutionary parties with which to lead the struggle to destroy the existing state and organs of democratic accountability ("workers' councils") with which to replace it.[10] By contrast, the transition from one form of capitalist organization to another does not require the bourgeoisie to develop similarly new institutional forms: the state is already dedicated to the defense of capitalism in a general sense, but the activity of the various state institutions needs to be decisively turned in a specific and different direction. In the British, case the dynamic behind the neoliberal turn came from a minority within the newly elected Conservative Party, which acted as the vanguard of the British capitalist class. As late as the aftermath of the 1983 General Election, Thatcher could still note: "There was revolution still to be made, but too few revolutionaries."[11]

What was the significance of Thatcher as an individual? In Alasdair MacIntyre's terms, was she one of "those actors who are essentially representatives of a social group or class, and who are therefore replaceable," or one of "those actors who are more than this, who cannot be replaced"? Of the figures from the Russian Revolution discussed by MacIntyre, did she more resemble Milyukov, "a mirror for the Russian bourgeoisie," or Lenin, "an expression of his party but more than this"?[12] In a partly justified response to the notion of an all-conquering "Thatcherism," which so paralyzed and disorientated the left during the 1980s, several writers have, from different standpoints, effectively placed Thatcher closer to Milyukov. According to Andy Beckett in his history of the 1970s: "Right up until the last days of the 1979 general election Margaret Thatcher was not the only possible answer to the questions the decade posed." To support this conclusion, he cites an assessment of her ascendancy by Alfred Sherman: "It was chance."

> Thatcher's rise was a series of accidents. If she had not been selected for Finchley in 1958, as a result of an electoral fraud committed without her knowledge; . . . if potential rivals for the party leadership such as Edward du Cann and Keith Joseph had not, in one way or another, ruled themselves out; if her leadership had not been ruthlessly managed by the wartime escaper and arch-intriguer Airey Neave, Thatcher would not have become prime minister. Again, if the Falklands war had turned out badly—as might easily have happened—she would not have survived as long as she did. But overarching all these contingencies, the precondition of Thatcher's success was Labour's continuing failure.[13]

Callaghan could have called the General Election for October 1978 and Labour would likely have won, but even if they had not and the Conservatives had taken office at the earlier date, the latter party would then have had to deal with the Winter of Discontent— a contest for which they were unprepared and which Thatcher herself believed would have destroyed the government before it had begun.[14] And, as Colin Hay has argued, Callaghan's caution in not calling an early election allowed Thatcher and her allies in the media to "construct" the "Winter of Discontent" as a crisis of governability, which gathered her support.[15] The opposite view has been taken by the Scottish writer James Kelman, who wrote shortly after Thatcher's removal from office: "If she hadn't been around somebody else would have been chosen. The very notion of 'Thatcherism' suggests that what is happening in this country began with her and will therefore end with her."[16] Beckett sees the period as involving a series of contingent events which could have had other outcomes. Kelman is deterministic, emphasizing the conditions of crisis which would have ultimately brought forth the necessary political leader-ship in an attempt to resolve them in the interests of capital. Both arguments have some validity, but both ultimately underestimate the role of leadership.

Gramsci wrote of the "form of self-deception" involved in "belittling" the class enemy—a folly of which, sitting in a fascist prison, he had good reason to complain:

> In one respect, this tendency is like opium: it is typical of the weak to indulge in reveries, to dream with their eyes open that their de-sires are reality, that everything will happen as they envisage it. On the one hand, impotence, stupidity, barbarism, fear; on the other hand, the highest qualities of fortitude and intelligence—the out-come of the struggle must not be in doubt, and victory appears to be already in one's grasp.... [But] if the enemy dominates you and you belittle him, do you acknowledge being dominated by someone you consider inferior? But how did he manage to dominate you? How come he defeated you and proved superior to you at precisely the decisive moment that should have revealed the degree of your su-periority and his inferiority? The devil must have thrown a monkey wrench into the works.[17]

Thatcher was in a minority among the leadership of her party which had itself been elected (as it would subsequently be reelected) by a minority of voters. She nevertheless had several advantages. One was the financial support provided by revenues from the export of North Sea oil, the price of which had soared as an unintended consequence of the Iranian Revolu-tion, and which began to make a serious impact on the balance of payments around the time of the 1979 General Election. If this windfall can genuinely be described as a happy accident in terms of her project, the same cannot be said for the fact that the Conservatives faced a compromised and incoherent Labour Party, a section of whose membership and voting base had shifted to the newly formed Social Democratic Party. It rather reflected the crisis of an entire social democratic tradition that depended on the continuing health of the capitalist system to provide reforms, the possibilities for which had now ended. Finally, the real enemy of the Conservative government, the broader labor movement, was in ideological and organizational turmoil, already disillusioned by the previous Labour government and weakened by unemployment (although offered some relief by the emergence of the economy from the depths of the 1981–82 slump).[18] Thatcher came close to defeat on several occasions during the first years of the 1980s. As late the early spring of 1982, even her natural supporters, editorialists in the *Times* and *Sunday Times* and commentators for the IEA, noted both the extent and range of opposition to her policies, their failure to transform the country, and their lack of fidelity to the principles of monetarism to which she supposedly adhered.[19] One Thatcherite acolyte, John Hoskyns, whose was head of the Downing Street Policy Unit in 1980, later claimed that if the steel strike of that year had ended in "humiliation" for the government, "it is quite possible that Thatcher would not now be a household name, nor would union reform, privatization or any other radical policies have been adopted."[20] Her position only became unassailable through two victories.

The first was over the Argentinean military in 1982. The "Falklands factor" did not have any lasting popular impact, although it was widely believed to have done so by writers around the then-influential journal *Marxism Today*. The real impact was to consolidate Thatcher's supremacy over the Conservative Party. The war was a gamble for Thatcher, not in the sense that there was ever much likelihood of the British forces losing; their relative weight compared to the Argentineans, the military balance of forces, was far too one-sided for that to be plausible. The real risk was that victory would come at the price of so many British casualties as to be publicly unacceptable. It did not.[21]

The second victory was over the National Union of Mineworkers (NUM) in 1985, which finally consolidated the neoliberal regime in Britain. In order to win, Thatcher was quite prepared to abandon market principles and use the state, in Georg Lukács's words, "as a weapon."[22] She later revealed that in 1990, when her government began to consider further pit closures as a prelude to privatization, she "never had regard to the commercial aspects alone." This, she claims, was partly from a sense of "loyalty and obligation" to the working miners who had scabbed on the 1984–85 strike, but there was another reason: "I knew we might have to face another strike. Where would we be if we had closed the pits at which moderate miners would have gone on working, and kept more profitable but left-wing pits open?"[23] Thatcher at any rate understood that the general interests of her class sometimes required the adoption of strategies which were contrary to particular economic doctrines.

These victories demonstrated that Thatcher was the genuine embodiment of the bourgeois vanguard, an anti-Lenin prepared to take risks before which more cautious but less decisive members of her class would have retreated or sought compromise. She was necessary to capital in Britain in a way that, say, Ronald Reagan was not to capital in the US, his role being that of a charismatic but replaceable front man for the collective leadership of neoconservative ideologues and corporate representatives which actually directed White House policy during his presidency.[24] In that sense, Kelman was wrong. Neoliberalism could not have been introduced at the speed and intensity it was without Thatcher or a similar personality. But Beckett is also wrong. Even if Callaghan had successfully sought reelection in 1978 as originally planned, or the Argentinean navy's missiles had been aimed with greater accuracy, the crisis in which British capitalism was engulfed would have forced whichever party was in office to move in neoliberal directions, albeit more slowly and with greater caution; there would be no return to the final years of the Golden Age, which Beckett is concerned to defend. Beckett is, however, right to note that Thatcher was able to carry out her program in part because the regime drew on the accumulated stock of material assets which had been built up in the postwar era. He is thinking particularly about council, or public, housing, but the point is of wider application:

> A similar dependency lay, almost never acknowledged, behind her social and economic reforms generally. Her freedom to make Britain more risk-taking and individualistic in some ways only existed because the country she had inherited, for all its flaws and tensions, was a relatively stable, unified place underneath: more equal in the late 1970s than it had ever been, still permeated by shared class assumptions, largely at peace—there had been few riots in Jim Callaghan's Britain. Her administration, supposedly dynamic and new, in fact lived off this social capital that stodgy old social democracy had produced.[25]

The extent to which neoliberalism has been successfully imposed in any country has depended on the prior extent to which the power of organized labor has been reduced. Where it was not, or insufficiently so, the project tended to stall, as a comparison of Britain and the USA, on the one hand, with France and Greece on the other would suggest. Only very rarely did even successful attacks involve destroying the trade union movement. The Chilean coup of 1973, the "other 9/11," is exceptional in this respect and it was only possible on a temporary basis. At the time, however, it was regarded as a tragic reversal of the reformist strategy adopted by Allende and Popular Unity, but not as foreshadowing any new development; Latin America had, after all, experienced numerous coups in the twentieth century, albeit few as violent as this. In the very important case of China, the ruling class was fortunate in that there was no movement to be destroyed—the reality of this so-called "workers' state" being an atomized labor force presided over by official trade unions that were an instrument of the ruling bureaucracy. Indeed, the emergence of the first genuine labor movement in China since the 1920s has been in response to the regime's neoliberal turn. In most cases, however, the attack on trade union power involved three chronologically overlapping strategies.

The first was to deliberately allow mass unemployment to grow by maintaining high interest rates and refusing to provide state aid to industries in the form of subsidies, contracts, or import controls. Interviewed by Adam Curtis in 1992 for his BBC documentary *Pandora's Box*, Sir Alan Budd said that he was concerned that some of the politicians "never believed for a moment that this was the correct way to bring down inflation":

> They did, however, see that it would be a very, very good way to raise unemployment, and raising unemployment was an extremely desirable way of reducing the strength of the working classes—if you like, that what was engineered there in Marxist terms was a crisis of capitalism which re-created a reserve army of labour and has allowed the capitalists to make high profits ever since.[26]

By January 1982, unemployment in Britain exceeded three million for the first time since the 1930s and remained at roughly this level until 1986: "Benefit payments were sufficiently low to cut many people off from the company of those who remained in work, which itself reduced the possibility of working-class solidarity, but they were not so low that they induced the desperation that might have come from the prospect of star-vation."[27] Unemployed people themselves were treated increasingly harshly as the recipients of benefits with ever-decreasing value and the subjects of bureaucratic regimes of ever-increasing complexity. The effect of growing unemployment on the workplace was to discipline trade unionists into ac-cepting what would previously have been unacceptable, including forgoing wage increases or even agreeing to reductions in existing wage levels ("give-backs") in order to prevent closures which were in many cases only post-poned. In some respects this internal discipline still persists. When workers express their concern over the possibility of redundancy, it is often treated as a proof of precarity when, as Kevin Doogan has pointed out, it is not the "likelihood" of job loss that is uppermost in their minds, but the "conse-quences"—the possibility of a catastrophic fall in income, inability to pay debts, bankruptcy, and homelessness, all accompanied by enforced interac-tion with state institutions whose default attitude towards the unemployed is suspicion or outright hostility.[28]

The second strategy, the success of which ensured that little effective resistance to closures took place, was to provoke decisive confrontations be-tween state-backed employers and one or two important groups of union-ized workers: postal workers in Canada (1978), car workers in Italy (1980), air traffic controllers in the USA (1981), textile workers in India (1982), and miners in the UK (1984–85). In 1981, the then general secretary of the Scottish Trades Union Congress, Jimmy Milne, denied that the current re-cession was comparable to that of the 1930s: "The Thirties happened after the severe defeat of the 1926 General Strike. Today the movement is largely undefeated and it is still unbroken."[29] This was true in the sense that there had been no single defeat comparable to that of the British General Strike; indeed, the so-called "Winter of Discontent" of 1978–79 in Britain had seen the highest level of strike days since 1926 in actions which were largely suc-cessful. Unlike the struggles of 1968–75, however, these strikes were not imbued with feelings of optimism and hope, but of pessimism and despair. The labor movement had been organizationally and ideologically weakened both by compromises with social democracy in office (the Social Contract in Britain, the Moncloa Pacts in Spain) and an inability to conceive of any alternative to it in opposition. The imposition of neoliberal regimes required imposing the type of defeat which had not yet occurred, but which the weakening of the trade unions made possible. These defeats then acted as examples to other unions, against a background of multiplying legal restraints and increasing employer intransigence. As the defeats mounted, Christopher Harvie records, "Unions and workers reacted with anger, bewilderment, and latterly fatalism."[30] And in some cases, the fatalism to which Harvie refers had set in even before the decisive contest of the Miners' Strike. The industrial journalist Keith Aitkin recalls the scene at the Chrysler-Peugeot car plant at Linwood the day its closure was announced on February 11, 1981:

> I was sent along as a young reporter to write a "colour" piece about local reaction. In the shops and the small supply businesses around the huge plant there was plenty of raw anger. Yet the reaction among the workers themselves, clutching their redundancy letters, was eerily taciturn: "phlegmatic" was the word I wrote that afternoon. Lunchtime football games went on as usual around the factory buildings, to the accompaniment of Radio One on the tannoy. I asked one young lineworker if I could see his letter, and he just shrugged.[31]

In none of these cases was victory for employers and governments guaranteed in advance; in every one victory was achieved not only by the unleashed power of the state—formidable though that was—but also the failure of other unions and their federal bodies like the AFL-CIO and the Trades Union Congress (TUC) to give effective support to unions under attack. Ruling classes rightly gambled that most sections of the trade union bureaucracy would instead give priority to the continued existence of their organizations, however much reduced in power, rather than offering effective solidarity to those under attack. The only event which would have resulted in an alternative vision of the future would have been the defeat of the government by the labor movement; in concrete terms, the victory of the NUM in the Miners' Strike. This was by no means the impossibility that tends to be argued by those who—openly or not—welcomed the actual outcome; there were crucial turning points at which the NUM could have achieved victory as late as six months into the strike.[32] Neoliberalism could have suffered a reverse in Britain, as it was later to do in France, and this would have spared many people from the ravages which in fact occurred.

What is less clear is whether resistance within Britain would have qualitatively shifted the balance in international terms to the extent of preventing neoliberalism from becoming established as the dominant regime of capitalist organization at the international level. Once the neoliberal order had been established in the USA and imposed on the transnational economic institutions which it controls, the model acquired a cumulative force: in the developed world, the need to compete with the USA compelled other states to try to adopt the organizational forms which seemed to have given that economy its advantage; in the Global South, states accepted conditions which restructured their economies in neoliberal ways in order to obtain access to loans and aid.

The third strategy was to establish new productive capacity, and sometimes virtually new industries, in geographical areas with low or nonexistent levels of unionization and to prevent as far as possible the culture of membership from becoming established; latterly the process was repeated in the very areas, like Glasgow, where unionization has previously been strongest. One of the reasons why unemployment remained high even though new jobs were being created was that these involved new entrants to the labor market such as married women and the young, rather than those who had lost their jobs. This was a more prolonged, molecular process than the first two strategies, and one in which the employers rather than the state took the lead, although the latter gave support through grants, subsidies, and tax breaks. If the classic example of this strategy was the movement of productive capital from the old "Rust Belt" industrial regions of the northeastern USA to the southern "Sun Belt," similar, less extreme versions of the same process took place in England (from the northeast and northwest to the "M4 Corridor") and Scotland (from Glasgow to "Silicon Glen" and the New Towns). By 1987 less than one male worker in ten in Glasgow was employed in manufacturing while nearly a quarter of all workers were women employed in public services.[33] The change involved is perhaps best understood in personal terms. Ian Jack recalls his father and the world he inhabited:

> He started work as a fourteen-year-old apprentice in a linen mill on five shillings a week and progressed variously through other textile factories in Scotland and Lancashire, into the engine-room of a cargo steamer, down a coal pit, through a lead works and a hosepipe

factory. . . . He ended his working life only a few miles from where
he had begun it, and in much the same way; in his overalls and
over a lathe and waiting for the dispensation of the evening hooter,
when he would stick his leg over his bike and cycle home. He never
owned a house and he never drove a car, and today there is very
little evidence that he ever lived. . . . Few of the work places survive. The cargo steamer went to the scrapyard long ago, of course,
but even the shipping line it belonged to has vanished. The coal pit
is a field. Urban grasslands and carparks have buried the foundations of the mills. The house he grew up in has been demolished
and replaced with a traffic island. The school which taught him the
careful handwriting has made way for a supermarket. In this way,
deindustrialisation has disinherited the sons and daughters of the
manufacturing classes; a benign disinheritance in many respects,
because many of the places my father worked were hell-holes, but
also one so sudden and complete that it bewilders me.[34]

What Jack calls "deindustrialisation" involved major occupational and
spatial shifts: to light manufacturing along the new seventy-mile corridor
from Ayr to Dundee known as Silicon Glen; to financial services centered
on Edinburgh; and to the oil industry centered on Aberdeen. The result was
to produce an economic structure in Scotland which increasingly resembled
that of Britain as a whole.[35]

In some respects, Aberdeen acted from the early 1970s as a test bed for
the type of changes which were to become generalized across Scotland and
Britain as neoliberalism advanced: a dominant industry (oil) in which long
hours were standard and from which trade unions were rigorously prevented
from entering; average earnings boosted by oil-related salaries but which bore
no relation to the earnings of the majority of the population; and an inflated
housing market whose benefits accrued to existing owners and those wealthy
enough to enter it.[36] Similar if less extreme conditions followed in Silicon
Glen in the wake of the US (Apollo Computer, Unisys) and Japanese (Mit-
subishi, NEC) software and light engineering companies which took over
from old employers like British Leyland at Bathgate and made Livingston a
boomtown in the 1980s. The employees most in demand were either skilled
workers who had already been trained by other firms or were school-leavers

uncontaminated by trade unionism. Approaches varied between the Americans and the Japanese. The former emphasized single-status working conditions and overall personal responsibility for quality control; the latter were more overtly disciplinarian, with a traditional division of labor; but both involved performance-related pay and, particularly in the American case, fierce hostility to any attempts at trade unionization.[37] By the late 1980s, 90 percent of companies in the other New Towns of Cumbernauld and East Kilbride had no non-manual workers in a union and over 60 percent had no manual workers in a union either; where membership was sufficiently high to have gained recognition, it tended to be on the basis of single-union deals.[38] In an article published in 2001, Christopher Harvie quotes one Motorola "manufacturing associate": "Unions? What would they have to worry about, the quality of the lemons in the iced-water machines?"[39] Unfortunately for the credibility of these claims, by the time Harvie's article appeared in print, it was clear what the unions would have to worry about: Motorola closing its mobile phone–manufacturing plant in Bathgate with the loss of three thousand jobs after pocketing £20 million in government grants.

These geographical shifts within nation-states were more common and more damaging to trade union organization than the threatened geographical shifts to locations in the Global South, which were often made by employers, but far less frequently carried out, not least because of the uncertainties over the ability of developing states to provide technological infrastructure and the cost in abandoning fixed capital which such relocations involved.[40] However, as Graham Turner notes, "it is the threat of relocation that proves just as powerful as the reality of a transfer somewhere cheaper."[41] These threats proved successful at least in part because of the way in which sections of the trade union bureaucracy and the left have exaggerated the extent of outsourcing and external relocation, the principle effect of which has been to further reduce the confidence of union members to resist.[42] Lynsey Hanley writes: "My husband, born in 1975 in the former shipbuilding town of Birkenhead, recalls from the eighties and nineties 'an atmosphere of total defeat.'"[43]

Where these three strategies were successful, they allowed corporate restructuring, the closing of "unproductive" units, and the imposition of "the right of managers to manage" within the workplace, which in turn ensured that wage costs fell and stayed down, so that the share of profits going to capital was increased. Conditions changed in the workplaces. In his memoir of New York during the 1960s and 1970s the author Edmund White recalled two office jobs he was forced to take in order to support himself while trying to establish himself as a novelist. The first, in the early part of the 1970s, was in Time-Life Books on Sixth Avenue:

> Officially we worked from ten until six but I could never get in until eleven and I kept expecting to be reprimanded or even fired, but nothing ever happened. In fact we had little work, and the whole week's worth could be dashed off during a panicky Friday afternoon. . . . I spent the whole day wasting time. A two-hour lunch. Endless coffee breaks with other writers and researchers.

This may sound idyllic in comparison with what was to come, but as White notes: "Nothing is more tedious than working in a big corporation. We had such a narrow range of activity and our tasks were so silly and infantile that we felt degraded." Later in the decade (chronology is not a strong point in White's otherwise engaging memoir), he describes the quite different experience of working in public relations with an unnamed but highly profitable chemical company as "by far the worst job I ever had as an adult. . . . We were supposed to be in the office from eight a.m. to eight p.m., at least, six days out of seven." The atmosphere was also different, as well as the hours: "Everyone in the building was afraid to make a decision, and the entire organization was paralyzed with fear."[44]

The neoliberal onslaught also opened up the possibility of three longer-term developments, to which I will return below. The first was to increase the probability that, when economic growth was resumed, working-class organizations would not be in a position to take advantage of increased profit rates by pushing for higher wages and better conditions: in other words, that any future boom would primarily benefit capital, not labor. In Britain, trade union density in 1979 was 55.4 percent; by 1983, 47.6 percent; by 1987, 43.4 percent; by 1992, 36.3 percent; and by 1997, 29.9 percent.[45] The second was that, while forcing wage levels to remain stagnant or decline in real terms was the desired outcome in one respect, it caused difficulties in another, namely restricted or falling levels of consumer expenditure: the answer, of course, was to create hitherto unknown levels of working-class debt. The third was to assist the social and liberal democratic parties to adapt to neoliberalism by weakening the main source of countervailing pressure from the broader labor movement, thus ensuring that fiscal and other changes favorable to capital would not be reversed. "Neoliberals aimed to develop a thorough-going re-education program for *all parties* to alter the tenor and meaning of political life: nothing more, nothing less."[46]

The successful onslaught on the labor movement by the vanguard re-gimes allowed all the other components of the neoliberal repertoire that Chris Harman calls "anti-reforms" to be implemented.[47] Some of these proved to be either irrelevant in practical terms or of a purely temporary significance and are now seen as intellectual curiosities. For example, mon-etarism, or governmental control of the money supply, was never seriously adopted by any state, least of all by the USA, which maintained an impres-sive record of deficit financing from the mid-1960s onwards that actually peaked during the vanguard neoliberal presidencies of Reagan and Bush the Elder. And in Britain, as Daniel Rodgers writes: "Monetarism turned out to be a bulldozer that could raze a building but could not erect one."[48] Any catalog of those policies which proved more enduring would have to include the following, although the list is by no means exhaustive: privatization of state-owned industries and utilities, flexible labor markets, outsourcing of non-core functions, deregulation of financial markets and the removal of exchange controls, abolition of protective tariffs and subsidies on essential goods, commodification of services once provided free at the point of use, the shift from direct and progressive to indirect and regressive taxation, and a monetary policy dedicated to the maintenance of low levels of inflation. But neoliberalism as a system incorporating these elements only emerged in a piecemeal fashion, after many false starts, accidental discoveries, opportu-nistic maneuvers, and unintended consequences. Aditya Chakrabortty has defended the idea that the Thatcherite project was preplanned in advance by citing a speech by Sir Keith Joseph from 1974 in which he argued against what he calls "over manning" in British industry:

> Nowadays, the smart thing to say about Thatcherism is that it was
> heavily improvised—that Joseph and Thatcher and the rest defined
> their ideology only after the first term. But reading that speech,
> made five years before Thatcher even moved into number 10, what

jumps out is how consistent the argument was: manufacturing, and the people who worked in it, had to be hacked down to size as a matter of economic necessity.[49]

But the claim that British industry was overmanned (or "feather-bed-ded") had been a standard component of the "what's wrong with Britain" discourse since the early sixties at least and was as likely to be invoked by liberals or the right of the Labour Party as any wings of the Conservative Party.[50] To prove the point about premeditation it would be necessary to demonstrate that the specific themes of neoliberalism had been worked out by the Thatcherite wing of the Conservative Party. This is unlikely to be possible.

Take, for example, privatization. This is usually treated as an example of how theory was turned into practice by the Conservative regime after 1979, not least by Margaret Thatcher, in whose autobiography it is retrospectively presented as a consistently held component of her program for transforming Britain.[51] There were two aspects: "the direct sale of public assets" and "government-enforced introduction of 'compulsory competitive tendering' first into local government and then into the National Health Service (NHS)."[52] There is no doubt that this led to major changes in social and economic life by the opening years of the twenty-first century, as Colin Leys details:

> Most people now worked for private companies, and what remained of the public sector has been remodelled on "business" lines, with "profit centres", performance-related pay, annual "market-testing", "outsourcing", "downsizing" and "productivity savings" targets—and in sectors like hospitals and the arts, appeals to charity and companies for donations. Conversely, people now bought their phone services, water supplies, gas and electricity, from other private companies. Buses, trains and train stations, airlines and airports were also now privately owned and operated, as were more and more government offices and, imminently, hospitals and clinics. Prisoners were detained in private prisons. Fees now had to be paid for many public services that used to be free—for example, dentistry, eye care, university education, the use of government statistics, museums and research libraries, musical instrument teaching in schools. Official terminology had been

changed to encourage the shift from a "producer" to a "consumer" culture: "customer" replaced "patient".... Cuts in public spending opened the way to other kinds of commercial penetration of the "life-world". Most major sports events had already become corporate ideological property. . . . The same was increasingly true of television shows, art exhibitions and conferences.[53]

Privatization offered longer-term advantages to individual capitalists (and to the state managers and politicians with whom they increasingly exchanged roles), if not to their states or the system as a whole: it allowed companies to expand markets into sectors from which they were previously excluded and established conditions for international mergers and acquisitions, which state ownership tended to deter.[54] It is for these reasons, as Göran Therborn notes, "Once put on track [privatization] was vigorously pushed by interested investment bankers and business consultants, turned into a condition of IMF-World Bank loans, and taken up as an ideological centrepiece by the right-wing media."[55] Similarly, for Michael Mann: "Neoliberalism made lesser progress in most other countries [than the UK and the USA]. Yet one of its policies, the privatization of publicly owned companies, did spread globally."[56]

But the privatization strategy was largely improvised in response to the adverse circumstances Thatcher encountered during her first term in office. Schemes for what was originally called "denationalization" had been part of the ideology of British New Right think tanks like the Conservative Party Public Sector Research Unit and the Selsdon Group since the late 1960s, but were marginal to Conservative Party policy on taking power: the 1979 manifesto hardly mentions privatization and only the National Freight Corporation was targeted for this fate. Was this because the Conservatives were concealing their real aims with a view to implementing them once elected? There is no evidence for this. The 1978 "Ridley Plan" was intended to break the power of the trade unions in the nationalized industries—rather than, at this stage, the public sector as a whole—in order to raise efficiency, productivity, and competitiveness, and above all eliminate the need for state subsidies: it did not propose wholesale privatizations and, indeed, even Conservative radicals considered utilities to be natural monopolies.[57]

The privatization strategy was therefore essentially a pragmatic response to the combined impact of two pressures on the government, which were

themselves aspects of the economic crisis that helped propel the Conservatives into office in the first place. One was the continued upwards pressure on
state spending caused by both the need for technological investment in the
public sector and high levels of unemployment; the sale of key industries and
services would both remove the need for the former and provide the Treasury
with revenue to meet the latter. The other was the continuing fact of minority
support for the Conservatives, despite two General Election victories made
possible by the British electoral system; the creation of mass share ownership
from the flotation of state-owned public assets seemed to offer the possibility of a "people's capitalism," whose adherents would henceforth look to the
Conservatives as their natural political home. Beyond the short-term cash
injection attendant on each sale, neither of these goals was achieved; the current costs of subsidizing the fragmented rail network, post-privatization, may
actually be greater than those formerly incurred by subsidizing British Rail,
while there is no evidence to suggest that either former tenants who bought
their council houses[58] or workers who bought shares in privatized companies
were any more likely to vote Conservative than before.[59] Anthony Heath and
his colleagues found in their study of the British General Election of 1983 that
the council house buyers who voted Conservative were already predisposed
to do so and that those who had previously voted Labour continued to do so
in the same proportion as those who continued as council-house tenants:[60]

> Initially at least, Thatcher's message proved popular with many
> working-class people. Among her supporters was Alan Watkins,
> who had risen from engineering apprentice in the 1960s to produc-
> tion manager of a small Coventry firm by the late 1970s. He voted
> Conservative in 1979 because "I liked this message of helping you
> to help yourself . . . and I felt the unions had too much power." For
> a man like Alan, who had worked hard to buy his own house and
> car, trade union membership offered little. He agreed with Marga-
> ret Thatcher when she proclaimed her intention to liberate Britain
> from "vested interests." Unlike Herbert Morrison in the 1940s,
> Thatcher did not have in mind profiteering businessmen.[61]

As Howker and Malik rightly observe, "right to buy constitutes the single largest piece of privatisation ever attempted by the British government—

larger, in fact, than all the others (trains, water boards, electricity suppliers, airports) put together."[62] "Right to buy," officially launched in August 1980, was in fact the expansion and promotion of an existing "right" which had existed in theory since council housing began in the nineteenth century and in practice since the 1920s, gathering in take-up since the 1950s. What was new were the extent of the discounts and mortgages which were provided.[63] Yet the ideological impact of privatization on the working class was more subtle than is usually supposed. The shift which most people in Britain were forced to make from rented council housing to private home ownership, for example, did not in itself signal a dilution of working-class consciousness; it did, however, mean that workers were in a weaker strategic position. As the Scottish novelist Alan Bissett notes of his friends: "They can't go on strike for longer than a day, because, well, *who's going to pay the mortgage?*"[64] Any prolonged industrial action by workers threatened their ability to meet debt repayments and consequently raised the prospect of repossession, bankruptcy, and homelessness. The situation led to caution in the face of neoliberal attacks, not conversion to the truth of neoliberal beliefs. Indeed, the way in which high interest rates tended to turn home ownership into a massive financial burden or even, in the era of negative equity, an outright liability was inclined to produce dissatisfaction with the system rather than acceptance of it. Where, then, was the basis of support for vanguard neoliberalism?

The End of the Vanguard Era

In 1989, as privatization and the other key components of the neoliberal system were fixed and became available for adoption or imposition, former US State Department official Francis Fukuyama announced in the pages of the *National Interest* that we had arrived at the End of History. In this truly empty homogenous future time, he assured his readers, economies based on market capitalism and polities based on liberal democracy would be the only viable options for humanity.[65] Fukuyama was fortunate in his timing for, as if to confirm his diagnosis, the Stalinist regimes which had claimed, however inaccurately, to show an alternative future began to collapse, first in Eastern Europe and then in the USSR itself, opening up a section of the world economy from which the market had previously been minimized, if not entirely excluded. At the same time as Fukuyama was predicting a New World Order in quasi-Hegelian terms, a British academic called John Williamson was preparing a rather less pretentious paper for the Institute for International Economics in Washington, outlining what he saw as the emerging consensus about policy reform in the US capital.[66] Although specifically dealing with Latin America, the ten key "policy instruments" that he listed—including privatization, deregulation, and trade liberalization—accurately summarized the economic approach which had come to dominate the First World, had made inroads in the Third, and was poised to overrun the rapidly disintegrating Second.

Of these two documents, the latter was incomparably the more realistic. Williamson later complained that his meaning had been distorted by the radical left, that he had never intended it to be a blueprint for exploitation and that indeed he was highly critical of the policies of Bush the Younger.[67] Socialists were right, however, to see in his modest discussion paper a codification of the doctrines upheld by the institutions of global capitalism, although the "Washington Consensus," as it became known, was too restrictive a term. It tended to refer to how the IMF and the World Bank operated in the Global South, demanding as the condition for financial support a series of "reforms," without recognizing that these policies had also been implemented earlier in the Western core of the capitalist system, where they were known locally by the names of the politicians most responsible for systematically introducing them—Thatcherism in Britain, Reaganomics in the USA, Rogernomics in New Zealand—but which are now collectively known as neoliberalism. In 1988, relatively early on in the establishment of neoliberalism in Britain—at a time when it was still known by the name of the local vanguard figure—Bob Jessop and his collaborators cautioned against seeing a single, universal process of restructuring at work:

> There is a danger that, by invoking the forces of "capital in general," such an account not only reduces Thatcherism to monetarism but also attributes a singular and unique logic to capital. This would leave unexplained the relative success or failure of such restructuring processes in different societies. And it would also fail to explain the different forms which economic and political restructuring takes in different countries. In Britain we find a particularly stark example of the neo-liberal

strategy but relatively clear-cut neo-corporatist patterns can be found in Sweden or West Germany (even under a Christian-Liberal regime) and more neo-statist strategies in Japan and France. There is no single logic of capital and it cannot therefore be used to explain the specific forms of restructuring in different societies.[68]

By the following year, it was clear that these claims for plurality were increasingly chimerical. The third and final explanation is to argue that the turn was simply a response to an opportunity provided by the removal of competition from the Stalinist states after 1989. The assumption here is that the welfare regimes in the West were provided in order to present an attractive face of capitalist democracy and could be withdrawn as soon as the supposedly competing system was no longer an alternative pole of attraction.[69] This argument has proved particularly attractive to those who still mourn the passing of Stalinism.[70] It is, however, as inadequate as the previous one, because—to an even greater extent—the timing is out of sync. Both the "proto-neoliberalism" of the Callaghan and Carter governments, and the fully fledged versions of Thatcher and Reagan took place at a time when, if anything, Stalinism was at the height of its global reach and power, with the triumph of the revolutions in Ethiopia (1974), Indo-China (1975), former Portuguese Africa (1975), Nicaragua (1979), and Zimbabwe (1980); the geopolitical counterpoint to neoliberalism was the Second Cold War.

Within a ten-year period, between the fall of the Berlin Wall in 1989 and the Battle of Seattle in 1999, all of the vanguard regimes of reorientation had been replaced by parties or, at any rate, individual politicians ostensibly committed to an alternative path: Chile (1989), New Zealand (1990), the USA (1992), Britain (1997), and Russia (1999). Yet as Alex Callinicos notes, "the hegemony of neoliberalism is demonstrated precisely by the fact that its policies survived the electoral defeat of the parties that inaugurated it."[71] This suggests two questions. First, why did nothing fundamental change? Second, since it did not, why could the neoliberal order not simply have been maintained by the original vanguard regimes? As Alain Badiou asks: "Once the whole world accepts the capitalist order, the market economy and representative democracy, these facts being equally objective and indubitable as universal gravitation, if not more, why carry on with the fiction of opposing parties?"[72]

CHAPTER 3

Social Neoliberalism

Regimes of Consolidation, 1992–2007

In his novel *The Line of Beauty*, Alan Hollinghurst makes one of his characters observe, as the British General Election of 1987 draws to a close, "The eighties are going on forever."[1] But they could not go on in precisely the same way. In some respects, the second phase of neoliberalism saw a continuation of trends which had already begun in the 1980s. Some were technological, in particular the maturation of information technologies and their link to telecommunications, with the expansion of new industries which followed. Some were aspects of economic policy, in particular the massive extension of deregulation in relation to capital and information flows and intellectual property rights.[2] At the very moment neoliberalism consolidated into a coherent program, it underwent a crucial mutation, which the adherence of previously reformist parties and movements made possible.

Social neoliberals were in fact the first people to describe themselves as neoliberals at all, at a time when the vanguard onslaught was still underway. The term first seems to have been used by a Democratic Party contender for the presidential nomination, Gary Hart, in 1984 and was adopted by the actual Democrat contender, Michael Dukakis, in 1988: "Neoliberalism was basically a creed aimed at suburban voters: it abandoned leftish stances on economic issues (Dukakis proposed no new taxes) but still took a 'civilized' European approach to cultural issues like gun control, the environment and the death penalty."[3] As Thomas Frank notes:

To the reader of today ... what stands out in their work is the distaste they expressed for organized labor and their enthusiasm for high-tech enterprises. The 1983 Neo-Liberal manifesto, for example, blamed unions for the country's industrial problems, mourned for all the waste involved in the Social Security program, and called for a war on public school teachers so that we might get a better education system and thereby "more Route 128s and Silicon Valleys." It was all so modern, so very up-to-date. "The solutions of the thirties will not solve the problems of the eighties," proclaimed a book-length account of this band of cutting-edge thinkers. "Our hero," announced one of the leaders of the bunch [Charles Peters], "is the risk-taking entrepreneur who creates new jobs and better products."[4]

The all-out frontal attacks on the labor movement and working-class conditions characteristic of the first stage of neoliberalism largely ceased by the late 1980s. In some cases, this was partly because the ruling class had become more cautious after overstepping the limits of what was possible through a general social offensive, for example in Britain with the poll tax. More commonly, strategies changed because the earlier onslaught had achieved the basic aim of weakening the labor movement, instilling among the trade union bureaucracy a generalized structural reluctance to engage in official all-out action. The achievement of this condition is perhaps the greatest service neoliberalism has achieved for capital.

Back in the mid-1980s, after the crushing of the British miners and Reagan's reelection, Adam Przeworski asked: "What kind of society would it be in which accumulation would be free from any form of political control, free from constraints of income distribution, from consideration of employment, environment, health of workers, and safety of consumers?"

It would be a society composed of households and firms, related to each other exclusively through the market. Social relations would become coextensive with market relations and the role of the political authority would be reduced to defending the market from attempts of any group organized as nonmarket actors (i.e., other than as household or firms) to alter the rationality of market allocations. Since social and political relations would be depoliticized, demands by nonmarket actors would find no audience. The tension between accumulation and legitimation would be overcome: accumulation would be self-legitimizing for those who benefit from it and no other legitimacy would be sought. . . . Household income would depend solely on the market value of the labor performed. Reproduction of the labor force would be reprivatized and the traditional division of labor within the household—between earners and nurturers—would be restored. Persons excluded from participation in gainful activities would have no institutional guarantee of survival. They might be isolated on "reservations," whether inner cities or depressed regions, where they could be forgotten or ignored. Workers would be disorganized as a class.

Przeworski noted that such a society had only been achieved in Chile under conditions of military dictatorship, and we know that since then Chile has returned to civilian rule and bourgeois democracy; the question was whether it could be achieved under the latter set of conditions.[5] The problem had greatly concerned the Austrian school. Neoliberals claim that the establishment of free market policies will automatically produce comparably beneficial effects in other areas of social life.[6] Not only are these claims false, neoliberalism also exacerbates all the inherent evils which capitalism involves in all its incarnations. Consequently, so long as citizens are able to vote, and as long as they have political parties prepared to represent their interests, however inadequately, for which to vote, there is always the possibility that the neoliberal order might be undermined. For Wolfgang Streeck:

> That is, so long as voters are still able to remove a government serving the capital markets. The *Marktvolk* can never be entirely sure of its position. The mere possibility that a less market-friendly opposition might come to power may cost the state dearly in confidence and therefore in money. The best debt state, then, is one governed by a Grand Coalition, at least in financial and fiscal policy, with tried-and-tested techniques to exclude deviant positions from the common constitutional home.[7]

Neoclassical solutions to this dilemma were twofold. The first was to ensure that only sympathetic politicians are in control of the state, if necessary by nondemocratic means. Hayek argued against making a "fetish of democracy" from *The Road to Serfdom* (1944) onwards, but his position is perhaps most clearly expressed in a justly infamous letter to the *Times* in 1978, where he wrote: "I have not been able to find a single person even in much-maligned Chile who did not agree that personal freedom was much greater under Pinochet than it had been under Allende."[8] The Chilean option is not, however, the preferred one, mainly because of the many inconveniences which military and still more fascist dictatorships tend to involve for bourgeoisies themselves.

The second solution was suggested precisely by the recognition that while formal democracy was desirable, substantive democracy was problematic. In 1939, Hayek recommended that economic activity should be removed as far as possible from the responsibility of politicians who might be expected to deploy it for electoral purposes.[9] And in this respect at least, neoliberalism has attempted to implement the program of its theoretical antecedents. Ellen Meiksins Wood rightly identifies the current attitude of the US ruling class toward democracy as consisting of two strategies: "One is to find electoral processes and institutions that will thwart the majority in one way or another. The other—and this is ultimately the most important—is to empty democracy of as much social content as possible."[10] The existence of these strategies has been openly admitted by the ideologues of neoliberalism. Philip Bobbitt, an adviser to the White House under Bill Clinton, has argued that we are entering a period in which the nation-state is being replaced by what he calls the "market state," a formation characterized by "paradoxes." I will return to Bobbitt in due course, but one of his paradoxes is that "there will be more public participation in government, but it will count for less, and the role of the citizen *qua* citizen will greatly diminish and the role of citizen as spectator will increase."[11] Przeworski thought not, in Western Europe where social democratic parties existed and furthermore retained high levels of electoral support:

> But in the United States, where about 40 percent of adults never vote, where parties of notables have a duopolistic control over the electoral system, and where barriers to entry are prohibitive, one must be less sanguine about the prospects. For suppose that the project is economically successful, even if for purely fortuitous reasons, and beneficial for a sizeable part of the electorate, that the

Right captures both parties, and the offensive enjoys the support of the mass media. . . . Such a prospect is not totally far-fetched.[12]

Perry Anderson has pointed out that an electoral base, even a much reduced one, is unlikely to be attracted by "the pure doctrine of the free market that is the animating spirit of neo-liberalism." But the "ideological supplements" offered by Thatcher and Reagan—respectively imperialist nationalism and religious fundamentalism—were as likely to alienate support as to cultivate it. What was required were "regimes of consolidation," formally characterized by social or liberal democratic rhetoric, which were able to incorporate the rhetoric of social solidarity while maintaining and even extending the essential components of neoliberalism.[13]

More fundamentally though, it was also apparent to more thoughtful members of the bourgeoisie that initial successes against the working class based on a strategy of all-out frontal attack had reached the limit of what was possible, particularly in Britain where the regime overreached itself by imposing a poll tax that provoked the first example of successful generalized resistance to the neoliberal program. Yet these same successes meant that it was possible to consider supporting, or at least tolerating, different parties from those of the right which had formed the original vanguard.[14] The social and liberal democratic parties brought an additional, more ameliorative element into the otherwise forbiddingly bleak repertoire of neoliberalism. This apparent supplementing of the naked laws of the market was originally marketed as a "third way" between traditional social democracy and neoliberalism.[15] It is more accurately described by Alex Law and Gerry Mooney as "social neoliberalism," since it involves not a synthesis of the two, but an adaptation of the former to the latter.[16] "While Thatcher wanted to marginalize trade unions as completely as possible, New Labour sought to mould them in its own image. Unions were again legitimized but their validity depended on their utility for business."[17]

The second explanation attempts to explain the time gap between initial propagation and ultimate adoption by claiming that the bourgeoisie turned towards neoliberalism under the political threat posed by the movements of 1968.[18] "As much as it targeted the kind of social compromise associated with the New Deal, neoliberalism also required the dismantling and effacing of the concrete political and social achievements of the 1960s. An array of hopes, ideas, and practices associated retrospectively with the cultures of the 1960s in the US and parts of Europe had to be extirpated or discredited."[19] In fact, the relationship of neoliberalism to the period between 1968 and 1975 is much more complex than this suggests. "1968" involved at least six overlapping moments.

There were overlaps between all of these. As Selina Todd has noted of the younger workers involved in the strike movement of the late 1960s and early 1970s in the UK: "Workers like them fused the older labour movement's commitment to workers' collective independence with the sixties ideals of personal autonomy and self-expression that were promoted in pop music, fashion and civil rights campaigns."[20] But there were also tensions between working- and middle-class women:

Judy Walker's was one in which working- and middle-class women were able to find common ground for campaigning. But the relationship between class and feminism was never without tension. Many working-class women disagreed with the middle-class feminist's belief that male behaviour was primarily to blame for women's exploitation.[21] The revolutionary possibilities represented by the May events in France and the worldwide series of insurgencies which followed was real enough, but had been brought to an end in the West by the mid-1970s, above all by the collaborationist politics of the trade union bureaucracy and the social democratic and communist parties.[22] The last moment in these revolutionary years was the containment of the Portuguese Revolution in November 1975; but outside of Chile, the neoliberal ascendancy began after this date.[23] Indeed, one of the conditions of possibility for the introduction of neoliberalism was precisely that working-class organizations had already been weakened to a point where they found it more difficult to successfully resist. The real fear of the British ruling class towards the end of the 1970s was not revolution but ungovernability. The problem here is that the ideology of the vanguard neoliberal regimes of Thatcher and Reagan was not simply opposed to the postwar settlement in economic terms, but to the increasingly successful movements for social liberation of the 1960s. The two could be combined as different examples of "indiscipline." Lord Hailsham, Lord Chancellor in the Heath government, once rolled up the following events into one faintly comic ball: "The war in Bangladesh, Cyprus, the Middle East, Black September, Black Power, the

Angry Brigade, the Kennedy murders, Northern Ireland, bombs in White-
hall and the Old Bailey, the Welsh Language Society, the massacre in the Su-
dan, the mugging in the Tube, gas strikes, hospital strikes, go-slows, sit-ins,
the Icelandic cod war."[24]

Thatcher criticized British society for simultaneously being insufficiently individualistic in economic terms, by collectively relying on com-
prehensive education, public housing, trade union organization, and other
"socialistic" innovations (for which the postwar settlement was responsible),
and being too individualistic in social terms, by rejecting deference, order,
and obedience to parents, employers, police, and authority in general (for
which the social liberalization of the sixties was to blame).[25] Her pronouncements to this effect are legion, but let one stand for them all: "We are reaping
what was sown in the sixties," she announced in 1982, appropriately enough
in the Daily Mail: "Fashionable theories and permissive claptrap set the
scene for a society in which old values of discipline and restraint are deni-
grated."[26] She wanted to reverse the equation, forcing the British to be free
in relation to economic activity, but unfree in relation to social morality and
state legality.

Yet, as Richard Vinen has argued, what this means is not that Thatcher
was opposed to the "post-war consensus," as both she and her opponents
claimed. In fact, Thatcher actually defended two key aspects of it: namely
the deeply conservative social values associated with issues of race, gender, and sexuality, and the Cold War NATO alliance with the US—both
of which had also been fundamental to mainstream Laborism. If anything,
it was the Labour Party which had moved to break with this aspect of the
consensus between 1979 and 1983, when it embraced identity politics and
unilateralism.[27] Failure to appreciate the continuities in Thatcher's politics
stems largely from the uncritical adoration of the welfare aspects of the
postwar settlement by the left: "Fetal rights, a balanced-budget amendment,
advanced nuclear armaments, tax and social-welfare cuts, and anti-commu-
nism do not necessarily combine. Reagan combined them, though his supporters did not do so consistently."[28]

As Owen Hatherley points out, social neoliberalism (he calls it "social
Thatcherism") did not begin with New Labour, but the post-Thatcher Conservative government: "From John Major's avowed intent to create a 'class-

less society' to New Labour's dedication to fighting for 'social inclusion', the dominant rhetoric has been neoliberalism with a human face."[29] This is true, but it is also important to note that Major was no more capable of carrying out the shift to social neoliberalism than Callaghan had been able to carry out the previous shift to vanguard neoliberalism: in neither case was their heart in it. The transition from regime of reorientation to regime of consolidation therefore involved a transition from what, in Gramsci's terms, was a war of maneuver to a war of position: the first involved a frontal onslaught on the labor movement and the dismantling of formerly embedded social democratic institutions ("roll-back"); the second involved a more molecular process involving the gradual commodification of huge new areas of social life and the creation of new institutions specifically constructed on neoliberal principles ("roll-out").[30]

Central to this shift were the social democratic parties that had traditionally seen their role as reforming, or even transcending, capitalism. How did they come to play the role of open, unapologetic supporters of the capitalist system, and in its most uninhibited form at that? In 1984, Andrew Gamble argued that social democracy would not succumb to neoliberalism, or what was then called a "social market economy," but would remain a danger to it:

> Either the Labour Party must be brought to accept it, or the Labour Party must never govern again. In the first case this would mean the Labour Party abandoning Clause IV; accepting the priority given to the control of inflation; renouncing protectionism whether in the form of tariffs, quotas or subsidies to shield any sector of the British economy from the need to be internationally competitive; and accepting a much smaller state sector, with lower taxation, selective rather than universal welfare provision, as well as the permanent weakening of trade union organisation and the institutions of popular sovereignty lessening their ability to intervene in the outcomes of free markets. No-one really expects the Labour Party to head down this road.[31]

It is probably true that no one, even on the revolutionary left, expected the Labour Party to embrace the policies listed here. More recently, Gamble has cautioned against "a tendency to reify neo-liberalism and to treat it as a phenomenon which manifests itself everywhere and in everything." In particular: "European social democracy . . . has plainly been influenced by neo-liberal ideas, but to suggest that it has become simply an expression of neo-liberalism, is too simple a judgement."[32] Pleas for greater complexity should usually be respected, but in this case his plea suggests an unwillingness to grasp the extent of the shift that has taken place. He is scarcely alone in this, of course. Here is *Guardian* journalist Martin Kettle:

> The historical aspect of the Blair era matters because it has become fashionable to treat it merely as a continuum from the Thatcher era which preceded it. This simply was not true. The Blair era—and we are really talking here about the Blair-Brown era—was much more an attempt to reassert social values and new forms of solidarity in the aftermath of Thatcher than an attempt simply to embrace Thatcher's possessive individualism.[33]

Gregory Elliott argues that social democracy evolved over three distinct periods: 1889–1945, 1945–1975, and 1975–present.[34] As a movement, it has always been fundamentally supportive of capitalism in practice, but during the first period it was at least programmatically committed to abolishing it. The second period coincided with the postwar boom and allowed the possibility of positive reforms for the working class without threatening the system, although as we have seen, these were also delivered by forces to the right of social democracy. Once the possibility of reform was removed, all that remained, for the leadership at any rate, was the commitment to capitalism and some residual rhetoric. Central to this process was the crisis of Keynesianism. In ideological terms, the collapse of the Stalinist regimes did not so much "prove" as confirm the already widely held belief that any alternative form of economy to neoliberal capitalism was impossible. Tony Judt has claimed that the collapse of Stalinism had a quite different effect on the left than the defeat of fascism or the fall of any traditional conservative regime has had on the right, because Stalinism, however much they might have opposed it, acted as a "residual belief system" for social democrats, by which they could distinguish themselves from mere liberal or Christian democrats: "For the Left, the absence of a historically-buttressed narrative leaves an empty space. All that remains is politics: the politics of interest, the politics of envy, the politics of re-election. Without idealism, politics is reduced to a form of accounting, the day-to-day administration of men and things." Such a situation is survivable for the right, but as Judt concludes, "for the Left it is a catastrophe."[35] In fact, as Alan Sinfield has pointed out, by 1989, virtually no one, especially not on the post-1968 revolutionary left, regarded the Stalinist regimes as "a model for socialism." The real ideological shock, although one which was more slow-acting, had been the earlier revelation that the welfare state in its post-1945 form was incompatible with capitalism, at least as anything other than a short-term expedient.[36]

Gerassimos Moschanos summarizes the current politics of the former social democratic parties as "the 'economic' state withdraws in favour of the market and the 'philanthropic' state timidly re-emerges to reduce the social costs to the market." But social costs are considered only in relation to the market:

> Today's social democrats, their room for manoeuvre greatly limited by a liberal international economic system *and* their own liberal options of the last two decades, seem resigned to *choosing between different forms of inequality.* . . . [F]or the first time since the Second World War social democrats do not possess a *politically plausible* social and economic strategy—that is, one both inspired by their own tradition and clearly distinct from that of their opponents.[37]

New Zealand was the first Western country where a neoliberal agenda was systematically applied, between 1984 and 1990, with the full panoply of techniques developed over the previous decade. In recognition of this achievement, it remains the only national application of neoliberalism apart from Thatcherism and Reaganomics to be granted its own honorific, "Rogernomics," after Finance Minister Roger Douglas.[38] The particular poignancy of this example, which foreshadowed later developments in Britain, was that the instrument for carrying through the agenda was the New Zealand Labour Party. In the British context, Pat Devine writes: "Thatcherism had destroyed the old historic bloc and created the basis for a new neoliberal era, it had not yet succeeded in creating a new historic bloc in which neoliberal principles and politics became the generally accepted ideological cement holding it together." In the case of Britain, "this was to become the historic mission of New Labour."[39] The process by which this took place contrasts with the prior emergence of the vanguard regimes of reorientation, but once again Britain is the paradigmatic case.

When Blair took office, he did not need to reconstruct the state on neo-liberal lines, as that had already been accomplished by his predecessor: he inherited the new structure readymade. As Blair wrote in his autobiography:

> I knew the credibility of the whole New Labour project rested on accepting that much of what [Thatcher] wanted to do in the 1980s was inevitable. The way she did it was often very ideological, sometimes unnecessarily so, but that didn't alter the basic fact: Britain needed the industrial and economic reforms of the Thatcher period.[40]

Relationships between the leadership and the party membership were also different. Like Thatcher, Blair was in a minority in the leadership of his own party, but could draw on the support of a membership which was prepared to support more radical changes in policy. But here the comparisons break down. Thatcher was supported by Conservative Party members who saw her as returning to traditional policies eroded by years of compromise with the trade unions and social democracy. Blair was supported by Labour Party members who were prepared to abandon traditional policies out of desperation at their apparent inability to win elections and the consequent need to compromise with the policies of the Conservatives, which were assumed to have a popular resonance. "Right-leaning politicians eulogised unfettered markets from ideological belief; left-leaning politicians were schooled to think that obeisance to finance was the price that had to be paid for power."[41] In many cases, the bitterness of this compromise was only made palatable by the self-delusion that the leadership was only pretending to embrace neoliberalism in order to gain power, after which the reforms they wished to see would be implemented. No such reversal took place, of course—if anything, the New Labour leadership embraced capitalism and capitalists more enthusiastically than representatives of the traditional right have ever found necessary.

Labour MP David Lammy wrote in 2011 that the riots which swept England in the summer of that year had to be seen in the context of "two revolutions":

> The first was social and cultural: the social liberalism of the 1960s. The second was economic: the free market, liberal revolution of the

1980s. Together they made Britain a wealthier and more tolerant nation. But they have come at a cost, creating a hyper-individualistic culture, in which we do not treat each other well.

Lammy is of course concerned to stress his admiration for both "liberalism" and "the creative genius of a market economy. . . . But these two revolutions, built around notions of market freedom, sell Britain short unless they are moderated by other forces."[42] Ed Howker and Shiv Malik prefer to talk about two "paradigm shifts." The first, in keeping with their general tendency to backdate developments to the postwar period, was "the post-1945 welfare era" and the second "the post-1979 neo-liberal era":

> Both reforms were impressive in their scope and success. Attlee transformed a nation ravaged by war, torn by seemingly insurmountable differences in education, class and life expectancy, and gave even the poorest within it genuine prospects. Then Britain was saved again, this time by Thatcher, from a spiralling economic tumult of unproductive industry. She led a renaissance in entrepreneurship. What's more, successive generations in British society have fought to protect the rights of people regardless of their gender or race or sexuality.

It is unsurprising, then, that these authors declare their belief in capitalism and assert that "the creation of wealth is not just desirable but vital—it's the underpinning of any decision that we take as individuals or as a society."[43]

The difference between regimes of reorientation and those of consolidation is perhaps best illustrated by their attitude toward the role of the central bank. Virtually since the onset of neoliberalism, a key ideological position has been what Edward Luttwak calls "central bankism," or the acceptance by governments that an independent national central bank would have responsibility for monetary policy.[44] And until the crises of 1997/8, 2001/2, and 2007/8 at any rate, monetary policy tended to involve an exclusive focus on maintaining low inflation. Under the Thatcher regime, the Bank of England acted in conformity with the wishes of the government, although the quasi-fiction of "independence" was useful for deflecting political blame.[45] New Labour could have simply continued with this relationship and Gordon Brown's initial act of transferring the power to set interest rates to the

Bank of England was partly an extension of it, one which had previously been proposed by a former Conservative chancellor, Norman Lamont, in his 1993 resignation speech: "I do not believe that even timing of interest rate changes should ever be affected by political consideration. Interest rate changes should never be used to offset some unfavourable political event. . . . The time has come to make the Bank of England independent."[46] But it was also to demonstrate New Labour's commitment to capital, particularly when accompanied within weeks by the removal of the Bank's powers to supervise and regulate financial institutions.[47]

Similarly, the capitalists who were most lauded by New Labour tended to be precisely those who had previously been featured as the most "parasitic" in labor movement demonology: bankers and financiers, now reborn as the wellspring of job creation and the source of private finance initiative funding. As Paul Mason reports:

> It was the Clinton and Blair administrations who designed the light-touch banking regulations that unleashed financial mania. It was as if they had a tacit deal with the financial sector: the market would be bent and regulated to achieve different, more "progressive" social ends than those imagined by the Thatcher-Reagan generation. In return, all regulation would be as light as possible on principle, and the giants of the finance system would be left alone to generate wealth for themselves.[48]

The complicity of social democracy in consolidating the neoliberal regime is one reason why Martin Wolf, while acknowledging the vanguard role of Thatcher and Reagan, is able to write: "But many of the leaders who made most of the difference were far from being committed liberals. Many were on the left."[49] Definitions of "the left" which, like Wolf's, include the likes of Deng and Clinton are not to be treated seriously; but it is true that many forces which had originally been genuinely committed to opposing local manifestations of the global order, like Solidarity in Stalinist Poland or the African National Congress in apartheid South Africa, ended by implementing neoliberal policies once in office.[50] Many more, like the British, New Zealand, and Norwegian Labour Parties, had at least been nominally committed to reforming the system on behalf of the working class. Their capitulation represented the final stage in the normalization of neoliberalism: the point at which it became accepted not as a temporary aberration associated with the program of a particular political party but the framework within which politics would henceforth be conducted. In Britain, the vanguardists of the Conservative Party certainly regarded the transformation of the Labour Party as one of their greatest achievements, precisely because it would ensure that the others would not be reversed.[51] Conservative intellectuals such as Ferdinand Mount and Simon Jenkins have rightly described the decades since 1979 as "the Blair-Thatcher years," a period dominated by the doctrine of "Blatcherism."[52] But perhaps the final word should go to the house journal of neoliberalism: the *Economist*. It noted that Blair's "lasting legacy" was the way in which no mainstream politician now pursues policies that are radically different from his: "New Labour's particular blend of free-marketry and social justice is now widely seen as the natural path of British politics, and few politicians of any stripe would dare veer far from it."[53] For New Labour, skills became "the answer to almost everything," "the new socialism, or at least the old social democracy," and, above all, "a substitute for the inadequacies of New Labour social policy as measured by the commitment to overt planned redistribution of wealth, income and education of the party's past."[54]

One of the key successes that neoliberalism has achieved for capital has, therefore, been to render inconceivable alternatives to the economic policies established by the initial regimes of reorientation—or at any rate, alternatives to their left. Conservative MP John Redwood noted of his time in the Conservative Research Department during the early 1980s: "In our policy discussions we would always include the question of whether the changes we were proposing could be made irreversible."[55] In Britain, for example, each successive phase of the neoliberal experiment saw the incremental abandonment of the repertoire of measures through which governments had traditionally influenced economic activity, beginning with Geoffrey Howe's abandonment of exchange controls in 1979 and concluding (to date) with Gordon Brown's transfer of the power to set interest rates from the Treasury to an unelected committee of the Bank of England. Perry Anderson described the former as the Thatcher regime's "first and most fundamental act on coming to power," but the same may be said of the second in relation to Thatcher's successor.[56] As the Italian journalist Antonio Polito wrote: "After the neo-liberal revolution the economy is by definition outside the range of politics."[57]

As Peter Burnham writes, "depoliticisation is a governing strategy and in that sense remains highly political"; it is a strategy which operates by "placing at one remove the political character of decision making." For Burnham, there are three forms of depoliticization:

> First, there has been a reassignment of tasks away from the party in office to a number of ostensibly "non-political" bodies as a way of underwriting the government's commitment to achieving objectives. . . . The second form . . . is in the adoption of measures ostensibly to increase the accountability, transparency and external validation of policy. . . . Finally, depoliticisation strategies have been pursued in an overall context favouring the adoption of binding "rules" which limit government room for manoeuvre.[58]

Consequently, as in a number of other areas, the satires written by William Burroughs in the 1950s now seem uncomfortably close to reality:

> The forms of democracy are scrupulously enforced on the Island. There is a Senate and a Congress who carry out endless sessions discussing garbage disposal and outhouse inspection, the only two questions over which they have jurisdiction. For a brief period in the mid-nineteenth century they had been allowed to control the dept. of Baboon Maintenance, but this privilege had been withdrawn owing to absenteeism in the Senate.[59]

Elections have not, of course, ceased for those charged with garbage disposal, outhouse inspection, and even Baboon Maintenance. As Alan Greenspan notes, in one of the many impressive if tactless outbreaks of honesty that appear in his autobiography: "The global economy—which must move forward if the world's standards of living are to continue to rise and poverty to retreat—requires capitalism's safety valve: democracy."[60] Under what Sheldon Wolin calls "inverted totalitarianism, . . . It is politics all the time but a politics largely untempered by the political." By this Wolin means both intraparty factional struggle and interparty competition, which reach their apotheosis in the USA in the selection process for presidential candidates and the subsequent presidential election, where electors are faced with "a choice of personalities rather than a choice of alternatives."[61]

The potential for such a development has always been present in capitalist democracy. During the 1930s, Antonio Gramsci distinguished between what he called "conjunctural" and "organic" phenomena. The former "do not have any very far-reaching historical significance; they give rise to political criticism of a minor, day-to-day character, which has as its subject top political leaders and personalities with direct governmental responsibilities." The latter, on the other hand, "give rise to socio-historical criticism, whose subject is wider social groupings—beyond the top figures and beyond top leaders."[62] What has changed is that the conjunctural is no longer an aspect of politics; it has become its essence. Consequently, most discussion of politics—in the developed world at least—is devoted to expending more or less informed commentary and speculation on essentially meaningless exchanges within parliaments and other supposedly representative institutions. Did the government fail to deliver on this promise? Have the opposition changed their position on that policy? In a situation where political differences become ever more marginal, issues of "character," "experience," "personality," "style," and the like assume a quite unwarranted importance: what else is left to talk about? Peter Oborne's discussion of party convergence in Britain incorrectly assumes the process is complete, rather than simply well advanced, but his essential point is valid:

> In practice the differences between the main parties are minor and for the most part technical. The contradiction between apparently bitter party competition on the political stage, and collaboration behind the scenes, defines the contemporary political predicament. One consequence of this mystifying discrepancy between reality and perception is that most reporting on British politics, which continues to articulate out-of-date assumptions about party political competition, has become unintelligible and meaningless.[63]

Debates, therefore, have the quality of a shadow play, an empty ritual in which trivial or superficial differences are emphasized in order to give an impression of real alternatives and justify the continuation of party competition. For Dan Hind, "The facts of biography substituted for programme."[64]

As a result, "Cameronism meant that middle-class people no longer felt guilty voting for a party that had previously looked homophobic, bigoted and old-fashioned."[65]

The most recent US electoral spectacle might appear to contradict this assessment, but at a deeper level confirms it. Barack Obama clearly benefited from popular rage at the social and economic disaster neoliberalism has produced for the majority of US citizens. His election, and even more so his reelection, has both discomfited racists in the US and given confidence to its non-white population. Whether it represents a break with the neoliberal order is, however, more questionable. Both Clinton and Obama are representatives of what Mike Davis calls "a culturally permissive neoliberalism whose New Deal rhetoric masks the policy spirit of Richard Nixon."[66] As Walter Benn Michaels wrote in the wake of Obama's victory over Hillary Clinton to become the Democratic Party presidential candidate:

> The real (albeit very partial) victories over racism and sexism represented by the Clinton and Obama campaigns are not victories over neoliberalism but victories for neoliberalism: victories for a commitment to justice that has no argument with inequality as long as its beneficiaries are as racially and sexually diverse as its victims. . . . In the neoliberal utopia that the Obama campaign embodies, blacks would be 13.2 percent of the (numerous) poor and 13.3 percent of the (far fewer) rich; women would be 50.3 percent of both. For neoliberals, what makes this a utopia is that discrimination would play no role in administering the inequality; what makes the utopia neoliberal is that the inequality would remain intact.[67]

As explained by James Bloodworth,

> The progress towards eliminating various forms of discrimination is welcome in its own right. However, on its own it is a change the economically privileged can live with. Put another way, identity politics is compatible with neo-liberal economics. It can co-exist with the corporate boss who makes more money in a week than his cleaner takes home in a year—as long as the chances of being the boss are assigned proportionally among different ethnic groups, sexualities, and genders. [68]

Jameson writes of the type of alternatives which used to be posed by
the regular rhythms of the business cycle which gave "the impression of a
political alternative between Left and Right, between dynamism and conservatism or reaction."[69] In many ways, modern politics has come to resemble the pre-labor movement Whig/Tory divide of the eighteenth and
nineteenth centuries, with two parties representing different divisions of a
sizeable wealthy class. On the one hand is the traditional New Right base of
businessmen, accountants, bankers, and estate agents, most of whom vote
Conservative, sometimes New Labour or Lib Dem. But this is now joined by
a "new new money" demographic (those working in the entertainment and
leisure industries, the media, marketing, advertising, the so-called "creative
industries," managerial-class public sector workers), most of whom vote Lib
Dem or New Labour, sometimes Conservative.[70]

For all practical purposes, members of the ruling class in the West are
united in accepting neoliberalism as the only viable way of organizing capitalism as an *economic* system; but the same class is divided in relation to how
capitalism should be organized as a *social* system. They may all be neoliberals now, but they are not all neoconservatives. In the US, both Democrats
and Republicans are openly committed to capitalism, but there are also real
divisions of opinion between them concerning, for example, gay rights or
environmental protection. Indeed, as James Davis writes, although "the social democratic and liberal left has embraced neoliberalism . . . the center-left
must also pay homage to ideas of justice and equality, most often directly at
odds with their concrete economic policies, or fear a loss of support to competitors further to the left":

> Increasingly, these contradictions between economic liberalization
> and social or economic justice cannot be avoided by center-left par-
> ties and this vulnerability provides an opportunity for the right to
> fragment and disorient the left. In part, for the mainstream right,
> immigrant scapegoating, along with attacks on multiculturalism
> and the economic position of the working class, is an electoral strat-
> egy that puts the left and social democratic opposition on the defen-
> sive. In periods of economic decline and insecurity, fear generated
> around these cultural and social issues helps to obscure coherent
> critiques of economic life.[71]

The increasing irrelevance of politics has given rise to several clear trends across the West, including increasing voter volatility and decreasing partisanship, indicating that many of those electors still involved casting their vote do so—appropriately enough—on a consumer model of political choice, where participation is informed by media-driven perceptions of which result will be to their immediate personal benefit. Unsurprisingly, the numbers prepared to carry out even this minimal level of activity are declining.[72] A British survey from 2004 showed that New Labour's triumphant reelection of 2001 was achieved on the basis of the lowest poll (59 percent) in any postwar election, although it has since sunk further. The lowest point prior to 2004 was the General Election of 1997, when the Labour Party, supposedly reunited with its electoral base, actually won with a lower share of the vote than it received in 1987, when it lost to the Conservatives for the third time in a row.[73]

The combination of increasing political convergence on the one hand and voter abstention on the other has led to a reconfiguration of the relationship between politicians and the state outlined at the beginning of this section. As Peter Mair notes, where once they were as concerned with "representation" as with "procedure," the emphasis has now shifted decisively to the latter, away from civil society towards the state:

> Parties have become agencies that govern—in the widest sense of the word—rather than represent; they bring order rather than give voice. It is in this sense that we can also speak of the disengagement or withdrawal of the elites, although while exiting citizens are often headed towards more privatized worlds, the exiting political leadership is retreating into an institutional one—a world of public offices.[74]

This argument is conducted in general terms, but the same point has been noted across the developed world, even in surveys officially commissioned by the state. "The most critical change in power relations in Norway," notes one, "is that democracy—fundamentally understood as representative democracy, a formal decision-making system employing election by a majority and directly-elected bodies—is in decline." This does not mean that interest in politics conceived in the broadest sense has necessarily declined:

> But it is for the most part being channelled through single-issue action groups and other forms of participation than party politics

and broad-based membership organisations. The new organisation form is the here-and-now-organisation—help for self-help groups, residents' associations, neighbourhood action groups, grief groups, next-of-kin groups, associations for people with different kinds of disabilities and single-issue lobby groups. [75]

Since in Europe it is not yet possible in the name of economic rationality to do away with the remnants of national democracy, especially the accountability of governments to their voters, the method of choice is to integrate national governments into a nondemocratic supranational regime—a kind of international superstate without democracy—and have their activities regulated by it. Since the 1990s, the European Union has been converted into such a regime. [76]

CHAPTER 4

Boom Economies?

L ooking back on Hayek's mission statement of 1949, "The Intellectuals and Socialism," Daniel Stedman Jones writes: "The most striking thing about [it] is how much of his pure ideological vision did come to pass in Britain and the United States after 1980. . . . It is hard to think of another 'utopia' to have been so fully realised."[1] David Harvey has argued that neoliberalism can be interpreted "either as a *utopian* project to realise a theoretical design for the reorganization of international capitalism or as a *political* project to re-establish the conditions for capital accumulation and restore the power of economic elites."[2] There are actually three elements in this formulation, not two. One is neoliberal theory ("a utopian project") which bears only a tenuous relationship to capitalist reality. The other two are different aspects of what Harvey describes as "a political project," restoring power to economic elites and reestablishing the conditions for capital accumulation, although they do not depend on each other. I have already rejected the first part of this definition on the grounds that there was no need to restore what had never been lost. What of the second?

Harvey is right to observe that neoliberalism "has not been very effective" in this respect.[3] If 1973 represented "the last year of the fifties" then the subsequent decline was not uniform in the four decades that followed: "In effect, these middle decades were a kind of Indian summer following the seventies, and it lasted such a long time—about quarter of a century, if you started with the end of the Reagan recession in 1982 and ended with the housing collapse in 2007—that it would be almost impossible to go back to where things stood before it all began and try to reset. Throughout the

Indian summer, the same key institutions continued to erode, with a lot of recession years and financial panics along the way. One way to see the Indian summer was as a series of bubbles."[4]

Wolfgang Streeck has argued that since the opening of the neoliberal era, capitalism has found three successive ways of "buying time" for the system: inflation, public debt, and finally private debt.[5]

The underlying problem is that it has failed to increase the rate of profit consistently. As Robert Brenner explains:

> During the long expansion of the 1990s, the average rate of profit in the [US] private economy remained 15–20 percent below that for the 1950s and 1960s, and a good deal more depressed than in Germany and Japan. From 1997, moreover, profitability plummeted in the US and across the world economy, even as the New Economy boom reached its zenith. Rather than setting the US and the world economy on a new course, the forces driving the New Economy actually exacerbated the fundamental problem making for long-term slowed growth—namely, persistent chronic over-capacity in manufacturing and related sectors making for reduced profit rates for the economy as a whole.[6]

Brenner correctly points to the failure of neoliberalism in achieving profit rates comparable to those of the "Golden Age," as have several other analysts. Robert Wade, for example, notes: "In much of the Western world the rate of profit of non-financial corporations fell steeply between 1950–73 and 2000–06—in the US, by roughly a quarter."[7] But this is not the decisive issue. As David McNally points out: "[The] great boom was the product of an exceptional set of socio-historical circumstances that triggered an unprecedented wave of expansion. But, prolonged expansion with rising levels of output, wages and employment in the core-economies is not the capitalist norm; and the absence of all these is not invariably a 'crisis.'"[8]

Constant use of the Great Boom as a reference point is problematic for two reasons.

First, it has led critics to expect that any subsequent boom must involve similar consequences for workers in terms of rising living standards, expanding welfare provision, and increasing class confidence. Since the period after 1974 had precisely the opposite characteristics, the temptation has been to read back from the condition of the working class to the condition of the capitalist system, and claim that the entire period has been, if not one of crisis, then at least one of stagnation. As Chris Harman notes:

> This does not mean that the world economy is doomed simply to decline. An overall tendency towards stagnation can still be accompanied by minor booms, with small but temporary increases in employment. . . . The present phase of crisis is likely to go on and on—until it is resolved either by plunging much of the world into barbarism or by a succession of workers' revolutions.[9]

But it is deeply implausible to think that a system as dynamic as capitalism could exist in a state of permanent crisis (or even stagnation) between 1973/4 and 2007/8—indeed, it would be difficult to understand why the events of the latter date could have had such significance had they not been preceded by a period of growth and expansion. There have been booms before, such as that of the 1920s, during which most workers did not benefit and indeed continued to be subjected to generalized attacks on their wages and conditions. One of the objectives of the neoliberal assault, after all, was precisely to weaken trade unions to the point where they would be unable to take advantage of any improvement in economic conditions.

Second, unlike Marxist economists, capitalists and managers do not tend to look back over a forty-year period to compare conditions then with their current situation. Moreover, as Duménil and Lévy write: "The objectives of managers depend on the social order in which management is performed." These objectives have changed: "After World War II, management basically aimed at growth (within corporations and in the definition of policies) and technical change. In neoliberalism, the main target became the stock market and capital income. . . . Neoliberalism biased managerial trends in favor of the financial component of management."[10]

On the contrary, they respond to demands from shareholders to produce immediate returns greater than their own performance compared with last year, or with those of their competitors from the current year. The decisive issue is instead whether the rate of profit is sufficiently high for them to continue to invest in production and be confident of an acceptable return.

Between 1982 and 2007–09, this was largely the case. In part this, was the result of the partial recovery from any recession caused by the destruction of some capitals and the rationalization and retooling of those which survived. More specifically, however, recovery was punctuated by a succession of short-term booms as a result of five factors, each of which had, however, in-built limitations. These factors overlapped with each other in time, but their maximum impact on the system occurred in this order.

The first and most fundamental was simply greater exploitation of the workforce, by increasing productivity on the one hand (making fewer workers work harder and longer) and decreasing the share of income going to labor on the other (paying workers less in real terms). According to Danny Dorling:

> From 1950 to 1973 across all the OECD nations, the average working week fell by half a day, so those at the bottom were allowed to toil less . . . . [A]ll these gains began to be reversed from around 1973, and by 2007 people were again working longer hours than they had been working in 1950. However, they were not producing as much in those hours spent working by 2007. . . . US productivity per worker fell by half between 1973 and the mid-1990s, not because people were working fewer hours, but because more were working longer hours less effectively at more demeaning, dirty, sometimes dangerous and often difficult jobs for lower real wages than most of their parents had worked for.[11]

Both were made possible by the relative success of the attack on the labor movement; both contributed to a partial restoration of the rate of profit; but both also had definite limits: the former was not physically sustainable on an indefinite basis and the latter restricted the realization of value created in production by reducing expenditure on commodities.[12]

The second is what Harvey calls "accumulation by dispossession."[13] There are several major difficulties with this notion.[14] Nevertheless, in this context, two of the processes Harvey identifies were important in the partial recovery of capitalism.

One was the expropriation of the remaining "commons" in the Global South, a process analogous to that of "primitive accumulation," which Marx identified as the founding moment of the system.[15] While no new value is created by this process, it does enable the release—or what might more appropriately be called the theft—of value which had previously been embedded in nature and hence unavailable for the purposes of accumulation, bringing into the circuit of capitalist production land, water, forests, minerals, and other resources which had previously either been inaccessible or in the hands of indigenous peoples.

The other was the privatization of state-owned industries and public services. Again, no new value is created, but neither is the process simply relocating resources within the system from the public to the private sector. Privatization provided resources which—potentially at least—could be used directly for production rather than in the process of realization or as part of the social wage. But here too there are limits to the process. There has been resistance, above all in Latin America, over the privatization of water. And, although there have been subsequent re-nationalizations in response to the current recession, the opportunities provided by opening up the hitherto closed Stalinist economies, or even the transfers from public to private ownership in the West and Global South, were essentially once-and-for-all operations, the scale of which will never again be repeated.

The third was the emergence of new centers of capital accumulation outside the established core of the world system in East Asia and, above all, in China, which contributed to a partial restoration of profitability. China in particular has played two crucial roles in the global economy: one, as a manufacturer of cheap consumer goods for Western and, above all, US import markets—a necessary complement to the suppression of working-class wage levels; the other, using the money earned from exports as the source of loans to the US through Treasury bonds, which are then loaned again to American companies and consumers. And there is of course a further, less material, role which China has played in reinvigorating capitalism, particularly in Europe, where it has been used as a threat: accept lower wages and work more flexibly for longer hours or see companies either close in the face of Chinese competition or relocate to China to take advantage of the supposedly super-exploitable workforce. But even given the vast reserves of labor that China possesses (which are far greater than any of the other emergent economies), labor costs will not remain at their current low levels forever, which will reduce the attractiveness of China as a site of investment and increase the cost of Chinese exports. More immediately, although the consequences are not yet clear, recession in the US and other Western markets, and the consequent fall in demand, will begin to erode China's trade surplus.[16] Indeed, there is pressure within China itself to encourage personal spending, in order to stimulate the internal market as a substitute for lost export revenue. Whether this is likely to be successful is another question, since the high levels of personal saving, particularly in the countryside, are not the result of an innate Chinese propensity towards financial prudence, but a function of the lack of social provision for healthcare or pensions which neither the Chinese state nor private capital are likely to provide under current conditions. What the Chinese state has done is to institute a massive program of public spending (4 million yuan) to stimulate the economy, with short-term success, at least.[17]

The fourth, itself a result of profit rates failing to consistently reach what capitalists considered acceptable levels, was a fall in the proportion of surplus value being invested in production and the rise in the proportion being saved, to the point where the latter is greater than the former. Not for the first time in the history of the capitalist system, the need to find profitable uses for surplus capital, where productive investment was insufficiently attractive, tended to draw industrial capitalists towards financial speculation.[18] Indeed, Duménil and Lévy have claimed that neoliberalism operates mainly or even solely for the benefit of the financial component of capital, which "managed the crisis according to its own interests, which prolonged the crisis" and which in turn "made it possible for finance to shift the course of history in its own interests." From this perspective they describe the US Federal Reserve adoption of a monetary policy of high interest rates under Paul Volcker as "the 1979 coup."[19] These authors are not alone in taking this view. The late Peter Gowan, for example, was a Marxist, but wrote of the US, following the onset of recession, that in the absence of serious rivals, it still has an opportunity to restructure its economy: "But such is the social and political strength of Wall Street, and the weakness of social forces that might push for an industrial revival there, that it would seem most likely that the American capitalist class will squander its chance."[20] Why the weakness of a section of US capital should be a matter of concern to socialists is not entirely clear, but even leaving aside the political implications, it is not true that financial and industrial capital can be separated in this way. As Neil Smith notes:

> Without industry producing commodities for profit, Wall Street would have nothing to invest, while producers in turn need Wall Street to float their stocks, issue credit, bankroll company take-overs, and so forth. Densely interlocking directorates weave these sectors together, and globalization, widely if not accurately seen as emanating from the financial sector, is just as much about the international reorganization and expansion of commodity production.

There are of course differences in the types of calculation involved in "the pursuit of industrial profit" do those in "the pursuit of interest lent."[21] As Al Campbell points out, "productive capital requires conditions appropriate for production (and sale) of commodities, financial capital desires an environment where it is permitted to do whatever it chooses in the pursuit of its own profits." The Great Depression of the 1930s showed productive capital that accumulation could no longer depend on a largely unregulated system. "Financial capital, on the contrary, largely continued to adhere to the liberal line that unregulated markets always work best, including financial markets."[22] The point at which productive capital came to share this view in the 1970s signaled the opening of the neoliberal era, but did not mean that it has become subordinated to financial capital, rather that their interests had converged. In April 2009, for example, the German luxury car manufacturer Porsche announced that it had made pretax profits of 7.3 billion euros in the six months leading up to January 31 at a time of collapsing car sales, an outcome due almost entirely to a windfall from share options which the company held in Volkswagen.[23] The new focus on finance had wider implications than the shifting focus of investment, which tends to be compressed into the term "financialization."[24] But among all the complexities of arbitrage, derivatives, hedge funds, and the rest, there are two essential points about financialization which need to be understood. One is that, financial speculation, like several of the factors discussed here, can increase the profits of individual capitalists at the expense of others, but cannot create new value for the system as a whole. The other is that, insofar as profits were raised, one aspect of financialization became more import-

ant than any other and consequently needs to be considered as a factor in
its own right.

The fifth and final factor was a massive increase in consumer debt. As
Mann points out, there were two ways in which US households had attempted to reverse their declining living standards from the early 1970s:
increasing participation in the workforce by women (up from 44 percent to
60 percent between 1973 and 2003) and working longer paid hours. Neither
of these was successful. In the case of the first, the increased income from
women was offset by the way in which employers lowered men's wages, so
although individual households may have benefited, average household income remained static, except at the upper end of the income scale. In the
case of the second, longer hours tended to be available for those at the upper
end of the income scale, effectively those members of the middle classes for
whom increasing their income was not a necessity. A third and increasingly
inescapable option, from the mid-1990s, was the acquisition of debt, secured
on the value of their house.[25] As David McNally notes, credit became crucially important in preventing the return to crisis only after the post-1982
recovery had exhausted itself. The East Asian crisis of 1997 and the dotcom
collapse of 2000–2001 signaled a "gargantuan credit expansion, increasingly fuelled after 2001 by record-low interest rates, [which] postponed the
day of reckoning."[26] Why? The assertion is often made that, although the ir-
responsibility of politicians and bankers may primarily be to blame for the
current crisis, some of the responsibility must lie with the individuals who
took on the debt: "If millions of Americans had just realised they were borrowing more than they could repay then we would not be in this mess. The
British public got just as carried away. We are the credit junkies of Europe
and many of our problems could easily have been avoided if we had been
more sensible and just said no."[27]

Has the accumulation of debt simply been a means for "consumers" to
add to their possessions as moralistic accounts like this imply? Insofar as
better-off working-class people have spent borrowed money on commodities which are above the minimum needed to reproduce their labor, it is a response to their situation under neoliberalism. As Madeleine Bunting notes,
"the overwork culture interconnects with the drive to consume" in that it
is only in the latter activity that people are treated with the respect denied

in the workplace: "The harder you work, the longer and more intense your hours, the more pressure you experience, the more intense is the drive to *repair, console, restore,* and *find periodic escape* through consumption."[28] But the main reason for increased debt has been the need to maintain personal or familial income levels.

The threefold strategy of allowing unemployment, disciplining labor, and relocating production could never be permanently effective in cowing resistance, but the effect was prolonged by the very nature of the neoliberal boom. Because such growth as did take place in the heartlands of the system was based on investment in services rather than manufacturing or other productive sectors of the economy, such new jobs as were created tended to be characterized by more insecure employment or underemployment: "Britain now holds the EU record in the proportion of people employed in such occupations as data entry and call centre reception; there are as many people 'in service' (e.g., maids, nannies, gardeners and the like) as there were in Victorian times."[29] As the British government's own statisticians recognize, these occupations are at the bottom of the pay scales; on average "personal service occupations earned £14,146 for the 2002/03 tax year."[30] But this was not the only reason. One of the characteristic features of neoliberalism is privatization, a consequence of which has been the charging for services that were once either paid for or subsidized out of general taxation. The levels of taxation to which working-class people are subject have not fallen; indeed they have increased as the sources of tax revenue have moved from income and property towards consumption, but they are now additionally required to pay for essential services which now take the form of commodities. As James Meek writes:

> We have no choice but to pay the price the toll keepers charge. We are a human income stream. . . . By moving from a system where public services are supported by general taxation to a system where they are supported exclusively by the fees people pay to use them, we are taken from a system where the rich are obliged to help the poor to a system where the less well-off enable services, like a road network, that the rich get for what is, to them, a trifling sum.[31]

This suppression of real wage levels among the working class therefore encouraged—indeed, one might say, necessitated—a massive expansion in borrowing. At the same time, debt also provided an alternative to struggle, in conditions where that was difficult or impossible. In the USA, between 2000 and 2004, household debt increased by 39 percent, but real disposable income did not, with workers relying on $675 billion of new borrowing rather than on salaries and wages, which only increased by $530 billion, to finance an overall $1.3 trillion increase in spending.[32] Kevin Phillips describes the process in relation to the USA: "The number of good jobs shrink, wages decline, consumer appetites remain constant or intensify, credit cards are pitched endlessly and misleadingly, the credulous sign up, and cards are issued. Rates and charges eventually change, pain begins, and on go the plastic shackles."[33]

In addition to the credit cards highlighted by Phillips, the variety of now over-familiar mechanisms also includes overdrafts, loans, mortgages, and, most insidious of all, loans secured *on* mortgages on the assumption that house prices would continue to rise indefinitely. As John Bellamy Foster and Fred Magdoff show:

> For those families on median-income percentiles (40.0–59.9), debt burdens have now reached their peak levels for the entire period 1995–2004. These families have seen their debt service payments as a percentage of disposable income increase by about 4 percentage points since 1995, to almost 20 percent—higher than any other income group. The lowest debt burden is naturally to be found in those in the highest (90–100) income percentiles, where it drops to less than 10 percent of disposable income.

As these authors point out: "All this points to the class nature of the distribution of household debt."[34] The British figures are similar. While New Labour was in office in the UK, total debt held by individuals rose from £570 billion to £1,511.7 billion, an increase of 165.2 percent. During the same period, the ratio of personal debt to disposable income rose from 101.6 percent to 173.1 percent—an increase of 71.5 percent which exceeds even the increase of 49.8 percent registered during the preceding period of Conservative government.[35] For Ivor Southwood:

> Permanent debt has come to shape this era of flexibility as much as insecure work, and the two are of course mutually supportive.

> Individual debt —due in many cases . . . to a combination of higher
> education and intermittent low-paid work, rather than the use of
> credit as a lifestyle-boosting steroid—manoeuvres the individual
> into a position of complicity with the very system which is despised.
> A population submerged in debt is relatively easy to manage.[36]

Crucially, the modern citizen is expected not to be ever free of debt but
to organize her life around the ongoing acknowledgement and faithful ser-
vicing of this debt. Indeed, being debt-free can be a major practical problem, as not having a history of credit and debt-servicing (a credit history and
rating) can be a serious obstacle to one's recognition as a person with legal
status for a variety of purposes.[37]

The impact of credit and debt is also exhausted, and the collapse of one
component of US housing, the so-called "subprime" market involving people who in many cases were never able to meet their payments, provided the
occasion for the return to recession conditions. As Andrew Kliman notes,
"the US housing crisis has its roots in the system of production. . . . The increase in home prices were far in excess of the flow of value from new production that alone could guarantee repayment of the mortgages in the long
run." Whether or not the expansion of credit constitutes a problem for capitalism depends on the relationship between it and expansion of the value
in production, which ultimately forms the basis of working-class incomes.
When the supply of new credit and the production of new value are roughly
aligned, growth of the former need not be a concern; but when, as between
2000 and 2005, the rise of after-tax income was slightly greater than a third
of the rise in house prices, the disparity proved unsustainable.[38]

Given that, *contra* Gordon Brown, the system was bound to reenter a period of crisis at some point, it is perhaps unfair to criticize neoliberalism for
failing to maintain the rate of profit permanently. It did, however, provide one
other major service to the capitalist class and the bourgeoisie more generally,
which are outside the terms of Harvey's definition, although it might be compatible with it if we recast the notion of *restoring power* to the ruling class in
terms of the *transfer of wealth and resources* to the ruling class and its hang-
ers-on. Richard Vinen has written in relation to the Thatcher governments
that he once believed their policies were "so obviously wrong-headed that
they were bound to result in signal disaster," but: "We should now have the

grace to recognise that the signal disaster never arrived and that, at least in its own terms, the government was often—though not always—successful."[39] The question surely is: for *whom* were they and the neoliberal experiment as a whole "successful"? As Sidney Pollard pointed out as early as 1990, of all the advanced economies, Britain had the highest inflation, the highest interest rates, and the highest unemployment, combined with falling output, declining national income, and the longest hours: "The exception was the one aim which, curiously, the government did not stress in its statements of policy, though it clearly played a large part in its programme; the transfer of income from the poor, and especially the poorest, to the rich, and especially the richest."[40] These transfers were a general phenomenon. Duménil and Levy note two movements in the fortunes of the ruling class: one involving a "relative deterioration" in their holdings at the beginnings of the crisis in the 1970s and the other "a restoration and more under the neoliberal banner." The latter is what they describe as a "tour de force accomplished by the dominant classes through neoliberalism, both in the absolute and relative to the other classes of the population," but it was one which involved diverting declining profits from productive investment.[41] As Alfredo Saad-Filho writes, in one sense, "the notorious inability of the neoliberal reforms to support high rates of investment or high GDP is really irrelevant. . . . It *has* been able to support much higher standards of consumption for the top strata of the population and its promotion of consumer debt." This, rather than the capacity "to promote growth, reduce inflation or even to increase the portfolio choices of the financial institutions," was the real consequence of neoliberalism.[42] The neoliberal program benefited individual members of the capitalist class by increasing their personal wealth at the expense of the living standards of the poor and the working class, as the following figures demonstrate.

The Gini coefficient expresses inequality as a number between 0 and 1, with 0 representing absolute equality (everyone has the same income) and 1 (or sometimes, as used below, 100) representing absolute inequality (one person has all the income and everyone else has none). As Branko Milanović writes, at a global level, "the Gini coefficient of the GDPs per capita of all countries in the world, after being roughly stable during 1960–78, has inexorably risen since 1978, from a Gini of about 46 to a Gini of 54 today—a huge increase of almost 20%."[43] Claims that neoliberal policies have reduced income inequality among nation-states and increased economic growth in the Global South depend almost entirely on the single case of China.[44] Although several analysts have claimed that China has achieved this by departing from the neoliberal model, these claims both underestimate the extent of Chinese neoliberalism and exaggerate the extent to which the developed world itself follows the policies it imposes on the Global South: the European Union Common Agricultural Policy or the American aerospace industry are no more run according to the principles of neoliberal theory than the Chinese Township and Village Enterprises.[45]

Inequalities have not only risen between nations, but within them. Take the USA, the society to which neoliberals always pointed as the model for all others to follow. Some statistics suggest the extent to which these increased bourgeois living standards have been accomplished at the expense of the working class. Between 1973 and 2000, the average real income of the bottom 90 percent of US taxpayers fell by 7 percent, while that of the top 1 percent rose 148 percent and that of the top 0.1 percent rose 343 percent, excluding capital gains.[46] In 1965, during the last full decade of the postwar boom, the ratio of chief executive officer income to that of an average worker was 35:1; by 1980, the opening of the first full decade of the neoliberal era, it had risen to 80:1, and by 2005 to 450:1.[47] To express the gap in another way, between 1968 and 2005 the salary of the highest-paid CEO in the USA went from 127 average workers and 239 minimum-waged workers to 7,443 average workers and 23,282 minimum-waged workers.[48] In Britain, even after ten years of Thatcherism, the average CEO of one of the FTSE top one hundred companies in 1988 earned "only" seventeen times the wage of an average worker; by 2008, it had risen to 75.5 times.[49]

Ajay Kapur and his colleagues at Citicorp argue the USA, Canada, and the UK are now a "plutonomy":

> When the top, say, 1% of households in a country see their share of income rise sharply, i.e., a plutonomy emerges, this is often in times of frenetic technology/financial innovation driven wealth waves, accompanied by asset booms, equity and/or property. Feeling wealthier, the rich decide to consume a part of their capital gains right away. In other words, they save less from their income, the well known wealth effect. The key point though is that this new lower

savings rate is applied to their newer massive income. . . . The consequent decline in absolute savings for them (and the country) is huge
when this happens. They just account for too large a part of the national economy; even a small fall in their savings rate overwhelms
the decisions of all the rest.

On this basis, Kapur calculates that the top 20 percent of earners in the
US are responsible for 70 percent of personal consumption.[50]

In a plutonomy there is no such animal as "the U.S. consumer" or
"the UK consumer," or indeed the "Russian consumer." There are
rich consumers, few in number, but disproportionate in the gigantic
slice of income and consumption they take. There are the rest, the
"non-rich," the multitudinous many, but only accounting for surprisingly small bites of the national pie. Consensus analyses that do
not tease out the profound impact of the plutonomy on spending
power, debt loads, savings rates (and hence current account deficits), oil price impacts etc., i.e., focus on the "average" consumer, are
flawed from the start. It is easy to drown in a lake with an average
depth of 4 feet, if one steps into its deeper extremes.[51]

Robert Yates interviewed a US former investment banker in his forties
who had lived in Britain for fifteen years:

He recognises that in his version of the city, the problems he reads
about in the papers have little impact. He wouldn't say he knew Britain, even London, particularly well. "I've lived here so long, but in
a way I know nothing about the daily things. Don't ask me about
the schools, the hospitals. Don't ask me very much about what goes
on *out there*." By "out there", he meant in the city at large, "and all
those places you read about, places in the north." In terms of wealth,
he would be around the middle reaches of the ultra-high net worth
individuals; compared to the Russian oligarchs, he and his friends, a
multinational set, were "more cultured, less rich!" he said, but probably more typical—in terms of numbers—of the plutocratic money
coursing through Britain. If he was not at home in London he would
be most likely to be abroad—often looking at art. He sometimes
stayed with friends in the country, he said, but this would be in the

highly circumscribed territory marked out by country house week-ends, mostly in the south-east of England. "My friends are all the same; they have no idea what's going on, *especially* the English ones, they know even less about 'out there'." He has a point. Sometimes overlooked, in our mania over the last decade for observing the rich incomers—and how divorced their lives appear to be from the main-stream of the population—is how these outsiders have taken their lead from native peers. Prospering in Britain has long equated to making a life *apart*, away from the public realm; and has been about acquiring habits—from schooling to leisure to eating—whose very point sometimes seems to be its difference from the average Briton's experience.[52]

Like neoclassicism before it, neoliberalism had always been an ideology. Both represented not disinterested theory but the articulation of particular class interests. Neoclassicism represented mainly the interests of a *rentier* subset of the bourgeoisie, described by radicals and Marxists before the First World War as being characterized by extreme individualism, and focused on the means of consumption rather than the means of production.[53] Neoliberal-ism in some respects reflects the way in which these attitudes have been generalized across the bourgeoisie as a whole. Loretta Napoleoni argues that we have entered a new "Gilded Age," similar to the one dissected by Thor-stein Veblen prior to the First World War, in which the ruling class has once again become a "leisure class."[54] As Steve Fraser notes, however, there is one marked difference between the previous gilded age and ours; in the former, there was organized mass resistance to the rule of capital: "The Knights of Labour, the Populist Party, the anti-trust movement, the cooperative move-ment in town and country, the nation-wide Eight-Hour Day uprisings of 1886 which culminated in the infamy of the Haymarket hangings, all ex-pressed a deep yearning to abolish the prevailing industrial order." Nothing like this accompanied the era of neoliberalism:

> Fast forward to our second Gilded Age and the stage seems bare indeed. No Great Fears, no Great Expectations, no looming social apocalypses, no utopias or dystopias—just a kind of flatline sense of the end of history. Where are all the roiling insurgencies, the break-

away political parties, the waves of strikes and boycotts, the infectious communal upheavals, the chronic sense of enough is enough?[55]

It is unsurprising, therefore, that no significant section of the international ruling class has abandoned its belief in the fundamentals of neoliberal capitalism: they have too much to lose. Colin Crouch has written of the need to accept that:

> political and economic elites will do everything that they can to maintain neoliberalism in general and the finance-driven form of it in particular. . . . They have benefitted so much from the inequalities of wealth and power that the system has produced, compared with the experience of strongly redistributive taxation, strong trade unions and government regulation that constituted the so-called social democratic period.[56]

For David Graeber,

> The response [of the elites] only makes sense from a political perspective. Financial elites, having shown the world they were utterly incompetent at the one activity they had claimed they were able to do—the measurement of value—have responded by joining with their political cronies in a violent attack on anything that even looks like it might possibly provide an alternative way to think about value, from public welfare to the contemplation of art or philosophy (or at least, the contemplation of art or philosophy for any other reason than the purpose of making money). For the moment, at least, capitalism is no longer even thinking about its long-term viability.[57]

But neoliberalism is also an ideology in a second sense, not only one which presents the perspective of a particular class as universal, but also one which seeks to explain or justify the discrepancy between theory and reality, between the promise of improved standards of living for all and the delivery of inequalities in which benefits are reserved for the rulers of society. Although the clearest expression of the view that "a fully free, capitalist system has not yet existed anywhere" is to be found in the writings of Ayn Rand and her acolytes, the sentiment is much more widespread than among the ranks of the objectivists or the libertarians with whom they affect to disagree.[58] Yet precisely because this vision is unrealizable, neoliberalism can never be satisfied; enemies are never completely overcome, if only because they must be constantly invoked to explain neoliberal failures: "Even after decades of neoliberal reconstruction, it is remarkable how many present-day policy failures are still being tagged to intransigent unions, to invasive regulations, to inept bureaucrats, and to scare-mongering advocacy groups."[59] As Neal Curtis notes, this is an essentially religious, even "evangelical" viewpoint: "Just as the evil in the world is not the fault of the Christian God, but our fault for not being sufficiently Christian, so the Market is not to blame for the faults of capitalism. It is our fault for not being economically liberal enough—for not matching up to its purity." From this perspective, "economic crises are not the fault of capitalism . . . but the fault of governments for not permitting the pure form of capitalism to bloom."[60]

Chris Lehmann discovers "another discomfiting respect in which the purist strain of libertarianism resembles the woolier brand of left dogma. Just as Marxist purists used to dismiss the horrors of Soviet rule as an epiphenomenal glitch in the working out of the materialist doctrine—the inconvenience of 'historically existing socialism'—so do today's market purists wave away all the abundant evidence of ruinous market externalities, from climate change to workplace deaths, en route to the utopia of wholly uncoerced capital exchange."[61]

James Davis notes the "highly unrealistic view of what the right has accomplished in the last thirty years" among neoliberals:

> Despite the ascendancy of neoliberal capitalism and the accompanying decline in the economic security of workers, the gutting of the welfare state, and the incremental fall in taxes owed by the rich and by corporations, the free market right nevertheless feels it has lost. This pessimistic view is useful inasmuch as it sustains siege mentality on the right and reinforces the idea that an alien social transformation is imminent. It is difficult to foresee a total reversal of the advancement of the position of women before the law and in the economy, for example, but it is possible to imagine that their position might be further enhanced. If the object of democratic social movements is the establishment of equality between all people then, as far as the right is concerned, the war will continue.[62]

CHAPTER 5

Broken Societies?

Neoliberalism has an inherently contradictory aspiration to create a population which behaves as sovereign individual consumers in the marketplace, obedient wage laborers in the workplace, and subordinate mass citizens before the state. David Marquand writes that "market and moral fundamentalists were brothers beneath the skin":

> For both, individual satisfaction was sacrosanct and both railed against collective constraints. Both disdained the bonds of community. Both were quintessentially utopian, dreaming of an impossible future of perfect freedom. . . . Above all, both were enmeshed in paradox. The first stood for libertarian individualism in the economy, but for order in a limited state and traditional morality in personal conduct. The second championed order in the economy, but libertarian individualism in the personal sphere. Market individualism assumed that free choice in the economy would go hand in hand with respect for traditional morality. Moral individualists assumed that the ethic of "doing your own thing" could be confined to the private sphere, while economic life was organized on (unspecified) collectivist lines. Not surprisingly, both assumptions turned out to be false. Hedonism was indivisible.[1]

As Elizabeth Wilson writes,

> the modernity of the nineteenth century was incomplete and contradictory. . . . Bourgeois leaders tried to enforce a rigidly conservative

moral code in order to stem the floodtide of immorality they feared might engulf them. This code was not in itself part of the logic of capital, consistent rather with the puritanism of a former time than with the pleasure-seeking impulses of consumerism."[2]

During the 1970s, US neoconservatives like Daniel Bell and Irving Kristol argued that individualism in economic life tended to lead to a corresponding disinhibition in social and cultural life, which the moral and legal codes of bourgeois society were designed to repress. As the twentieth century had progressed, however, the mechanisms of social restraint had increasingly been dismantled, allowing the emergence of personality types which sought expression, even to the point of opposing bourgeois society itself as a barrier to this.[3] Bell and Kristol both wrote in response to what they saw as the excesses of the 1960s, but the dominance of neoliberalism has only intensified these contradictions to an unprecedented degree. As Martijn Konings notes: "During the 1970s progressive thinkers sounded remarkably similar to conservative thinkers." He is thinking particularly about Christopher Lasch:

> The trajectory that took Bell from progressiveness to neoconservativism appeared to reflect less a change of heart than an objective political logic: it was as if he was prepared to draw conclusions that others shied away from. Neoliberal discourses saw the progressive-liberal subject in much the same terms as Lasch did, as worshipping false gods, as expecting credit without being willing to work for it. But the problem as they saw it was precisely the subject's susceptibility to progressive-liberal ideas, and their solutions to the governance crisis centered on the need for a decisive break with progressive-liberal ideas. Lasch did not display much awareness of the political valence and uses of his own analysis, failing to recognize that the punitive sentiments and judgmental impatience he expressed were more typically targeted exactly at him and his progressive brethren and that an entire political logic was being built on that logic.[4]

As several very different authors have noted, a market which entrenches personal fulfillment through consumer choice as the ultimate value destabilizes not only those forms of identity which have traditionally helped support the capitalist system, like the family and the nation, but the very personal constraints which allow accumulation to take place.[5] As John Gray writes:

> The price of Thatcher's success was a society in many ways the opposite of the one she wanted.... In a television interview in January 1983 Thatcher declared her admiration for Victorian values and her belief that they could be revived. Actually, the country of Thatcher's nostalgic dreams was the Britain of the fifties, but the idea that unleashing market forces could re-create this lost idyll was strikingly paradoxical. The conservative Britain of the fifties was a by-product of Labour collectivism. Thatcher tore up the foundations of the country to which she dreamt of returning. Already semi-defunct when she came to power in 1979, it had vanished from memory when she left in 1990. In attempting to restore the past she erased its last traces.[6]

Michael Portillo, doyenne of the late-Thatcherite Right:

> viewed the Thatcherite social revolution as having two parts, but admit that only the first was achieved. First, people were to be allowed to keep more of their own money, through lower taxes on income, and correspondingly the state would do less. That she accomplished. Second, she intended that citizens should take much more responsibility. Those who became successful would be expected to do more for their communities. The altruistic tasks they took on would not only provide more efficient services to the public than the state could accomplish, it would also create better citizens and a healthier society. Of course, we remember the greedy people who emerged during the Thatcher years (the "loadsamoney" syndrome) and that damaged her. But she certainly did not approve of them. I have to admit to Margaret Thatcher's failure to complete her revolution. But she believed in a person's inalienable obligation to society.[7]

What is interesting is that these positions were essentially maintained by Blair, with appropriate genuflections in the direction of anti-sexism and anti-racism. Addressing the leadership of Rupert Murdoch's News Corp while still in opposition, he rejected "rigid economic planning and state control," and also "a type of individualism that confuses ... liberation from prejudice with a disregard for moral strictures. [The left] fought for racial and sexual equality, which was entirely right. It appeared indifferent to the family and individual responsibility, which was wrong."[8]

Precisely because of their adherence to these aspects of the postwar consensus, Thatcher and Blair were congenitally incapable of recognizing that the decline of "discipline and restraint" was not the result of correctible moral failings (Thatcher) nor the advocacy of incorrect attitudes on the left (Blair), but a trend inherent in the long-term development of capitalism which their own policies would exacerbate.

For William Davies, "What we witness, in the case of a World of Warfare addict, a social media addict or, for that matter, a sex addict, is only the more pathological element of a society that cannot conceive of relationships except in terms of the psychological pleasures that they produce." If "other people are only there to please, satisfy and affirm an individual ego from one moment to the next," then, as Davies remarks, the result is a vicious circle in which "it becomes harder and harder to find the satisfaction that one desperately wants."[9]

This vicious circle was exacerbated by the failure of neoliberal policies to achieve what they promised in material terms for the majority of people and the resulting increases in poverty and inequality on the one hand, and of the illnesses, family breakdown, and crime which they tend to bring on the other.

"Long before," argue Richard Wilkinson and Kate Pickett,

> the financial crisis which gathered pace in the latter part of 2008, British politicians commenting on the decline of community or the rise of various forms of anti-social behaviour would sometimes refer to our 'broken society.' The financial collapse shifted attention to the broken economy, and while the broken society was sometimes blamed on the behaviour of the poor, the broken economy was widely attributed to the rich.[10]

Wilkinson and Pickett go on to argue that both breakages are in fact primarily caused by the growth of inequality, which is to say, by the rich: "Although it does look as if neo-liberal policies widened income differences ...

there was no government intention to lower social cohesion or to increase violence, teenage births, obesity, drug abuse and everything else. . . . Their increase is, instead, an unintended consequence of the changes in income distribution."[11]

As Tony Judt points out, privatization has "no discernible collective advantage," for three reasons: it is inefficient, as public services had to be sold off at rock-bottom process to persuade the private sector to take them on, in addition to the fees paid to banks for conducting the transactions in the first place; second, it involves "moral hazard," as the state will either eliminate or at least reduce the possibility of risk; and, third, in more general terms, the state still had to regulate the services even afterwards.[12]

The real ideological consequences of privatization occurred in two other ways.

The first is that when public services like health and education are privatized (or simply run as if they were private companies), those aspects of service provision which are not purely functional for capital, such as social justice in the case of the former and personal development in that of the latter, tend to be reduced.[13] In education, there is an additional ideological component. As Sheldon Wolin notes, privatization "represents more than a switch in suppliers;" it also involves a "culture of competitiveness, hierarchy, self-interest. . . . Each instance of the private inroads into public functions extends the power of capital over society." Even under capitalism, education involves not only the acquisition of literacy and other skills, but empowerment, insofar as students develop the ability to think independently: "Privatization of education signifies not an abstract transfer of public to private but a takeover of the means to reshape the minds of coming generations, perhaps to blend popular education and media culture so as better to manage democracy."[14] One example can be found in what school students learn about the meaning of personal relationships: "The high performing school is an organisation in which the personal is used for the sake of the functional: relationships are important, the voices of students are elicited and acknowledged; community is valued—but all primarily for instrumental purposes within the context of the market-place."[15]

The second consequence of privatization is that when the state retreats from ownership and control it is much easier to present the effects of recession as outside the reach of human intervention, except through participation in the market. "Separating industry off from the state and subjecting it to the market can depoliticise the attacks on workers that accompany the crisis," explains Chris Harman, "shifting the blame to the seemingly automatic, natural forces of the market."[16] At the same time, once the market is naturalized in this way, it can also have a consoling effect on those who suffer from its operations: "Frederick Hayek knew that it was much easier to accept inequalities if one can claim that they result from an impersonal blind force," writes Slavoj Žižek. "The good thing about the 'irrationality' of the market and success and failure in capitalism is that it allows me precisely to perceive my failure or success as 'undeserved,' contingent."[17]

As Ben Wilson writes, this attitude is best summed up by the adoption of the doctrine of situational crime prevention (SCP) which has been influential on both the Home Office and private security firms:

> [SCP] comes from the starting point, like that of the Hayekian economists, that, left in freedom, we make rational choices on the market. ... It is the quintessence of individualism.... For we are all consumers who make choices. Most often, nice people buy things as the law dictates rather than steal them. This is for a variety of reasons (social expectation, upbringing, a belief in morality, etc.) but mostly because of lack of opportunity and a rationally made decision that the detrimental consequences of theft (losing your job, losing respect, etc.) outweigh the beneficial. In many ways it is like our decisions as consumers: we are exposed to numerous temptations on the high street or online and we choose the ones to give into.

As Wilson notes, "it is a pessimistic view of the individual," but it is one that is shaping the urban landscape. "SCP holds that everyone is a potential criminal and the world is a crime scene waiting to happen. That includes you." Furthermore, even if we do not choose to commit crime, we can be guilty of encouraging it by refusing ("choosing") not to take the necessary security precautions.[18]

Criminals, Incompetents, Intruders

Individuals may not blame capitalism as a system or themselves as participants in the system for their personal dissatisfactions, but this does not mean that they have dispensed with the need to find someone or something to blame; but whom? If, as Thatcher pointed out in a famous interview, "there is no such thing as society," but only a "living tapestry of men and women and people," then there can be no such thing as social groups, social classes, or, more to the point, social conflict.[19] But conflicts nevertheless continue to occur, with consequences set out by Zygmunt Bauman:

> Any turn of events that plays havoc with the expectations suggested by a person-focussed ideology is perceived and "made sense of," in the same ideology of privatisation, as a personal snub, a personally aimed (even if randomly targeted) humiliation; self-respect, as well as feelings of security and self-confidence, are its first casualties. The affected individuals feel debased, and since the ideology of privatisation assumes the presence of a culprit behind every case of suffering or discomfort, there ensues a feverish search for the persons guilty of debasing them; the conflict and enmity that arises is deemed personal. The guilty ones must be located, exposed, publicly condemned and punished. "Them" are as individualised as "us" in the ideology of privatisation.[20]

David Graeber echoes Baumann in arguing:

> [w]e have a real-estate bubble on the basis of the finance system, because every single super-rich person in the entire world has to have a house in London, so they're selling bits of London and the southeast. Why is it appealing? On the one hand, you have a creative, subservient working-class. You get the best servants here. Second of all, it's security; you have political safety, whereas if you come from Bahrain, Singapore, Macau, in those places something could still happen. The historical defeat of the working classes has now become the UK's export product. So people recognise that, but of course they resent it, so they take it out on the poor foreigners rather than the rich ones. Then the metropolitan elite preach tolerance, and of course they are hated; they are hated as the brokers of that system.[21]

Frank Field MP described these changes to the Home Affairs Committee in 2003 as a "movement from class politics to the politics of behaviour."[22]

To explain this apparent discrepancy, politicians (including Field) and the media have elevated two categories to the forefront of explanation: the Criminal and the Incompetent. These have been exemplified on the one hand by the armed burglar lying in wait to seize the property of the terrified readers of the *Daily Mail* and on the other by the social worker, alternatively unjustifiably removing children from one family or incomprehensibly failing to rescue them from another, to the uncomprehending fury of readers of the *Sun*. In circumstances where economics clearly is involved, as in the current crisis, scapegoats can be found who conform to these stereotypes; Bernie Madoff belongs to the ranks of the former, Sir Fred Goodwin to those of the latter. But there is also a third: the Intruder, characteristically an asylum seeker or illegal immigrant, who adds to the ranks of the Criminals while being housed and protected by the Incompetents, enslaved as they are to doctrines of Political Correctness.

The political implications are ominous. Alan Sinfield once wrote that "the larger danger of Thatcherism," which can here be taken as a surrogate for neoliberalism as a whole, was not so much its victories over trade unions or social democracy, but "its eventual failure to satisfy or control the emotions it arouses. . . . The rhetoric of Law and Order and victimization of subordinate groups, with which it attempts to make plausible its social and economic policies, provoke forces of retribution and stimulate expectations that may find terrible kinds of satisfaction."[23] It is this which has helped feed the growth of fascism in Europe, but this may not be the most frightening consequence. Fascism, even under the mask of respectability worn by the Front National in France or by the British National Party, can be identified, isolated, and crushed; and in Britain at least there has been a tradition of successfully doing so, from the mobilizations of the Anti-Nazi League and Rock Against Racism in the late 1970s to those of Unite Against Fascism and Love Music Hate Racism today. A bleaker, because more insidious, scenario would be for racism and xenophobia to become treated as commodities which can be chosen by consumers, not as part of a far-right project, but routinely, like cars or foreign holidays. A possible consequence, one not far removed from contemporary reality, was portrayed by the late J. G. Ballard in his final novel, *Kingdom Come*, where one of his typically detached heroes interrupts an act of "religious cleansing" in which a Muslim family are evicted from their house by a crowd of suburban consumers: "I accepted that a new kind of hate has emerged, silent and disciplined, a racism tempered by loyalty cards and PIN numbers. Shopping was now the model for all human behaviour, drained of emotion and anger. The decision by the estate-dwellers to reject the imam was an exercise of consumer choice."[24]

The changes in the form of property ownership brought about by neoliberalism, which did not in any fundamental sense alter capitalist relations of production, nevertheless had effects on human subjectivities. Hannah Arendt once suggested that the most terrifying aspect of Nazi and Stalinist rule was not that the conception of human nature they held were true, but that it could be made true.[25] Some writers, including the late Pierre Bourdieu, have argued that this is also true of neoliberalism.[26] And indeed, if it were possible to create societies in which people think of themselves primarily as consumers, individually responsible for their fate, employment prospects, health, and even personal happiness, then we would have reached the apotheosis of neoliberalism, the final perfection of the type of human that Michael Kidron called "Market Being."[27] This is unlikely to happen for a number of reasons, to which I will return below, but the damage which is being done to actual human beings in the attempt has been considerable and continues to this day.

Not education but money and power are the ends to which people should aspire:

> Thus educators, poorly paid and relatively powerless in the real world of politics and economics, are not really respected even in their fields of expertise. The best and brightest do not become teachers. People know that if teachers were smarter they would not have chosen such an unimportant field; they would make their own way in the world. Those talented eggheads and dreamers who do understand this and become teachers anyway are especially to be mistrusted, motivated as they are by alien ideas, thinking they are better than the rest.[28]

"The only way to explain this", writes David Graeber,

> is not that they are somehow confused about their self-interest, but that they are indignant at the very idea that self-interest is all that

politics could ever be about. . . . The moment that we realize that most Americans are not cynics, the appeal of right-wing populism becomes much easier to understand. It comes, often enough, surrounded by the most vile sorts of racism, sexism, homophobia. But what lies behind it is a genuine indignation at being cut off from the means for doing good. Take two of the most familiar rallying cries of the populist right: hatred of the "cultural elite" and the constant calls to "support our troops." On the surface, it seems that these would have nothing to do with each other. In fact, they are profoundly linked. It might seem strange that so many working-class Americans would resent that fraction of the 1 percent who work in the culture industry [more] than they do oil tycoons and HMO executives, but it actually represents a fairly realistic assessment of the situation: an air conditioner repairman from Nebraska is aware that while it is exceedingly unlikely that his child would ever become CEO of a large corporation, it could possibly happen; but it's utterly unimaginable that she will ever become an international human rights lawyer or drama critic for *The New York Times.* . . . If an air conditioner repairman's daughter does aspire to a career where she can serve some calling higher than herself, she really only has two realistic options: she can work for her local church, or she can join the army.[29]

The Scottish playwright Alan Bisset recalls such a process of atomization taking place in his youth:

I grew up on a new-build housing scheme in Falkirk called Hallglen. In 1975, the year of my birth, my parents were among the first people to move there. It looked just like *Gregory's Girl*, the council homes gleaming an identical white. There were grass parks, ash parks, swing-parks, woodland, shops owned by local people, two bars, even a nightclub (which I'm reliably told, attracted folk "from as far away as Airdrie"). It was a great place to grow up, a testament to imaginative social housing. My memory of the early eighties was of parties: street parties, house parties, gala days, the adults rolling around singing the hits of the sixties and Corries songs, while their children were upstairs on the Atari.

Come the Nineties and the fences were five, six, seven feet high. Nobody walked in and out of their neighbour's gardens. The street parties had all stopped. Envy of the neighbours became all-pervasive,
and so the arms race: two cars per household, TVs in every room,
double-glazing, patios, garden extensions, conservatories, satellite
dishes. It's not that there was no warmth and friendliness any more,
but put it this way: people no longer come all the way from Airdrie
to the pubs and clubs of Hallglen because nobody really bothers to
leave the house anymore.[30]

Upon this atomized landscape are erected new ramparts of reaction.
David Blacker writes about "the pitiful cretins holding signs warning the
government away from their medicare (a government program):"

These are people who have half-internalized the idea that turning
against one another and competing for crumbs is somehow more
enabling than collective action against the gluttons at the high
table. Old tricks of divide and conquer such as racism, xenophobia, religious clannishness (which yields a sense of belonging and
"metaphysical comfort"), and sometimes purely Madison Avenue–
manufactured aesthetic preferences, like the designed distaste for
protesting "hippies," further confuse the crumb-seekers. The de-
pressing irony appears to be that the only people who "believe"
in neoliberalism—and then only half-way—are the ones who are
actively victimized by it, the ones against whom it is wielded as a
propaganda weapon.[31]

Such tactics operate in a context were

[a] generalized sameness is inevitably one result of the global scale
of the markets in question, and their dependence on the consistent
or predictable actions of large populations. It is attained not by the
making of similar individuals, as theories of mass society used to
assert, but through the reduction or elimination of differences, by
narrowing the range of behaviours that can function effectively or
successfully in most contemporary institutional contexts.[32]

Structural change lies behind this affective experience. As Giovanni

Arrighi, Terence K. Hopkins and Immanuel Wallerstein note, "[t]he history of the capitalist world economy since 1973 has been the history of its adjustment to the social upheavals of the previous five years." This includes "cultural and political backlash of the 1970s and of the 1980s against everything that 1968 stood for," but also of the need to:

> ... distinguish carefully between the movements and ideologies of 1968 and the underlying structural transformations that preceded and outlived those movements and ideologies. These structural transformations are the outcome of secular trends of the capitalist world-economy, and as such cannot be reversed by any unfavourable conjuncture that might ensue from their open manifestation.[33]

In effect, what firms learned in the 1970s was to put the individualization of both customers and products at the service of commercial expansion. Diversified consumption entailed hitherto unknown opportunities for the individualized expression of social identities. The 1970s and 1980s were also a time when traditional families and communities were rapidly losing authority, offering markets the opportunity to fill a fast-growing social vacuum, which contemporary liberation theorists had mistaken for the beginnings of a new age of autonomy and emancipation. The possibilities for diversified obsolescence they inflicted on first-generation consumer durables also helped to motivate renewed work discipline among traditional workers and the newcomers to paid employment, not least the women.[34] The novelist J. G. Ballard diagnosed the transition thus:

> People certainly lost interest in the future. And, partly, I think, the prosperity in the sixties and seventies induced a kind of infantilism. People stopped dealing with a timescale that lay outside their immediate present. They began to have no sense of what had happened yesterday or what would happen the day after tomorrow. So people became immersed in the fulfilment of their own needs and their own satisfactions. They literally lost interest in the future. But by the same token, they also lost interest in the past.[35]

Stuart Hall and his collaborators on *Policing the Crisis* identified the new restructuring thus:

A glance at some of the new magazines which were the product of this era—like *Playboy* or *Playgirl*—will suggest how easily free sex could be harnessed to the services of the status quo. There are many indications that capitalism itself required some restructuring of the tight bonds of family life—though the backlash in defence of the family, when the Women's Movement pushed their critique to the limits, suggest that, like all the other liberatory trends, this one was also designed to stop short within well-designed limits. Looking back [from 1978], we can see now that the "crisis of authority" associated in the early days of affluence with its advanced party "youth," was the first symptomatic reaction by the old guard of a dominant culture to a rupture in *its own traditional forms*. Those who identified capitalism with its earlier ethic resisted the onset of the new ethic in the name of the defence of traditional wisdoms and way of life. They were thus obliged to regard the advocates of the "cultural revolution" as constituting a conspiracy foisted on society from outside (mainly, as usual, from the United States). They could not see that the bonds of a more austere bourgeois moral regime were being partly dissolved *from inside*, as a by-product of capitalism's own contradictory "maturity."[36]

Mark Greif, borrowing from Marcuse, draws a distinction between *liberation* and *liberalization* in relation to sex: "One of the cruel betrayals of sexual liberation, in liberalization, was the illusion that a person can be free only if he holds sex as all-important and exposes it endlessly to others—providing it, proving it, enjoying it." As Greif points out, the betrayal was not always intentional: many radicals simply inverted the age-old moralistic argument about the need to restrain sexual activity because of its overwhelming power:

> This misformulation of liberation became as damaging as it did only because another force turned out to have great use for the idea that sex is the bearer of the richest experiences: commerce. The field of sex was initially very difficult to liberate against a set of rival norms that had structured it for centuries: priority of the family, religious prohibitions, restraint of biology. Once liberation reached a point of adequate success, however, sex was unconscionably easy to liberate

further, as commerce discovered it had a new means of entry into private life and threw its weight behind the new values.[37]

Perry Anderson, writing of the same process, notes that:

> [s]ince the sixties, a more or less bohemian counter-culture had developed in the US, rejecting conventional mores and beliefs. Radicalized by opposition to the war in Vietnam, it had served as a convenient target for Nixon to rally a silent majority of law-abiding patriots to his cause. With the fading of war in Indochina as an issue, depoliticization of this area set in. From the late seventies onwards, much of what was once a counter-culture migrated into a less rigidly regimented, vaguely bien-pensant sector of mainstream bourgeois life itself, where market forces normalized flouting of traditional taboos into profitable forms of repressive de-sublimation. This mutation, of which Clinton could be taken as a tawdry emblem, catalysed a vehement reaction in the ranks of low-denomination religion, pitting no longer a "silent" but a "moral" majority—in reality another minority, of evangelicals—against godless subversion of right living. Self-conceived as conservative, these groups became over time shock troops of Republican electoral mobilization, propelling contrary forces—sympathy for LGBT would be a short-hand today—into the Democratic camp.[38]

Identity and autonomy, championed at first on the left, were soon co-opted by the neoliberal right. Liberating individualism was transformed into exploitable atomization, creative self-expression replaced by a depoliticized, desocializing consumerism that enabled the rise of a new oligarchy. The most enduring political legacy of the New Left is not to be found in leftwing movements, but in the radical right's institution-smashing insurgency.[39]

As Hall and his colleagues point out, although the counterculture "produced no material political force . . . what it *did* produce was a specter of 'the enemy' in the mind of its opponents."[40]

As Peter Hitchens writes:

> The Left are right to put part of the blame for the current riot of selfishness on the shoulders of Lady Thatcher. They are right to perceive a moral emptiness in her government, which showed no interest in moral and cultural issues, in family breakdown, the decay of

marriages, the collapse of discipline and learning in schools.[41]

Viv Albertine's diary of the late punk period describes the same phenomenon in a very different setting:

> 1981: There are two kinds of people in the "punk" scene. There are the psychopathic, nihilistic extremists and careerists, who are very confident because they have no fear, lack empathy and don't care what others think of them. The second kind are drawn to the scene by the ideas—I hope the latter will endure much longer than the first type, who are just like the collaborators during the Second World War, just want to be on the side that's winning. It's new to me, this mercenary streak in people. I didn't notice it in my teens, but now I'm in my twenties I notice it more. Or maybe this attitude only started to rear its head after Margaret Thatcher became prime minister in 1979.[42]

Mark Lilla has written of how "the Jacobin spirit" embodied in the Tea Party "dovetails with the spirits of Woodstock and Wall Street":

> For half a century now Americans have been rebelling in the name of individual freedom. Some wanted a more tolerant society with greater private autonomy, and now we have it, which is a good thing—though it also brought us more out-of-wedlock births, a soft pornographic popular culture, and a drug trade that serves casual users while destroying poor American neighborhoods and destabilizing foreign nations. Others wanted to be free from taxes and regulations so they could get rich fast, and they have—and it's left the more vulnerable among us in financial ruin, holding precarious jobs, and scrambling to find health care for their children. We wanted our two revolutions. Well, we have had them. Now an angry group of Americans wants to be freer still—free from government agencies that protect their health, wealth, and well-being; free from problems and policies too difficult to understand; free from parties and coalitions; free from experts who think they know better than they do; free from politicians who don't talk or look like they do (and Barack Obama certainly doesn't). They want to say what they have to say without fear of contradiction, and then hear someone

on television tell them they're right. They don't want the rule of the people, though that's what they say. They want to be people without rules—and, who knows, they may succeed.[43]

"The deliquescence of bourgeois society has come about not through the abolition of capitalism but as a result of capitalism operating without restraint."[44]

Anderson writes of how, by the 1970s,

> the bourgeoisie . . . in any strict sense, as a class possessed of self-consciousness and morale—was extinct. . . . In place of that solid amphitheatre is an aquarium of floating, evanescent forms— the projectors and managers, auditors and janitors, administrators and speculators of contemporary capital: functions of a monetary universe that knows no social fixities or stable identities.

And this had led to changes in behavior. Rightly dismissing sociological notions about the *embourgeoisement* of the working class, Anderson instead identifies a quite different process, "a general *encanaillement* of the possessing classes."[45]

As Angela Nagle notes, "The Sadean transgressive element of the 60s' has become the 'style of the new right.'"[46] But, as John Micklethwait and Adrian Wooldridge write, "the battle between libertarians and traditionalists is about class as well as values. In particular, it is a battle between business conservatives and social conservatives":

> These two categories often overlap: many social conservatives are small-business owners (and vice-versa). But there is also a difference of emphasis. Business conservatives are focussed on making money. Social conservatives are worried about what kind of society America is becoming. Business conservatives belong to country clubs. Social conservatives wear plaid trousers and read the Bible literally. . . . Even in the South, where most businesspeople are socially conservative, they often shy away from ideological controversies—not least because they are bad for business.

As these authors note, there is "a logical contradiction between trying to be the party of both the free market and the heartland," above all because "the more successful the [Republican] party is at implementing its economic creed, the more quickly it devours its own demographic base."[47]

This hybrid of cultural liberalism and free-market economics is not restricted to the US. "Thatcher might have won elections," notes Robert Elms:

> but culturally we won. Look at Britain now: it's a society where racism is absolutely frowned on; where gay marriage is accepted. It's totally different from that Little England that Thatcher tried to hold onto. This period from the mid-seventies to the early nineties was the last time pop and politics sat together and where pop meant anything politically.[48]

One of the most telling aspects of this development is the Equality Act (2010), which received royal assent on April 8, shortly before the General Election which resulted in the Conservative-Liberal Democrat Coalition taking office. Conceived by the New Labour government as a means of consolidating and rationalizing all the legislation relating to inequality from the Equal Pay Act 1970 through to the Equality Act (Sexual Orientation) Regulations 2007, the Act originally included a new duty for public bodies to take account of "socio-economic disadvantage" when making decisions about how to perform their functions.

Jefferson Cowie notes in this regard that:

> As fundamental as inclusion, identity and diversity were, an emphasis on gender and racial equality alone tended to allow jobs, pay and labor rights to fall out of the equation, leaving workers with a set of individual rights to non-discrimination amidst a more brutal economy—a multicultural neo-liberalism. . . . Popular depoliticization has allowed economic elites nearly uncontested control over civic life, making postmodern politics the cultural handmaiden of the neo-liberal order.[49]

As Peter York writes, the cult of authenticity has "taken on board the styles and slogans of a mass of post-war liberations and welded them to the most iron-clad capitalism possible."[50] Similarly, for John Pilger:

> The award of the Nobel Prize to the first black American president because he "offered hope" was both absurd and an authentic

expression of the lifestyle liberalism that controls much political debate in the west. Same-sex marriage is one such distraction. No "issue" diverts attention as successfully as this . . . . The truth is that what matters to those who aspire to control our lives is not skin pigment, or gender, or whether or not we are gay, but the class we serve.[51]

As the musician Sylvain Sylvain observed towards the end of the 1980s: "Today maybe you can be gay, but you can't be communist."[52] Carl Cederström and Peter Fleming write:

All those elements of personality that were once barred from work—sexuality, lifestyle, fashion tastes, obsessions with pop stars and health food—have now become welcome, if not demanded on the job. If you're gay, that's great! If you hate capitalism, wonderful! If you are of Nepalese ethnic descent, perfect! For there is no better call centre worker than one who can improvise around the script, breathe life into a dead role and pretend their living death is in fact the apogee of life.[53]

It was groups like Wham!—or more accurately their forerunners in the 1960s and 1970s, with all their talk of fighting the system, standing up to the establishment, being who you wanted to be and living life on your own terms—who opened up the door for Mrs. Thatcher. By undermining the institutions that had dominated British life for decades, by emphasizing the importance of self-gratification, and by celebrating the value of the individual, Lennon and his contemporaries made it much easier for younger voters, in particular, to embrace her free market message.[54]

Doreen Massey writes of:

the way in which so many of the radical challenges it made to the post-war hegemony (feminism, the rejection of an undifferentiated "public," the acknowledgement of heterogeneity, the stress on flexibility and flow rather than rigidity . . .) have been in a thousand ways recuperated into the current hegemonic project, taken up in ways we never meant, turned to use as flexibilised labour, selfish individualism, and arguments against collectivism and the state. "Liberation" turned into lifestyle capitalism. Cries of "yes but . . ." and "we never meant that" do not have much political appeal. And so we find ourselves wrong-footed, and yet further disarmed."[55]

Megan Erickson takes the specific example of schooling. Take the anarchist anti-school vision associated particularly with Paul Goodman but shared far more widely: "Rebelling against the institutional part of public institutions is the defining characteristic of this response to structural inequality. Goodman sees schooling as social control, the individual thwarted, taxes squandered on 'wars, school teachers, and politicians.'" But as Erickson notes, the US school system is already highly decentralized, and "the values of freedom, autonomy, and choice are in perfect accordance with market-based 'reforms,' and with the neoliberal vision of society on which they're based."[56]

The outcome of these changes is the "rebel consumer…who, adopting the rhetoric but not the politics of the counterculture, convinces himself that buying the right products individualizes him as transgressive. Purchasing the products of authority is thus reimagined as a defiance of authority."[57]

Consider Eduardo Paolozzi's publicly funded mosaics at Tottenham Court Road underground station, completed by the Scottish artist in 1982, just as the first phase of neoliberalism was getting going, and dismantled in 2015 as part of the Crossrail project. Much of the discussion around this act of vandalism centered on the artistic value of the artworks, but as Ian Martin notes:

> Arguments about the aesthetics of Paolozzi's mosaics missed the point, it seemed to me, which has less to do with the merit of the art itself and more to do with what, in the long run, it turned out the art was for. Paolozzi's legacy had stood intact for three decades. Not just as 1,000 sq m of charming, optimistic art, but as 1,000 sq m of commercial retardant. You can't paste an ad on to a wallful of public art. You can't fix one of those irritating micromovies over it, telling a vacuous five-second story about investments or vitamins or hair. The Paolozzi mosaics went up as decorative art, just as privatisation was about to explode like a dirty bomb all over the public realm. What survives at Tottenham Court Road station is a brave, forlorn little seawall set against a stormtide of corporate advertising.[58]

CHAPTER 6

Market States?

The other area where theory and reality have been at odds is in relation to the role of states. Friedrich von Hayek saw an important component of what he called "true" individualism as being voluntary submission to the rules of the market:

> The willingness to submit to such rules, not merely so long as one understands the reason for them, but so long as one has no definite reason to the contrary, is an essential condition for gradual evolution and improvement of rules of social intercourse; and the readiness ordinarily to submit to the products of a social process which nobody has designed and the reasons for which nobody may understand is also an indispensable condition if it is to be possible to dispense with compulsion.[1]

And if this "indispensable condition" is not met, compulsion will of course have to continue and the power of the state be increased. Since neoliberalism has been met with resistance as well as submission, we have seen an extension of the type of legal constraints earlier imposed on trade unions to social movements concerned with, for example, Third World debt or the environment. The limitation on the number of strikers allowed to picket outside a workplace, for example, has its analogue in the more recent proliferation of restraining orders issued against demonstrators outside research laboratories or company headquarters.

Unintended or not, renewed rounds of the kind of state intervention supposedly rejected by neoliberalism in theory were required to deal with the social problems neoliberalism generated in practice. One of the key reasons for the development of the security state is, therefore, the assumption that citizen-consumers will behave in noneconomic market ways. In David Edgar's coupling, "the free" cannot be trusted to be "the good," and as such, in Andrew Gamble's reformulation of the prewar German slogan, "the free economy" necessarily implies "the strong state"; it is because in both cases the former term signifies an atomized society.[2] The neoliberal state cannot simply be that of economic management but must also be that of social control. Thus, although Neil Smith is right that "the neoconservative moment has passed" as a result of the debacle in Iraq, this only refers to a very narrow aspect of neoconservatism as a particularly "adventurist" strategic option for US imperialism.[3] Neoconservatism as a necessary repressive accompaniment to neoliberalism in domestic terms is still alive and well. "The anarchy of the market, of competition, and of unbridled individualism . . . generates a situation that becomes increasingly ungovernable," writes David Harvey. And in the face of "social anarchy and nihilism," he notes, with perhaps excessive restraint, "some degree of coercion appears necessary to restore order."[4] The turn to neoconservatism in this sense will now become even more marked, as the unemployed, single parents, migrants, refugees, and asylum seekers will find themselves the target of a cynical scapegoating strategy to divert hostility away from those responsible for the crisis towards those who will suffer the most as a consequence of it: a classic case of blaming the victims of neoliberalism, in this case to shift responsibility for the failures of neoliberalism to resolve the problems created by capitalism. Unchecked, the future may well be as foreseen by George Steiner at the fall of the Berlin Wall, combining repression and commodification: "The knout on the one hand; the cheeseburger on the other."[5]

Privatization notwithstanding, neoliberal capitalism could not dispense with states' services—a truth upon which the chief executives of many an ailing financial institution has had occasion to reflect since September 2008. Unlike their neoclassical predecessors, however, neoliberals tended to emphasize anti-state rhetoric, whatever their record in practice. As a result, some critics of neoliberalism argue as if the latter really do see states and markets as antipodes and consequently invert the supposed value judgement involved, treating the state as a welcome restraint on market excesses rather than a destructive interference with market creativity. Tony Judt, for example, highlights the way in which totalitarian regimes always destroy all intermediary institutions between the state and the citizen, and claims that neoliberal regimes have a similar ambition, although in their case it is to remove any institutions which lie between the market and the consumer. In both cases, he argues, the objective is to produce atomized individuals unable to mount collective resistance. For Judt, however, the triumph of neoliberalism has changed the significance of the state, which he claims "is now an intermediary institution.... When the economy, and the forces and patterns of behaviour that accompany it are truly international, the only institution that can effectively interpose itself between those forces and the unprotected individual is the national state."[6] But, as we have seen, the opposition of interventionist state and free market is false. In Bernard Wasserstein's words, "Neoliberalism rejected the state of the social democratic compromise, not the state in general."[7] Indeed, in some respects states under neoliberalism have accrued even more power to themselves than they did during the Keynesian era. The measures of nationalization and state control in response to the present crisis are, therefore, not a return to state interventionism, since it has never ceased. Indeed, even though the neoclassical and neoliberal schools both see an important role for states—enabling market activity on the one hand, disabling collective opposition on the other—their actual role in direct economic terms has gone much further than either theoretical tradition allows.

Both the size of states and the level of state expenditure remain substantial, as Wasserstein notes in the context of the longer-term history of capitalism:

> The tentacular extension of the state, mainly as the result of two wars and the costs of social welfare, health and education, showed no signs of easing in the late twentieth century in spite of the "neo-liberal" trend.... The proportion of workers in public employment grew from between 2 and 5 per cent in west European countries in 1913 to between 15 and 30 per cent by the 1990s. From the mid-1990s, however, growth in public expenditure as a proportion of GDP eased in most countries. In "Euroland" total government outlays peaked at 49 per cent in 1995 and then declined to 45 per cent by 2000.[8]

Much of this expenditure was directed towards forms of state activity long-established during the preceding social democratic era. As far as the economy is concerned, the arms industry saw no diminution of government largesse in either Britain or the USA, and more targeted assistance was made available for companies deemed too important to the economy ("too big") to fail. Chris Harman points out that "states have intervened more to deal with crises since the 1970s than in the 1960s and 1950s for the simple reason that the crises have been much more severe," as these examples from the USA show:

> The US state helped bail out Chrysler when it came close to going bust in 1979; it took charge of negotiations in the 1980s to prevent US banks being dragged under by unpayable debts from Latin American countries. In 1998 it propped up the Long-Term Capital Management hedge fund and, most recently, through the Federal Reserve Bank, it has tried to limit the damage caused to the financial system by the mortgage crisis.[9]

What, then, has changed under neoliberalism? It is not the amount of state expenditure and areas of state intervention that have changed, but where money is spent and how activities are carried out. The process has been one of "reorientation rather than decline."[10] As Costas Lapavitsas explains: "What has vanished irretrievably is the notion—characteristic of postwar Keynesianism—that economic intervention should aim at achieving full employment and securing social welfare."[11] Philip Bobbitt has predicted the new orientation of the "market state" as these shifts take place:

> It will require more centralised authority for government, but all governments will be weaker, having greatly contracted the scope of their undertakings, having devolved or lost authority to so many other institutions, including deregulated corporations, which are in but not of the state, NGOs . . . which are in but not of the market, and clandestine military networks and terrorist groups, which set up proto-markets in security and function as proto-states at war.[12]

John Clarke and Janet Newman have argued that, in effect, this is already happening as the state follows a strategy of "dispersal": "The state delegates—through a variety of means—its authority to subaltern organisations that are thus empowered to act on its *behalf*."[13] The result has involved new relationships with private capital, as Simon Jenkins details for the British case:

> As the economy shifted from manufacturing to services, new candidates came forward for state custodianship. Some were genuinely new nationalised industries, such as the Crown Prosecution Service (replacing private solicitors), the Child Support Agency, the Housing Corporation and the provider wing of the NHS, corporatising what were myriad charities and foundations. Others emerged from the booming world of regulation. . . . Firms with anonymous names like Serco, Capita, Carillion and Jarvis build and run Britain's roads, railways, hospitals, schools, pension services, speed cameras and congestion charges, and are believed by the Treasury to be "private." Yet they are merely capitalist redefinitions of state-financed activities.[14]

Welfare provision best illustrates the point. Actual levels of spending have been maintained, partly because of resistance to attacks, but also because there are limits beneath which expenditure on the social wage cannot drop without endangering the process of accumulation.[15] But beneath headline spending figures, the services have been reconfigured. Care of children, the elderly, and people with disabilities or long-term illness, for example, has increasingly been passed from the state to the family—which generally means the female members of the family—with these "informal" arrangements then subject to evaluation by state agencies: "While the state has withdrawn in some ways, its powers and apparatuses have been extended in others—transferring 'responsibilities' but simultaneously creating the capabilities of surveillance and enforcement to ensure that such responsibilities are being fulfilled."[16]

The main distinction, in Britain at least, is in the attitude towards the constitutional form of the state; more specifically, towards what is known in Britain as devolution. One consequence of the Labour Party victory in the British General Election of May 1997 was the implementation of several long-awaited constitutional reforms, key among which were the devolution settlements in Scotland and Wales, and the restoration of local government in London. Many commentators who are otherwise highly critical of the New Labour government regard these measures as unambiguously positive and perhaps its only genuinely radical achievement.[17] Yet devolution is not only a way of meeting popular aspirations without threatening the economic order; it is also potentially useful to social neoliberalism. "Neoliberal politics actually favours both administrative decentralisation and the maximisation of local autonomy," writes David Harvey, for whom these "are primary vehicles for producing greater inequality."[18] Indeed, in a British context in particular, devolution is one of the strategies that specifically distinguishes social from vanguard neoliberalism, but it is one made possible only by the earlier success of Thatcher's centralizing drive in imposing counterreforms.

On the one hand, the more politics is emptied of content, the more social neoliberal regimes need to prove that democracy is still meaningful—not of course by extending the areas of social life under democratic control, but by multiplying the opportunities for citizen-consumers to take part in elections for local councillors, mayors, members of the Welsh and London Assemblies, and the Scottish, European, and British Parliaments. High levels of electoral participation in these elections would have been used to claim the active consent of the governed, but voter turnout has continued to fall as electorates have proved reluctant to play their allotted roles in the ritual, to the extent that the same establishment politicians who oversaw the hollowing-out of the democratic process now complain, with characteristic hypocrisy, that citizens are neglecting their civic responsibilities. Devolution, in other words, has not reversed the growing public withdrawal from official politics and, in that sense, has failed as a neoliberal strategy of legitimation.

On the other hand, devolution is also part of a neoliberal strategy of delegation and in this respect has been much more successful. Here, responsibility for implementing anti-reforms is spread beyond governing parties and central state apparatuses to elected bodies whose policy options are severely restricted both by statute and reliance on the Treasury for most of their funding. As Colin Leys notes:

> In effect, local political authorities are left to do what they feel they can within the constraints set by the market in their areas. Provided it is done in such a way that local people feel they have an appropriate share of whatever national resources there are, this option has the merit of relieving the central government of some of the responsibility for decisions that are in any case more and more severely constrained.[19]

Take devolved government in London as an example. Doreen Massey claims that there are still possibilities for reform at the local level:

> "Neoliberalism" is sometimes written about as though there is an automatic transmission belt from some ethereal sphere of greater forces to "how it plays out on the ground." It is not so. There are indeed pressures and constraints, often of immense power, but there are also agents who play along, or resist, or struggle mightily. There is room for political intervention.

Massey claims that the Greater London Authority (GLA) was a site of resistance, at least while Ken Livingstone was mayor; but after listing a series of admirable but largely symbolic or gestural policies (opposition to racism, support for Hugo Chávez), she is forced to admit: "There is no simple transmission belt for neoliberalism. And yet it is made here." Indeed, her substantive discussion shows precisely how the GLA has contributed towards the making of neoliberalism in the British capital city, even under Livingstone's leadership.[20]

The distribution of responsibility for decision-making downward to the localities is likely to continue and gather further momentum following the onset of recession and still greater spending restraints. In Britain, the process may actually be assisted by the parliamentary expenses scandal first revealed by the *Daily Telegraph* during the spring of 2009. The guilty men and women, among whom Conservative leader David Cameron has been the most insistent, are now attempting to mobilize mass revulsion at their own activities by calling for decision-making responsibility to be devolved still further, from professional politicians to individuals, families, neighborhoods, and even local councils.[21] Some naive social democrats have simply accepted this at face value. Ed Howker and Shiv Malik, for example, write that

> the closer people are to the power that's exercised on their behalf, the better that power will be administered in a democracy. . . . For this reason, the decisions by the coalition government to channel power to local communities—through the election of police chiefs and more local referendums—are very welcome; so too are undertakings to ensure greater transparency at all levels of government.'[22]

The *Guardian*'s Patrick Wintour says of Labour frontbencher Stella Creasy:

She insists the evidence shows that where people are involved in re-configuring services there can be better results and savings. "I think the biggest challenge for the left is not going to be money. I think it is going to be control, and being willing to devolve more power to local level, but devolve again and argue: 'If we are going to resolve this, you as a user need to have not just more say, but more responsibility.' But I think this is where the public are."[23]

On "cooperative" councils: "But in these times of an unprecedented public funding squeeze," asks Kate Murray, "isn't co-operative commissioning just a way of shifting responsibility for making cuts?" In spite of the fact that Lambeth Council's annual budget will have shrunk by a third, amounting to £90 million by 2015, Council leader Steve Reed replied: "We can deliver better public services by empowering citizens whether we have twice the amount of money we do or half the amount. This is not a cuts-led agenda but one we are implementing at a time of cuts."[24]

For Ambalavaner Sivanandan:

> What decentralisation means . . . is not devolving power from central government to local government, but from local government to private enterprise. What empowerment means is to hand over the running of local services to voluntarism and social enterprise and private firms, with local authorities playing an enabling role. That is the best-case scenario, but often social enterprise makes businesses of voluntarism and private enterprise makes businesses of social enterprise.[25]

Greg Sharzer describes "localism" as "the petty bourgeoisie's war of position":

> In place of the historical traditions of class struggle, the petite bourgeoisie's voluntarist ethos allows localism to promote small lifestyle choices and a proper moral outlook. Community and voluntary simplicity provide a neat fit with localism's criticism of size, and an implicit judgment of working class behaviours and appetites. Darker streaks of catastrophism and Malthusianism infuse it with terror when necessary.[26]

Participatory budgeting (PB) was first practiced by the Workers' Party after it won control of Porto Alegre in 1989, but was quickly picked up in the more developed world, notably by the Toronto Community Housing Corporation since 2001. As Greg Sharzer writes:

> PB is a resolutely localist project. It promotes community values and activism and encourages democratic control over the market. But it's also a way to reconcile tenants to neoliberal policy. . . . Rather than organizing to resist the cutbacks, the process framed them as inevitable. . . . PB advocates suggest many ways to get more people to participate. However, these are framed as technical, not political problems. In other words, it's okay to ask how budgeting works but not what the goals are.[27]

As Phillip Blond writes, "The welfare state, I believe, began the destruction of the independent life of the British working class . . . making the populace a supplicant citizenry dependent on the state rather than on themselves."[28]

Cameron has been urged to "delegate the axe," as the process is called by two enthusiasts for decentralization: "Local politics would take some of the pressure of rising expectations. Councils could no longer complain about central interference, league tables and challenge funding. The government would be relieved of blame for every penny rise in council tax."[29]

Neoliberal attitudes towards the mass of the population are an uneasy combination of private suspicion over what they might do without state surveillance and repression, and public disquisitions on the need to listen to The People, provided of course that politicians are being asked to listen to the right sort of people with the right sort of demands—in other words, longer prison sentences and more restricted immigration, rather than higher taxation for the rich or military withdrawal from Afghanistan. In the case of devolution, the assumption is that the people most likely to participate in local decision-making will be members of the middle class, who can be expected to behave, *en masse*, in ways which will impose restrictions on local taxation and public spending, and thus maintain the neoliberal order with a supposedly popular mandate.

As a result of these two pressures—some devolution of power and extreme fiscal retrenchment—Bobbitt predicts, "the welfare state will have greatly retrenched, but infrastructure security, epidemiological surveillance,

and environmental protection—all of which are matters of general welfare—
will be promoted by the state as never before."[30] These changes demonstrate
the fundamental difference between classical liberalism and neoliberalism.
Mark Olssen writes that in the latter, the state creates "the appropriate market
by providing the conditions, laws and institutions necessary for its operation"
and "an individual who is an enterprising and competitive entrepreneur," the
link between them signaled by:

> ... a change in subject position from "homo economicus," who nat-
> urally behaves out of self interest and is relatively detached from the
> state, to "manipulatable man," who is created by the state and who is
> continually encouraged to be "perpetually responsive." ... It is not
> that the conception of the self-interested subject is replaced or done
> away with by the new ideals of "neo-liberalism," but that in an age of
> universal welfare, the perceived possibilities of slothful indolence
> create necessities for new forms of vigilance, surveillance, "perfor-
> mance appraisal" and forms of control generally.[31]

As this suggests, it is in the areas of repression and surveillance that
the power of the state has heightened to a degree previously unimaginable,
except under conditions of total war last experienced between 1939 and
1945. In 1981, very early in the establishment of the neoliberal order, Henri
Lefebvre predicted that a consequence of neoliberalism would be "the administration of daily life," to the point where the state obtained "a state of
total knowledge—the past, present and future of each member (individual
or group) registered, described, prescribed by perfectly informed 'services,'
down to the smallest move, the smallest payment, the most insignificant of
social and individual acts." Without resistance, "this science-fiction scenario
will gradually become our familiar landscape," in which state or private bureaucracies "will treat daily life . . . quite simply as a conquered country."[32]
Attempts to downplay these developments tend on the one hand to claim
that new information technologies can also be used by citizens to record evidence of state activity and on the other that it is not so much the state ("big
brother") which is carrying out surveillance and tracking activity as different domains of society.[33] It is true that certain incidents that the state would
wish to cover up can be revealed by the use of the camera facility on mobile

phones, as in the killing of Ian Tomlinson during the 2009 G20 demonstrations in London; but the relative weight of organized resources is all on the other side and, as this episode reminds us, it has the capacity for violent repression, as well as surveillance. Equally, in the situation where many of the functions of the state have been institutionally "delegated" or "dispersed," how useful is it to maintain the absolute separation of "state" and "society"?

Why has this tendency been such an integral part of neoliberalism? In a British context, Jenkins claims that there were two strands to Thatcherism, realized in two distinct "revolutions": "The first revolution set out to liberate the 'supply side' of the British economy, and to give new spirit and confidence to private enterprise." If the first revolution was one driven by "political will," the second was an expression of "power": "Thatcher centralised government, enforced Treasury discipline and regulated both public and private sectors to an unprecedented degree. Where state ownership retreated, state control advanced."

Both aspects have continued: "[Blair] signed up for the first Thatcher revolution in Opposition and to the second as soon as he was in power."[34] Jenkins is an intelligent Conservative critic, but his admiration for the first Thatcher revolution blinds him to the way in which it made the second inevitable, not because of the mistaken views of Thatcher and her political offspring, but from the consequences and contradictions of the very economic and social "freedom" that Jenkins supports.

As Gramsci wrote,

> a particular political act may have been an error of calculation on the part of the leaders of the dominant classes, an error which historical development, through the parliamentary and governmental "crises" of the directive classes, then corrects and goes beyond. . . . Mechanical historical materialism does not allow for the possibility of error, but assumes that every political act is determined, immediately by the structure, and therefore as a real and permanent (in the sense of achieved) modification of the structure. The principle of "error" is a complex one: one may be dealing with an individual impulse based on mistaken calculations or equally it may be a manifestation of the attempts of specific groups or sects to take over hegemony within the directive grouping, attempts which may well be unsuccessful.[35]

For David Graeber:

> When historians write the epitaph for neoliberalism, they will have
> to conclude that it was the form of capitalism that systematically
> prioritized political imperatives over economic ones. That is: given
> a choice between a course of action that will make capitalism *seem*
> like the only possible economic system, and one that will actually *be*
> a more viable long-term economic system, neoliberalism has meant
> always choosing the former.[36]

In 2012, as the last of the essays which form the basis of this and the preceding chapter was being published, a book by David Priestland appeared in
which he claimed that patterns of domination in human history involve the
successive ascendancy of three groups, "the aristocrat and soldier, the sage
or priest [and] the merchant," each of whom have taken turns to rule over a
fourth group consisting of "the worker or peasant." The dominance of the
third ruling group, the merchants, occurs relatively late in history:

> The merchants' rise to political and cultural power began in sev-
> enteenth-century Holland and England and reached a febrile high
> point in Jazz Age America, before spectacularly imploding in the
> 1930s. It was only in the 1980s, when his aristocratic, bureaucratic
> and worker rivals were much diminished, that the merchant began
> his rise once again, to dominate the world order.[37]

Priestland effectively identifies the entire neoliberal period as one
dominated by "the pervasive merchant system" but, unlike the cases of the
aristocrat-warrior or sage-bureaucrat: "The disadvantages of the rule of the
merchant ... are often less apparent":

> In compelling everybody, in all spheres of human endeavor, to
> operate according to the ethos of short-term efficiency and drop-
> of-a-hat flexibility, the merchant risks destroying the other caste
> values that are essential to human well-being—whether it is
> the artisan's pride in creativity and skill, the worker's defense of
> community, or the sage technocrat's commitment to long-term,
> coordinated development. Along with this intolerance for other
> ways of doing, being and living, merchant rule brings growing

economic insecurity, corrosive inequality and potential environmental catastrophe.[38]

There is nothing with which I would wish to disagree in this assessment; yet among detriments which neoliberalism has caused for humanity, and to which Priestland rightly draws our attention, it is also worth noting that it represents a paradox for capitalism. The relative success of neoliberalism as a ruling-class strategy, particularly in weakening the trade union movement and reducing the share of profits going to labor, has helped to disguise that some aspects of this mode of regulation are proving unintentionally damaging to the system. Ross McKibbin wrote of then British chancellor of the Exchequer, George Osborne: "He wishes to serve the interests of the rich, but has a very narrow conception of what those interests might be, which is why there is no plan B."[39] Both points are certainly true, but "serving the interests of the rich" is not the same—or at least, not always the same—as "serving the interests of capital" and may in certain circumstances be in contradiction to it. In David Boyle's elegy for the end of traditional middle-class life, he quotes Paul Woolley, former stockbroker, academic, and a ferocious critic of the efficient market hypothesis:

> This is the death of prosperity.... I think capitalism is being driven over a cliff, and the funny thing is that the people who are driving it are meant to be the custodians for capital, and they've got the wrong instruction book.... All the tools they are using are predicated on a dud theory. They are doing the precise opposite of what they should be doing.[40]

If this is so, and I think it demonstrably is, then simply doing what these people want is unlikely to produce beneficial results, although it may help increase the wealth of individual capitalists. "Sometimes," write Michael Howard and John King, "government policies will go awry, with zealous retrenchment and the promotion of neoliberal measures that are economically inappropriate." But inappropriate for whom? If capitalists are able to insist that governments act in their individual interests, no matter what the collective costs, then, as these authors write: "Not surprisingly ... there will be a tendency for neoliberal excess."[41]

Capitalists are generally uninterested in the broader social interest, which we might expect; but they are also generally incapable of correctly assessing their *own* overall collective class interests, which might seem more surprising—although as we have seen, it is a long-standing phenomenon, observed by many of the great social theorists from the late eighteenth century onwards.[42] As a result, capitalist states—or more precisely, their managers—have traditionally acted to make such an assessment; but in the developed West at least, neoliberal regimes are increasingly displaying an uncritical adherence to the short-term wishes of particular business interests. Nor is this the only emergent problem: the increasingly narrow parameters of neoliberal politics, where choice is restricted to "social" rather than "economic" issues, has encouraged the emergence of far-right parties, usually fixated on questions of migration, which have proved enormously divisive in working-class communities, but whose policies are in other respects by no means in the interests of capital.

The self-destructive nature of neoliberal capitalism has nothing necessarily to do with the removal of restrictions on markets. The rise of neoliberalism made it fashionable to quote a passage from Karl Polanyi's *The Great Transformation*, the most famous sentence of which reads: "To allow the market mechanism to be the sole director of the fate of human beings and their natural environment, indeed, even the amount and use of purchasing power, would result in the demolition of society."[43] The assumption is invariably that neoliberalism is in the process of realizing Polanyi's nightmare: reversing the second part of his "double movement"—the social reaction against markets—and unleashing the mechanisms which he saw as being so destructive of society and nature. Leaving aside the fact that capitalism was always capable of producing social atomization, collective violence, and environmental destruction, even in periods when the state was far more directly involved in the mechanisms of production and exchange then it is now, there are two problems with this position. First, rhetoric apart, capitalists no more favor untrammeled competition today than they did when monopolies and cartels first appeared as aspects of the emerging system in the sixteenth century. Second, one would have to be extraordinarily naïve to believe that the neoliberal project has been about establishing "free" markets in the first place, although this myth has been assiduously perpetrated by social democratic parties who, eager to disguise their own capitulation to neoliberalism, emphasize their opposition to the marketization of all social relationships, even though no one—except perhaps the followers of Ayn Rand—seriously imagines this is either possible or desirable.[44] In what follows I will mainly draw on the experiences of the UK and the US, since these were the first nation-states in which neoliberalism was imposed under democratic conditions (i.e., unlike Chile or China) and where it has in many respects gone furthest.

There have always been tensions between capitalists and state managers. As Fred Block writes:

> The possibility exists that state managers, to improve their own position, will seek to expropriate, or at the very least, place severe restrictions on the property of the dominant classes. This threat is the root of the emphasis in bourgeois ideology on the need to prevent the emergence of a Leviathan state that swallows civil society. Yet since the bourgeoisie or other propertied classes cannot survive without a state, these classes have little choice but to seek a *modus vivendi* with the state managers. In social formations dominated by the capitalist mode of production, the dominant historical pattern has been the development of a *modus vivendi* that is highly favorable to the owners of capital.

Yet this *modus vivendi* is permanently under threat, since state managers have both to facilitate the process of capital accumulation and ameliorate its effects on the population and environment: "The consequence is that many of the state actions that have served to strengthen capitalism have been opposed by large sections of the capitalist class because they are seen as threats to class privilege and as steps towards a Leviathan state."[45] The attitude Block describes returns us to the Factory Acts and capitalist responses to them described by Marx in 1867. Has the capitalist class, then, finally succeeded in "binding Leviathan," to quote the title of an early British neoliberal text?[46]

On one reading, the relationship between neoliberal regimes and capital has since the 1970s prevented states from acting effectively in the collective, long-term interest of capitalism, leading instead to a situation where, according to Robert Skidelsky, "ideology destroys sane economics."[47] It is true that neoliberal regimes have increasingly abandoned any attempt to arrive at an overarching understanding of what the conditions for growth might be, other than the supposed need for lowering taxation and regulation and raising labor flexibility. Apart from these, the interests of the total national capital is seen as an arithmetical aggregate of the interests of individual businesses, some of which, to be sure, have rather more influence with governments than others. These developments have led to incomprehension among remaining Keynesians of the liberal left. "It is the decay of power," writes Will Hutton:

> The center fragments and power devolves to myriad new forces that often exercise their power with narrow obsessions in mind. Who now speaks for the whole? Who keeps a macro view, mediating competing interests and conflicts and has the courage to make decisions based on a strategic view of all our interests, not just sectional ones?[48]

Insofar as there is a "strategic view," it involves avoiding any policies which might incur corporate displeasure, however minor the inconveniences they might involve for the corporations, which of course includes regulation:

> Despite the importance of the corporate sector, allowing firms the maximum degree of freedom may not even be good for the firms themselves let alone the national economy. In fact, not all regulations are bad for business. Sometimes, it is in the long-run interest of the business sector to restrict the freedom of individual firms so that they do not destroy the common pool of resources that all of them need, such as natural resources or the labor force. Regulations can also help businesses by making them do things that may be costly to them individually in the short run but raise their collective productivity in the long run—such as the provision of worker training.[49]

Why is this happening? The reason is not simply because of successful lobbying and PR on behalf of individual businesses or industries, pernicious and pervasive though these increasingly sophisticated activities undoubtedly are.[50] Corporations have always done this: Why are state managers now so predisposed to respond positively to their efforts? The answer is in the way in which neoliberalism has reconfigured politics.

The necessary distance between the state and capital (or between state managers and capitalists) that Smith, Marx, and Schumpeter from their different political perspectives all regarded as being essential for the health of the system is being minimized. Ironically, China may be one of the few areas where this is not the case. Slavoj Žižek writes, "Arguably the reason why (ex-)

Communists are re-emerging as the most efficient managers of capitalism: their historical enmity towards the bourgeoisie as a class fits perfectly with the progress of contemporary capitalism towards a managerial system without the bourgeoisie."[51] In a US context, however, Doug Henwood writes that "policy is now made through a Wall Street lens of maximizing profits over the next few quarters, and the long term can take care of itself," which in turn suggests that "the distinction between the American ruling class and its business community—with the ruling class presumably operating on a time scale of decades rather than quarters—has largely collapsed."[52] Henwood's point about the regime adoption of timescales associated specifically with financial capital is important as it indicates the short-termism involved:

> It is hard to say at any moment whether the state is guiding capitalism, or capitalism leading the state by the nose. Neither has leisure or taste for long-term planning; both are reduced to hasty, improvised decisions, to get them out of one awkward corner into another—hand to mouth tactics with no more distant perspective than the next election or the balance sheet for the next shareholders' meeting.[53]

Reflecting on the "brutal hire and fire culture" of the banking sector, Joris Luyendijk asks:

> Why would people on a trading floor worry about the risks or ethics of the complex financial products they were selling, let alone about the long-term financial health of their own bank? Why would they even think about it as "their" bank, knowing that they could be out of the door in five minutes—either fired without prior warning or poached by a competitor. Why would a risk manager or compliance officer in such an environment sound the alarm? Why not screw your client given that it is all perfectly legal and you are under immense pressure to "perform."

He concludes: "This was beginning to look like a blueprint for short-termism."[54] "Short-termism is not new to corporate life," writes Phillip Inman: "For decades analysts have lamented how executives obsess about hitting quarterly targets to please shareholders and secure their bonuses. This is compounded by the shareholder's representative—the fund manager—

seeking to hit their own quarterly targets." Citing the arguments of the Paris-based think tank the OECD, he suggests: "A government needs to step in . . . because no boardroom can act alone, especially when the short-term measurement of success is so ingrained in the financial system. All public companies submit to it, and do little to support reform while the personal rewards remain bountiful."[55]

Three factors are important in producing this tendency. The first involves the constraints on policy, particularly economic policy, which have tightened throughout the neoliberal era; and these are not merely ideological constraints, but increasingly and cumulatively practical. In Britain, for example, as previously noted, MP John Redwood noted of his time in the Conservative Research Department during the early 1980s: "In our policy discussions we would always include the question of whether the changes we were proposing could be made irreversible."[56] Each successive phase of the neoliberal experiment saw the incremental abandonment of the repertoire of measures through which governments had traditionally influenced economic activity, beginning with Geoffrey Howe's abandonment of exchange controls in 1979 and concluding (to date) with Gordon Brown's transfer of the power to set interest rates from the Treasury to an unelected committee of the Bank of England. Perry Anderson described the former as the Thatcher regime's "first and most fundamental act on coming to power," but the same may be said of the second in relation to Thatcher's successor.[57] As the Italian journalist Antonio Polito wrote: "After the neo-liberal revolution the economy is by definition outside the range of politics."[58] The consequence has been a "depoliticization" of the political wing of the state managers. As Peter Burnham writes, "depoliticization is a governing strategy and in that sense remains highly political"; it is a strategy which operates by "placing at one remove the political character of decision making." For Burnham, it takes three forms:

> First, there has been a reassignment of tasks away from the party in office to a number of ostensibly "non-political" bodies as a way of underwriting the government's commitment to achieving objectives. . . . The second form . . . is in the adoption of measures ostensibly to increase the accountability, transparency and external validation of policy. . . . Finally, depoliticization strategies have been pursued in

an overall context favoring the adoption of binding "rules" which limit government room for maneuver.[59]

The Irish novelist Colm Toíbín recalled how, in 1985, while covering the trial of the Argentinean generals on charges of crimes against humanity, he met two Americans in Buenos Aires. These turned out to be representatives, respectively, of the World Bank and the IMF, in the country to dictate terms for the resolution of the economic crisis. They had little patience with these attempts to bring the uniformed criminals of the former regime to justice: "My American friends said it was a waste of money and a waste of time. Argentina, economically, they said, was a basket case, in desperate need of root and branch reform. The trial was, at best, a distraction."

It was an encounter with demonstrators protesting job losses and wage cuts that revealed even more clearly their attitude to ordinary Argentineans:

> One of the guys I was with grew really angry, could barely contain himself in the taxi. This was the last thing Argentina needs, he said. Protests like this were not just a waste of time, they were irresponsible. The country was going to have to go through years of hardship, he said, to get to a position where it could begin again. There were no choices. Argentina was not just broke, it owed a fortune and the costs of public service were outlandish. Protesting would not make the slightest difference.[60]

John Lanchester reports:

> "The thing about organisations like the IMF is they simply don't care what your circumstances are," I was told by an Argentinian financial Minister who's dealt directly with the organization during negotiations in the early noughties. "You might have particular historic reasons why a programme existed, targeting child poverty, or slum sanitation, or whatever, but they made clear they had no interest in that. They were just waiting for you to stop talking so they could tell you what to do. It was the same package of solutions for everyone irrespective of local history and conditions or social problems. Just take it or leave it and shut up."[61]

Yanis Varoufakis gives a similar example

> There was point blank refusal to engage in economic arguments.
> Point blank. . . . You put forward an argument that you've really
> worked on—to make sure it's logically coherent—and you're just
> faced with blank stares. It is as if you haven't spoken. What you say
> is independent of what they say. You might as well have sung the
> Swedish national anthem—you'd have got the same reply.[62]

The late Peter Mair wrote of the way in which political parties have
moved their locus from "society to the state," becoming in the process "agencies that govern" rather than "represent."[63] As politicians become a professional caste whose life-world is increasingly remote from any other form of
activity, economic or otherwise, and therefore more "autonomous," they
simultaneously become more committed to capitalist conceptions of the national interest, with business as an exemplar. Elections have not, of course,
ceased to take place; but they take the form of what Sheldon Wolin calls
"inverted totalitarianism": "It is politics all the time but a politics largely untempered by the political."

By this he means both intraparty factional struggle and interparty
competition, which reach their apotheosis in the USA in the selection process for presidential candidates and the subsequent presidential election,
where electors are faced with "a choice of personalities rather than a choice
of alternatives."[64] Consequently, in the developed word, discussion of politics largely offers more or less informed commentary and speculation on
the trivial exchanges within parliaments and other supposedly representative institutions. Peter Oborne's discussion of party convergence in Britain
incorrectly assumes the process is complete, rather than simply well advanced, but his essential point is valid: "In practice the differences between
the main parties are minor and for the most part technical. The contradiction between apparently bitter party competition on the political stage,
and collaboration behind the scenes, defines the contemporary political
predicament."[65]

Debates therefore have the quality of a shadow play, an empty ritual in
which trivial or superficial differences are emphasized in order to give an
impression of real alternatives and justify the continuation of party competition. Nancy Fraser compares Franklin Roosevelt's denunciation of "the
malefactors of wealth" in a radio broadcast of 1936 with Barack Obama's

feeble contribution to a televised presidential debate in 2012 when he essentially refused to draw any substantive economic distinctions between himself and Mitt Romney. As Fraser argues, this is not simply a matter of individual personality, for "Obama's weakness is hardly unique. . . . It is the broader pattern—the across-the-board collapse of political Keynesianism that must be explained. Faced with the failure of an entire political stratum to make any serious attempt to stop an impending train wreck, we cannot restrict ourselves to hypotheses centered on individual psychology."[66]

Instead, as Fraser herself notes, we have to focus on the weakening of the labor movement, since one of the inadvertent roles which it historically played was to save capitalism from itself, not least by achieving reforms in relation to education, health, and welfare. These benefited workers, of course, but also ensured that the reproduction of the workforce and the conditions for capital accumulation more generally took place. In this respect social democracy occupied a similar place to the precapitalist elites identified by Schumpeter as necessary to rule on behalf of a congenitally incapable capitalist class. But with the weakening of trade union power and the capitulation of social democracy to neoliberalism, there is currently no social force capable of either playing this "reformist" role directly or pressurizing non-social democratic state managers into playing it.

The second factor, opposed to the "depoliticization" of politicians, is the "politicization" of the nonpolitical wing of the state managers: the civil servants. As the political parties became less distinct from each other, the officials required to implement their increasingly similar policies are required to turn themselves more completely into extensions of the parties themselves. In the US, the politicization of the civil service has always been a more significant factor than in the UK, but even there the neoliberal era saw a heightening of the existing tendency. What Monica Prasad calls "the permeability and lack of technocracy" of the US state bureaucracy compared to the French or British may have some advantages for capital but generally "hinders the separation of policy making from political considerations" and leads to "the politically motivated choice of budget projections." These tendencies were exacerbated by the Civil Service Reform Act of 1978 which "further weakened the autonomous basis of the government bureaucracy."[67] In the UK, following hard on the heels of the United States as always, there has since 1979, and especially since 1997, been a more generalized influx of private-sector appointees into the civil service, which Oborne describes as being increasingly "emasculated" as a result, to the point where it has been effectively subject to a "corporate takeover."[68] But even in relation to the permanent home civil service, the expectation is that senior civil servants in particular will not attempt to point out the difficulties involved in governmental policies or even consider alternative ways of delivering policies, but simply present arguments to justify them, regardless of the empirical data, except where those policies contravene the neoliberal order. And in this, the markets will find allies in the capitalist state, or more precisely in the state managers, who are beginning to reassert their autonomy from politicians. A notable example was the response of Mervyn King, at the time governor of the Bank of England, to suggestions by then Prime Minister Brown that the British government stimulate economic growth through tax cuts or increased public spending. King's rejection of any such proposal was made in answer to the Treasury select committee and received instant assent from those nominally in charge of the British state, whose views he had been criticizing. Described by Liberal Democratic economic spokesman Vince Cable as "a very British coup d'etat," King's intervention was in fact perfectly normal behavior by a leading state manager.[69] His assertion of the prerogative of state institutions to subvert the will of elected politicians appeared dramatic only because the politicians in question had previously been so subservient to the wishes of capital that no such demonstration had previously been required. The only exceptional aspect of the affair was that the statement was made in a public forum rather than conveyed in an internal memorandum, the means by which previous Labour prime ministers had been informed that their aspirations were unaffordable.

Colin Leys argues that there are four "enabling conditions" for this abandonment of evidence: "the replacement of the culture of Royal Commissions by the culture of 'grey' literature; the loss of critical independence on the part of the academic research community; the de-politicization of the electorate; and the return to respectability of irrational beliefs."[70]

One of these conditions, the "depoliticization of the electorate" is itself a third and final factor in producing chronic short-termism in neoliberal regimes. Except it is not so much "depoliticization" as abstention by sections of the electorate who no longer have any parties for whom to vote. Many of those electors still involved in casting their vote do so—appropriately enough—on a consumer model of political choice, where participation is informed by media-driven perceptions of which result will be to their immediate personal benefit. Unsurprisingly, the numbers prepared to carry out even this minimal level of activity are declining.[71] The key point, however, is that those who do vote are more likely to belong to the middle classes—the real middle classes, that is, not the imaginary middle classes whose endless trials so exercise headline-writers for the *Daily Mail*—who tend to have a more focused view of their material interests and deploy more interventionist strategies for maintaining them than those bearing the brunt of austerity.

The middle class consists of three broad groupings, two of which are historically of very long standing: the traditional petty bourgeoisie and the professions. Both of these consist, in different ways, of the self-employed, although there are of course enormous differences in income and social status between representative figures of the first group, like a shopkeeper, and that of the second, like a doctor. The third group, emerging almost entirely within the twentieth century, is "the new middle class," itself with two components: members with a managerial and supervisory role, and those who function as semiautonomous employees. Both occupy what Erik Olin Wright called "contradictory" class locations.[72] In addition to the objective occupational divide within the new middle class, there is also a subjective political divide across it. Members tend to align themselves politically on the basis of whether they work in the public or private sectors, with the former orientating on social or (in the US) liberal democratic politics and the latter on conservatism.[73] It is not, however, the occupation which produces the political allegiance, but the allegiance which tends to make certain occupations attractive.

What is the significance of the growth of the new middle class and the nature of its occupational and political divisions for our subject? The middle classes are often portrayed as incapable of independent action, forced to vacillate politically until forced to choose between or divide between the bourgeoisie and the proletariat. The classic presentation of this case is in Trotsky's writings on Germany from the last days of the Weimar Republic; but this analysis, for all its brilliance, was intended to explain an extreme and atypical situation.[74] In normal circumstances, where civil war is not on the agenda, the room for maneuver of the middle classes is greater than Trotsky and those who have uncritically followed him suggest. Indeed, the leadership and much of the rank and file of the new "left" social movements came from professional and new middle class fractions, particularly in the welfare and "creative" occupations.[75] But new middle-class activists can be both liberal ("left") on social issues and neoliberal on economic ones.[76]

Since neoliberalism emerged as the dominant form of capitalist organization in the mid-1970s, what we might call the "right," private-sector orientated wing of the new middle class has begun to assert itself as an independent social force. In the mid-eighties, Mike Davis noted the rise of what he called "overconsumptionism," by which he meant not the expenditure habits of the very rich, but rather "an increasing political subsidization of a mass layer of managers, professionals, new entrepreneurs and rentiers who, faced with rapidly declining organization among the working poor and minorities during the 1970s, have been overwhelmingly successful in profiting from both inflation and expanded state expenditure." These groups (to whom Davis also added "credentialed technicians") constituted nearly a quarter of the US labor force by the late 1970s and have continued growing since. The political basis for the transition from Fordism to overconsumptionism in the USA was "neither militant labor nor reactionary capital, but insurgent middle strata," which during the 1970s began to mobilize against the social gains of the previous decade, above all against integration and bussing.[77] John Kenneth Galbraith observed that the beneficiaries of neoliberalism were the majority—not of the population or even the electorate, of course, "but of those who actually vote . . . the Contented Electoral Majority . . . rule under the rich cloak of democracy, a democracy in which the less fortunate do not participate." And as he correctly notes, this minority-majority are "very angry and very articulate about what seems to invade their state of self satisfaction."[78] What kind of issues might provoke their anger and stimulate their articulacy? According to Davis: "The most powerful 'social movement' in contemporary Southern California is that of affluent homeowners, organized by notional community designations or tract names, engaged in the defense of home values and neighborhood exclusivity."[79]

Galbraith identified three possible factors which might overturn the culture of contentment among the beneficiaries of neoliberalism. These were economic crisis, military failure, or urban revolt:

> Recession and depression made worse by long-run economic desuetude, the danger implicit in an autonomous military power and growing unrest in the urban slums caused by worsening deprivation and hopelessness have been cited as separate prospects. All could, in fact, come together. A deep recession could cause stronger discontent in the areas of urban disaster in the aftermath of some military misadventure in which, in the nature of modern armed forces, the unfortunate were disproportionately engaged.

"Military misadventure" has been followed by "deep recession," while "growing unrest" is unlikely to be far behind.[80] The problem is that the direction into which this combination of catastrophes will push the professional and new middle classes is underdetermined. It makes more effective use of public services than the working class, but this also means that it can be seriously affected by cuts in state provision. Michael Hughey argued early in the Reagan years that:

> If their general reaction to recent economic difficulties may be taken as an indication, the liberalism of the new middle classes does not run deep enough to threaten their purses and can in any case be readily abandoned if it does. But if segments of the new middle classes will sacrifice the poor and their own liberalism to bolster their personal economic fortunes, they are not likely to silently endure threats to their way of life as a result of more extensive tax cuts. As the tax cuts are extended, the new middle classes are beginning to discover that they are themselves the primary beneficiaries of a number of threatened government services and that having government on their backs is not an altogether uncomfortable burden.[81]

Although the neoliberal boom after 1982 enabled the issue to be avoided, the return of recession from 2008 has made it inescapable. One response would simply be for the professional and new middle classes to appropriate part of the state for themselves. In Britain, for example, responsibility for implementing neoliberal anti-reforms is being spread beyond governing parties and central state apparatuses to elected bodies whose policy options are severely restricted both by statute and reliance on the Treasury for most of their funding, as previously discussed. Neoliberal attitudes towards the mass of the population involve an uneasy combination of private suspicion over what they might do without state surveillance and repression, and public disquisitions on the need to listen to The People, provided of course that politicians are being asked to listen to the right sort of people with the right sort of demands—in other words, longer prison sentences and more restricted immigration, rather than higher taxation for the rich or military withdrawal from Afghanistan. In the case of devolution the assumption is that the people most likely to participate in local decision-making will be members of the middle classes, who can be expected to behave, *en masse*, in ways which will impose restrictions on local taxation and public spending, and thus maintain the neoliberal order with a supposedly popular mandate. "While overall inequality has increased," note three political scientists of the USA, "the pressure for redistributive policies has been sharply mitigated by the fact that the income inequality of *voters* did not increase."[82]

Monica Prasad has suggested that, ironically, one reason for the rise of neoliberalism in the USA was a paradoxical outcome of the successful demand for greater democratic accountability during the 1960s and 1970s. This led to the weakening of both congressional committees and party structures, and produced a new breed of "entrepreneurial politicians" interested in highlighting issues popular with specific audiences which would provide them with a stable following:

> Making the state more responsive to society thus made state actors more responsive to *nonpoor majorities* and sources of campaign financing, and less able to protect the interests of disadvantaged minorities—an ironic outcome, given the leftist motivations of the 1960s changes in state structures that were intended to give politics back to the people. Because economic policies such as targeted programs put the interests of majorities at odds with the interests of the poor, giving power to the people meant weakening autonomous state structures that had served as a bulwark against social sources of power, and these social sources of power led to the enactment of politically saleable market-friendly policies.[83]

A model for "returning power to the people" along these lines was built early on in the neoliberal experiment in the US. One feature of what was called "the New Federalism" of the early 1990s was "shifting control of social programs back to state and local levels," which "would also entail a shift in accountability for the administration of these programs." As Hughey points out, behind this lay a "Machiavellian design . . . for Republicans have not forgotten the protest marches of the 1960s" and this would lead to criticism or opposition being "redistributed among state capitals."[84] The most fully developed version can be found in California. Since the mid-1970s, politics in the world's fourth biggest economy have been characterized by a combination of falling voter participation among working-class and minority groups, and a targeted use of local referendums on "propositions." The latter have been designed to defend property values by blocking integrated schooling and urban development, and by preventing progressive taxation.[85] Proposition 13 was passed in 1978 and signaled the commencement of the neoliberal era in the US by capping taxes on property, even though house values were rising. As a result, the burden of taxation fell disproportionately on income tax, even though for most workers salaries and wages were stagnant or falling—and even increasing income tax requires a two-thirds majority in both houses of the state legislature. It was the self-interested behavior of a mobilized middle-class that brought California to fiscal crisis in 2009, after which the usual remedies of cutting public services, including child health care, were offered as a solution to the structural inability of the state to raise the necessary levels of taxation. Paul Krugman predicted at the time that the paralysis of California may foreshadow the future of US politics as a whole.[86] And in turn, the US may foreshadow the future of politics in the rest of the world, a development for which there are historical precedents.

Another aspect is the emergence of gated communities with inhabitants below the level of the bourgeoisie. In these, residents have to sign an agreement where the developer stipulates what types of activity are permissible and expected. Ironically, these can be quite as complex, prescriptive, and designed to control the behavior of inhabitants as those which local councils used to impose on their tenants. In return, occupants are provided with private services such as trash disposal. The obvious development, which has already become a reality in parts of the US, including—naturally—California, but also Florida and Minnesota, is that the occupants will withdraw from local taxation on the grounds that it involves them in paying for services which they do not receive while simultaneously paying separately for those which they do. As Anna Minton writes, this is analogous to the way in which "privately funded business districts and private places . . . undermine the public, democratic nature of city life, creating a different culture and atmosphere in places." The rules and charges imposed in gated communities are effectively laws and taxes:

> These trends apply equally in luxury gated communities and in social-housing estates, where residents may be asked to pay extra for private-security patrols, warden services and maintenance. This is all part of the same withdrawal from locally elected government, which provides services for the whole of an area and all of its people, in place of private services which are privately paid for and are not open to all.[87]

Yet only the very upper echelons of the middle class can afford this level of social withdrawal. We are likely to see, therefore, increased struggles for access to resources at local levels in which sections of the middle class attempt to monopolize these for themselves. In Britain, this will occur most blatantly in the field of education, as middle-class parents move from targeting schools as the most suitable for their children to establishing their own on the basis of government funding that would otherwise have been invested in the state sector. How large a proportion of the professional and new middle classes will pursue this path, rather than one of defending the welfare state and public provision more generally, will depend on the strength of a working-class movement advocating the latter as an alternative.

A New Phase of Capitalist Development or a "Third Period" of Neoliberalism?

John Bellamy Foster has argued that the possibility of a rational capitalism of the type supported and defended in their different ways by Keynes and Schumpeter is now a thing of the past.[1] Foster probably goes too far: but what is emerging is a symbiotic relationship between one increasingly inadequate regime response to the problems *of* capital accumulation discussed here and another increasingly extreme response to the most irrational desires and prejudices produced *by* capital accumulation. In the most recent novel by the Scottish science fiction author Ken MacLeod, the author imagines a situation in the near future where the ruling classes of the world take coordinated legal and military action in a passive revolution ("the Big Deal") to smash the dominance of financial capital, restore that of industrial capital, and essentially put an end to the neoliberal era.[2] This aspect of the novel is far more incredible than the alien encounters that occur elsewhere in its pages. Clearly, in situations of absolute, immediate crisis, short-term emergency measures would be introduced in the same way as the effective nationalization of banks and other financial institutions took place in both the US and UK during 2008. But these were minimal interventions to prevent outright collapse and save the institutions (and the practices which brought them to the point of crisis in the first place) without using them for any coherent strategic end, let alone any broader social purpose, and of course on the basis that they would be reprivatized as soon as possible.[3]

Let me be clear what I am not saying. I am not suggesting that it should be the work of socialists to propose solutions to the crisis of capitalism. It is always necessary to argue for reforms, of course, but the idea that the application of Keynesian solutions would restore the Golden Age of the postwar welfare state is simply illusionary and underestimates the extent to which those years were the result of a unique set of circumstances. Booms will continue to occur, as they did between 1982 and 2007, but the beneficiaries will become fewer and fewer. Consequently, I am not predicting that developments discussed here mean that capitalism will simply collapse under the weight of its own internal contradictions either. Scenarios of this type, from those predicted by Rosa Luxemburg onwards, have been proven false in the past and there is no reason to suppose that they will be any more accurate in the future. Indeed, a collapse not brought about by the conscious intervention of the oppressed and exploited would not be to their advantage in any case, but simply a step towards the barbarism to which Marxists from Engels onwards have seen as the consequence of failing to achieve a socialist society. And this is no mere slogan: the condition of central Africa today indicates the presence of actually existing barbarism as the daily reality for millions. Events in the developed world are unlikely to take this form, at least until environmental catastrophe becomes irreversible, but rather involve a gradual and, for all but the very poorest, almost imperceptible worsening and coarsening on their conditions of life.

What I am suggesting is that neoliberalism as a strategy has almost been too successful as a method of capitalist regulation. It has finally brought about the situation that Schumpeter feared, where creative destruction has no limits or boundaries, where, as Franco Moretti writes, "the good Burger will never have the strength to withstand the creative destroyer, and counter his will"; thus, "the impotence of bourgeois realism in the face of capitalist megalomania."[4] As we shall now see, however, this is not the only punishment which capitalism is in the process of bringing upon itself.

As noted in the *Financial Times* in relation for the Arab Spring, "The economy itself must be depoliticised."[5] Stanley Aronowitz writes of the US context:

As unions represent a declining proportion of the labor force, they see themselves as unable to resist encroachments by capital that overthrow American workers' once permanent assumption that their living standards will continue to rise. Saddled with debt—home mortgages, tuition payments for their children, car payments and other bills—and without strong union support, workers feel that the income loss they risk in challenging corporate capital is too steep a price to pay. When a minority of workers occasionally rebel against them, as happened in a contract struggle with Chrysler, both company and union leadership waste no time warning the rebels that rejection of the "best offer" may mean plant closure.[6]

This results in right-wing reaction; as Jeremy Engels writes, "The Tea Party cashes in on American's rage against the consequences of neoliberalism in order to defend the neoliberal status quo."[7]

Does the left have an alternative? Even before the recession, the attitudes of the liberal, the social democratic, and even the Marxist left were characterized by pessimism and a consequent scaling-down of aspiration. Joseph Stiglitz, the now repentant former chief economist at the World Bank, harks back to the Great Depression and notes that now, as then, "the system of capitalism is at a crossroads. . . . In the 1930s, capitalism was saved by Keynes, who thought of policies to create jobs and rescue those suffering from the collapse of the global economy."[8] Further to the left, Naomi Klein also supports a reformed capitalism informed by Keynesian measures:

> I am not arguing that all market systems are inherently violent. It is eminently possible to have a market-based economy that requires no such brutality and demands no such ideological purity. A free market in consumer products can coexist with free public health care, with public schools, with a large segment of the economy—like a national oil company—held in state hands. . . . Keynes proposed exactly that kind of mixed, regulated economy after the Great Depression, a revolution in public policy that created the New Deal and transformations like it around the world.[9]

As a Marxist, David Harvey might be expected to take a more uncompromising position, but he too looks back to the same remedies, citing

Roosevelt's message to Congress of 1935, in which he "made clear his view that excessive market freedoms lay at the root of the economic and social problems of the 1930s Depression." Harvey rightly notes that "Roosevelt's entirely reasonable conceptions sound positively radical by contemporary standards" and later commends his arguments as "one place to start" for those dedicated to creating an "open democracy, dedicated to the achievement of social equality coupled with economic, political and cultural justice."[10] Robert Pollin asks: "Given the evident failures of unleashed capitalism and the equally evident limits of leashed capitalism during the Golden Age, should the left not again be advancing a case for full-throttle socialism?" A good question; but Pollin considers an affirmative answer "unrealistic," even if "desirable," and says instead that "the left needs to figure out how to make a revived version of leashed capitalism workable."[11]

The attraction of these arguments is obvious. It suggests that not only are there alternative policies to those of neoliberalism, but that they have the advantage of being associated with a period of unparalleled prosperity, at least in the developed world, and they do not involve the risks of revolution. They do involve, however, three major problems.

First, these policies do not constitute a program. As Paul Mason writes: "The problem for neoliberalism's critics is that they now have no coherent world view to take its place." Alternatives are "scattered within the writings of neo-Keynesians, the anti-globalisation left and the Stiglitz critique of neoliberalism," but have "no concrete programme in the face of the crisis."[12]

Second, to the extent that they do constitute a program, elements of it have already been adopted by the bourgeoisie as part of its pragmatic response to the crisis. The rescue of, for example, Northern Rock was in response to a potential business failure of a size which no government could allow, particularly given the consequences which followed the US government's refusal to save Lehman Brothers. Therefore, when Labour MP Ronnie Campbell declared in the House of Commons that he intended to open an account with the newly nationalized Northern Rock on the grounds that it was now "the people's bank," he was simply proving the truth of T. S. Eliot's adage that humankind cannot bear very much reality.[13] The reality in this case being that, between nationalization in February 2008 and October of that year, Northern Rock cut 1,500 jobs and, as the result of a policy which saw it become twice as likely as competitors to repossess properties, carried out a fifth of the nineteen thousand repossessions in Britain.[14] These measures have absolutely nothing progressive, let alone socialist, about them, as several of the more sober commentators, by no means all on the left, have noted.[15] Martin Wolf, whom I quoted above demanding cuts in state spending in general and public sector pay in particular, has also admitted: "This is a Keynesian situation that requires Keynesian remedies. Budget deficits will end up at levels previously considered unimaginable. So be it."[16]

Similarly, Rupert Murdoch's mouthpiece Irving Stelzer appeared on *Newsnight*, a flagship BBC politics program, during March 2008 calling for "fiscal stimulus" and misquoting Richard Nixon to the effect that "We are all Keynesians now."[17] Rescuing the banks was acceptable, even to the *Economist*, because it was carried out on a "pragmatic, not ideological" basis.[18] Bailing out the banks, as opposed to directly stimulating consumer demand, is not a Keynesian solution, but let that pass; the key point is the pragmatic acceptance by neoliberal ideologues of the need for state intervention in markets, which is shared by capitalists themselves. "The irony is the extent to which the US government has had to come to the rescue and provide a socialist solution to capitalistic problems," commented Martin Sorrell of advertising giant WPP, while acknowledging "the advantage in certain circumstances of state directed capitalism."[19]

Third, to the extent that they do constitute a program and that it is more radical than that already being put in place by capitalist states, to what extent could it actually be implemented? Leaving aside the not unimportant question of whether states outside the USA have the financial capacity to intervene to the necessary degree, many of the mechanisms through which national or international interventions formerly took place no longer exist. Boris Kagarlitsky has argued that it is precisely the "irreversibility" of the neoliberal reforms, the abolition of the mechanisms for regulation, the absence of procedures for agreements to be amended or for signatories to withdraw, which now poses the greatest danger to capitalism: "However much it might wish to do so, the bourgeoisie will not be able to escape from its own institutional trap without help from outside." And who will provide this help? "Just as in the 1930s, the only way this conflict can be resolved is through a dramatic strengthening and radicalization of the left."[20] But why

should the left wish to help the bourgeoisie restore the system only to prepare the ground for a further crisis?

I stressed earlier that the ability of state managers, politicians, and capitalists to introduce neoliberal measures was directly or indirectly dependent
on their success in weakening the labor movement. Any hope of reversing
neoliberalism, let alone of moving towards socialism, will therefore depend
on rebuilding that movement and doing so on a basis which is independent
of political parties committed to the existing order. Ultimately, then, the issue is one of class power, but it is precisely this conclusion which even critics of neoliberalism find difficult to accept. Many see the working class as a
residual element, at least in the West. "With the working class a minority,"
write Polly Toynbee and David Walker, "those on low incomes are despised,
whether they work or don't work."[21] But even those who concede its continued existence doubt its ability to act as the potential gravedigger of capitalism. "Today," writes Andrew Gamble, "as the capitalist wagon careers out
of control down the track, spilling its load and its passengers, there are few
gravediggers in sight."[22] The first claim, about the size of the working class,
relies on the widely held but nonetheless incorrect belief that the majority
of workers in service industries belong to the middle class.[23] In her foreword to the Power Report, Dame Helena Kennedy notes that the "political
insiders" who contributed to the inquiry "tell us class has disappeared into
a meritocratic land of opportunity when what has happened is a reconfig-
uring of class with new margins, growing inequality but increasingly ugly
consequences." Kennedy recounts an episode which suggests the absurd but
logical terminus of the "disappearing working class" thesis:

> I remember seeing the writing on the wall back in the days of Mrs.
> Thatcher when a young woman who helped look after my children
> remarked that my mother and family did not seem working class,
> having seen my background described in a newspaper. I asked her
> who she thought were working class and she said people who did
> not work.[24]

It is the second claim, about the capacity of the working class, which
requires more serious consideration, since it is skepticism over this issue
which has prompted calls for new class alliances. Larry Elliott and Dan At-

kinson, for example, propose what they call a New Populism against the New Olympians of international finance, an alliance consisting of "small business people and farmers, ... independent middle-class professionals and shopkeepers." In addition, it would include two other groups

> with significant blocks of members: manufacturing and export businesses and trade union members. . . . Those owning, running and working in industry know better than anyone the virulence with which New Olympianism has blighted the economy. Both union members and managers have much to gain from a more sensible attitude to industry.[25]

Previous attempts by the left to identify the activities of particular fractions of capital as the source of exploitation and oppression, rather than the system itself, do not inspire confidence in this analysis. Whether the opposition is supposedly between patriotic and cosmopolitan capital, competitive and monopoly capital, or—as in the current case—financial and industrial capital, the tendency is first to align, then to submerge the interests of labor beneath those of one ("progressive") section of the warring brotherhood. But however much they may fight among themselves, all sections of the capitalist class have benefited from the restraints which neoliberalism has imposed upon labor. And the "manufacturing and exporting" wing of capital continues to do so, for one response to the crisis in Britain has certainly been cooperation between trade unions—or rather their bureaucracies—and employers; but this has been entirely to the advantage of the latter, involving workers accepting pay freezes, pay cuts, as in Honda, or in the most extreme case, periods of working for nothing, as in British Airways. Managements have claimed that these are the only alternatives to job losses and have of course congratulated union officials for "sensibly" and "pragmatically" accepting these claims.[26]

This has not been the only response. Neoliberalism has always been resisted in its heartlands, even after the 1980s defeat of the labor movement. As the example of the poll tax in Scotland suggests, ruling-class initiatives did not go unopposed. The Home Office Citizenship Survey (England and Wales) in 2001 asked participants whether they had engaged in what the survey called "civic activities" over the past twelve months. It found that 38 percent had participated at least once during that time, the most popular activity being signing a petition, but 18 percent had attended a public meeting or rally. The British Social Attitudes survey has different figures, but shows the percentages of people taking part in demonstrations doubled between 1986 (6 percent) to 2002 (12 percent), an increase largely due to the rise of the antiwar movement.[27] Indeed, all the major issues to have arisen in Britain since the late 1980s, from the poll tax to the Criminal Justice Bill, from hospital closures to the sell-off of council housing, from the British National Party to asylum seekers, and above all the imperialist wars in Afghanistan, Iraq, and Gaza, have involved people in responding either to attacks on their communities or to geopolitical injustices.

The problem has been that, although trade unions have certainly been involved, trade union action has been minimal. The point is not that trade unions have ceased to take action over workplace issues: public sector workers (and those in privatized industries such as the railways) in particular have continued to defend both their wages and conditions and the services they provide with heroic resilience through several decades of neoliberal attrition. Aside from this, the major form of resistance has been the international revival of occupation as a defensive tactic to prevent closure or ensure the payment of previously agreed pension and redundancy agreements.[28] The return of the sit-in has partly been a response to the restrictions, both legal and ideological, which neoliberalism has imposed on the labor movement, a case of forging a weapon from the limited resources left by the very success of the ruling class and turning it against them. Yet, welcome though these developments are, it is not clear how far it is possible to generalize this tactic outside of manufacturing, where it can apply the greatest pressure on employers, by cutting off the supply of parts to customers or simply denying the owners the ability to sell off land, plant, or machinery: it is less apparent how the same effect can be achieved by occupying a bank or a call center. And this is the fundamental reason why many critics of neoliberalism do not see the working class as the source of an alternative to neoliberalism or capitalism more generally. Even those who reject the claim that workers have come to accept neoliberalism argue that most workers are not unionized and those that are belong to declining sectors of the economy. The majority have increasingly precarious employment (they are "flexible," in ruling-class language), which acts as a disincentive to organization.

The extent of precarity should neither be exaggerated nor underplayed. For most of the history of capitalism, precarity has been the normal experience of most of the working class. The only period in which stable employment has been the norm, across the developed world at least, has been since the onset of the Great Boom and, despite widespread belief to the contrary, this is one of the few aspects of this otherwise wholly exceptional period in the history of capitalism to have continued into the neoliberal era. What has changed is that certain categories of financial, managerial, and administrative employment that previously had the greatest security have now become more vulnerable, not least because of the extent of corporate rationalization and downsizing that tended to follow the acquisitions and mergers boom of the 1990s and 2000s.[29]

A more serious problem than precarity is simply the failure to unionize, let alone achieve recognition in the many workplaces where workers have permanent contracts, either formally or in effect. Of the factors which are supposed be obstacles to effective unionization, there is little evidence that small workplace size (at least above that of the family firm), or the increasingly complex relation between or within firms caused by outsourcing and contracting out, or jobs particularly associated with women or ethnic minorities necessarily involve barriers to organization; much depends on how committed and imaginative trade unions are in recruiting.[30] There is no reason why non-union workplaces should remain un-unionized and although it would be foolish to pretend that there are not huge difficulties in the way, it would be equally foolish to believe these are insurmountable. Unionization took place in Britain during the 1930s following the great defeat of the 1926 General Strike—think of light engineering and car manufacturing in the East Midlands and around London, for example—and, although the process was hardly automatic, mass membership was established relatively quickly. Perhaps even more pertinently, the great unionization movements in the USA during the 1930s were motivated by the desire of a workforce to participate in the consumerist paradise of the 1920s boom from which they were excluded by low wages, but, even more important, by their resistance to the discipline of the foremen and pressure of keeping up with the production line.[31] These conditions are quite similar, in terms of both financial exclusion and the nature of the workplace regime, to those which currently prevail in the great telemarketing or financial services office-factories. Nostalgia for the shipyards and its corollary, despair over the call centers, are therefore not only useless, but also quite unnecessary. In this context it is necessary to remember the maxim taught to Walter Benjamin by Bertolt Brecht: "Take your cue not from the good old things but the bad new ones."[32] There is no objective reason why these workplaces cannot be organized in the same way as Singer's or any other iconic name was before them. And here the exceptions to defeats which characterized the popular front disasters of the 1980s and 1990s may be relevant, those cases where workers fought back with militancy and without recourse to nationalism, but by building workplace solidarity and community support. These either found no wider echo at the time, as in the Lee Jeans occupation in Greenock (1981), or occurred too late to reverse the defeatism which had already infected the trade union movement after 1985, as in the Timex dispute in Dundee (1994) and Glacier's occupation in Glasgow (1996). But these strikes and occupations may have greater significance in the present period than they did at the time, because there now exist far greater opportunities for generalization. It is instructive to compare the success of the small-scale but extremely effective occupation of the Prisme factory in Dundee during 2009 with the failure to save the Diageo plant in Kilmarnock, where the campaign relied on the same failed popular front strategy—that is, attempts to ally with a "progressive" section of capitalism—criticized earlier in this section.

One of the central problems, not merely of neoliberalism, but the capitalist system it seeks to defend, is that it is ultimately incapable of improving or even maintaining the condition of the majority. It is in this contradiction that hope lies. For most people under the neoliberal order, economic life has become more uncertain, political life more meaningless, social life more fragmented, and cultural life more degraded. Since, contrary to the neoliberal viewpoint, human beings are not just greedy little bundles of appetite armed with effective demand, they are rebelling and will continue to rebel against these assaults on their humanity. And in this context, it is important to remember that we have not returned in all respects to our starting point in the late 1970s. At least some of the people who might have previously been persuaded to accept a supposedly temporary deterioration of their living conditions in order to restructure capitalism for the greater good are considerably less likely to be fooled again, given the way in which over thirty years of sacrifice has benefited only those at the top of society and furthermore failed to prevent a recession. As Alan Bissett writes:

> My friends' hatred of the rich is now palpable. It's not because they themselves didn't become rich, but because they've realised that the system was rigged all along. Having rejected socialism for most of their adult lives, having rejected even the very *existence* of a working class, they now burn with fury at a system which purports to be meritocratic but which in reality works against them. Their arrival into the "middle class" had become an illusion, sustained by easy credit and an economy requiring conspicuous consumption to sustain itself.[33]

At the same time, the hold of social democracy over the working class, the idea that it still represents an alternative to the openly capitalist parties rather than belonging to their ranks, has been weakened by years of social neoliberal government. Terrible though the experiences behind these developments have been, they represent potentially positive changes in consciousness, if the left is capable of offering an alternative. Therefore, although the resumption of economic crisis in 2007 provides an opportunity for the rulers of the world to adapt neoliberalism or replace it in the interests of continuing their one-sided class war, the conjuncture is equally apt for those who oppose all manifestations of the capitalist order to try to bring it to an end. The nature of the outcome depends as much on the actions of the readers of this book as those of anyone else.

REFERENCES

Adorno, Theodor. "The Stars Down to Earth: The *Los Angeles Times* Astrology Column: A Study in Secondary Superstition." In *The Stars Down to Earth and Other Essays on the Irrational in Culture*, edited by Stephen Crook. London: Routledge, 1994 [1957].

Alesina, Alberto, and Enrico Spolaore. *The Size of Nations.* Cambridge, MA: MIT Press, 2003.

Al-Kazzaf, Hari. "Western Demos Make Big Impact on Islamic World." 2002. www.spectrezine.org/war/Egypt.htm.

Althusser, Louis. "Contradiction and Overdetermination." In *For Marx*, 87–128. London: New Left Books, 1969 [1962].

Althusser, Louis. *Machiavelli and Us.* London: Verso, 1999 [1976].

Amin, Samir. *Class and Nation, Historically and in the Current Crisis.* New York: Monthly Review Press, 1980.

Amis, Martin. *Money: A Suicide Note,* Harmondsworth, UK: Penguin, 1985.

Anderson, Benedict. *Imagined Communities: Reflections on the Origin and Spread of Nationalism.* London: Verso, 2006.

Anderson, Benedict. "The New World Disorder." *New Left Review* I/193 (May/June 1992): 3–13.

Anderson, James. "The Modernity of Modern States." In *The Rise of the Modern State*, edited by James Anderson. Brighton, UK: Harvester, 1986.

Anderson, James. *Observations on Slavery: Particularly with a View to Its Effects on the British Colonies in the West Indies.* Manchester, UK: J. Harrop, 1789.

Anderson, Perry. *Considerations on Western Marxism.* London: New Left Books, 1976.

Anderson, Perry. "Jottings on the Conjuncture." *New Left Review* II/48 (Nov/Dec 2007): 5–37.

Anderson, Perry. *Lineages of the Absolutist State.* London: New Left Books, 1974.

Anderson, Perry. *The Origins of Postmodernity.* London: Verso, 1998.

Andreasson, Stefan. "Economic Reforms and 'Virtual Democracy' in South Africa and Zimbabwe: The Incompatibility of Liberalisation, Inclusion and Development." *Journal of Contemporary African Studies* 21, 3 (September 2003): 383–406.

Anonymous. "A Supplement, Containing an Account of the Present State of Agriculture, and the Improvements Recently Introduced." In *The Gentleman Farmer: Being an Attempt to Improve Agriculture by Subjecting It to the Test of Rational Principles*, Sixth edition, by Henry Home, Lord Kames. Edinburgh, UK: Bell and Bradfute, 1815 [1776].

Appleby, Joyce. *The Relentless Revolution: A History of Capitalism.* New York: W.

W. Norton, 2010.

Arendt, Hannah. *The Origins of Totalitarianism*. London: André Deutsch, 1986 [1951].

Armstrong, David. "On Revolutionary Chickens and International Eggs." *Review of International Studies* 27, no. 4 (Oct 2001): 669–674.

Arnold, Wayne. "China's Economic Recovery: A Tribute to Keynes." *The National* (Dubai) (August 2, 2009).

Arrighi, Giovanni. *Adam Smith in Beijing: Lineages of the Twenty-First Century*. London: Verso, 2007.

Arrighi, Giovanni. "The African Crisis." *New Left Review* 15 (May/June 2002): 1–38.

Arrighi, Giovanni. *The Long Twentieth Century: Money, Power and the Origins of Our Times*. London: Verso, 1994.

Arthur, Christopher. 'Capital, Competition and Many Capitals: A Reply to Finelli." In *The Culmination of Capital: Essays on Volume III of Marx's Capital*, edited by Martha Campbell and Geert Reuten, 128–48. Houndmills, UK: Palgrave, 2002.

Ascherson, Neal. "How Far Can We Fall? The Credit Crunch: Part One: What Does It Mean?" *Sunday Herald* (Glasgow) (July 27, 2008).

Ash, Timothy Garton. "This Epochal Crisis Requires Us to Resolve the Paradox of Capitalism." *Guardian* (London) (May 7, 2009).

Ashman, Sam, and Alex Callinicos. "Capital Accumulation and the State System: Assessing David Harvey's *The New Imperialism*." *Historical Materialism* 14, no. 4: 107–131.

Bacon, Francis. *The New Organon*, edited by Lisa Jardine and Michael Silverthorne. Cambridge, UK: Cambridge University Press, 2000 [1620].

Bageant, Joe. *Deer Hunting with Jesus: Dispatches from America's Class War*. New York: Three Rivers Press, 2007.

Bagehot, Walter. "Adam Smith as a Person." In *Works*, vol. 3, edited by Forrest Morgan. Hartford, CT: Travelers Insurance Company, 1889 [1876].

Bagehot, Walter. *Physics and Politics, or, Thoughts on the Application of the Principles of 'Natural Selection' and 'Inheritance' to Political Society*. London: Henry S. King, 1872.

Balibar, Etienne. "The Nation Form: History and Ideology." In *Race, Nation, Class: Ambiguous Identities*, Etienne Balibar and Immanuel Wallerstein, 86–106. London: Verso, 1991.

Ballard, J. G. *Extreme Metaphors: Interviews with J. G. Ballard, 1967–2008*, edited by Simon Sellars and Dan O'Hara. London: Fourth Estate, 2012.

Ballard, J. G. *Kingdom Come*. London: Fourth Estate, 2006.

Ballard, J. G. *Miracles of Life: Shanghai to Shepperton: An Autobiography*. London: Harper, 2008.

Ballard, J. G. "Rosetta Brooks. Myths of the Near Future." In Ballard, *Extreme Metaphors* [1988].

Ballard, J. G. "Toby Litt. 'Dangerous Bends Ahead. Slow Down': J. G. Ballard on

Kingdom Come." In Ballard, *Extreme Metaphors* [2006].

Banaji, Jairus. "The Fictions of Free Labour: Contract, Coercion, and So-Called Unfree Labour." *Historical Materialism* 11, no. 3: 69–95.

Barker, Colin. "A Note on the Theory of Capitalist States." *Capital and Class* 4 (Spring 1978): 118–26.

Barker, Colin. "The State as Capital." *International Socialism,* second series, no. 1 (July 1978): 16–42.

Batatu, Hanna. *The Old Social Classes and the Revolutionary Movements of Iraq: A Study of Iraq's Old Landed and Commercial Classes and of Its Communists, Ba'thists, and Free Officers.* Princeton, NJ: Princeton University Press, 1978.

Batson, Andrew. "China Rises on Power of Stimulus." *Wall Street Journal* (July 17, 2009).

Bauman, Zygmunt. "Happiness in a Society of Individuals." *Soundings* 38 (Spring 2008): 19–28.

Bayly, C. A. *The Birth of the Modern World, 1780–1914: Global Connections and Comparisons.* Oxford: Blackwell, 2004.

Beattie, James. *An Essay on the Nature and Immutability of Truth, in Opposition to Sophistry and Scepticism.* Edinburgh: William Creech, 1770.

Behr, Rafael. "The Shadow Power List." *New Statesman* (February 14, 2013): 24–27.

Beilharz, Peter. *Trotsky, Trotskyism and the Transition to Socialism.* London: Croom Helm, 1987.

Beissinger, Mark. "Nationalisms That Bark and Nationalisms That Bite: Ernest Gellner and the Substantiation of Nations." In *The State of The Nation: Ernest Gellner and the Theory of Nationalism,* edited by John A. Hall. Cambridge, UK: Cambridge University Press, 1998.

Bell, Daniel. *The Cultural Contradictions of Capitalism.* London: Heinemann Educational Books, 1976.

Bendix, Reinhard. "Tradition and Modernity Reconsidered." *Comparative Studies in Society and History* 9, no. 3 (April 1967): 292–346.

Bendix, Reinhard. "What Is Modernization?" In *Developing Nations: Quest for a Model,* edited by Willard Beling and George Totten. New York: Van Nostrand Reinhold, 1970.

Benjamin, Walter. "Diary Entries, 1937." In *Selected Writings,* Volume 3, *1935–1938,* edited by Howard Eiland and Michael W. Jennings. Cambridge, MA: Belknap Press of Harvard University Press, 2002.

Benn Michaels, Walter. "Against Diversity." *New Left Review* II/52 (July/Aug 2008): 33–36.

Bensaïd, Daniel. *Marx for Our Times: Adventures and Misadventures of a Critique.* London: Verso, 2002.

Berlin, Isaiah. "Introduction." In *Roots of Revolution: A History of the Populist and Socialist Movements in 19th Century Russia,* Franco Venturi. London: Weidenfeld and Nicholson, 1960.

Bessis, Sophie. *Western Supremacy: The Triumph of an Idea?* London: Zed Books, 2003.

Blackburn, Robin. *The Making of New World Slavery: From the Baroque to the Modern, 1492–1800*. London: Verso, 1997.

Blatty, William Peter. *The Exorcist*. London: Corgi Books, 1972.

Block, Fred. "Beyond Relative Autonomy: State Managers as Historical Subjects." In the *Socialist Register 1980*. London: Merlin, 1980: 227–42.

Blond, Phillip. *Red Tory: How the Left and Right Have Broken Britain and How We Can Fix It*. London: Faber and Faber, 2010.

Bois, Guy. "Against the Neo-Malthusian Orthodoxy." In *The Brenner Debate: Agrarian Class Structure and Economic Development in Pre-Industrial Europe*, edited by T. H. Aston and C. H. E. Philpin. Cambridge, UK: Cambridge University Press, 1985 [1978].

Boltanski, Luc, and Eve Chiapello. *The New Spirit of Capitalism*. London: Verso, 2005.

Boswell, James. *The Life of Samuel Johnson*, edited by Mowbray Morris. London: Macmillan, 1791.

Bourdieu, Pierre. "Neo-liberalism, the Utopia (Becoming a Reality) of Unlimited Exploitation." In *Acts of Resistance: Against the New Myths of Our Time*. Cambridge, UK: Polity, 1998.

Bourne, Randolph S. "Unfinished Fragment on the State." In *Untimely Papers*, edited by James Oppenheim. New York: B. W. Huebsch, 1919.

Bowcott, Owen. "The New British Empire? UK Plans to Annex South Atlantic." *Guardian* (September 22, 2007).

Bracewell, Michael. *The Conclave*. London: Martin Secker and Warburg, 1992.

Branson, Noreen. *History of the Communist Party of Great Britain, 1941–1951*. London: Lawrence & Wishart, 1997.

Braudel, Fernand. *Civilization and Capitalism, 15th–18th Century, vol. 1: The Structures of Everyday Life*. London: Fontana Press, 1985.

Braudel, Fernand. *Civilization and Capitalism, 15th–18th Century, vol. 2: the Wheels of Commerce*. London: Fontana Press, 1985.

Braunmühl, Claudia Von. "On the Analysis of the Bourgeois Nation State within the World Market Context: An Attempt to Develop a Methodological and Theoretical Approach." In *State and Capital: A Marxist Debate*, edited by John Holloway and Sil Picciotto. London: Arnold Edward, 1978.

Brenner, Robert. *The Boom and the Bubble: The US in the World Economy*. London and New York: Verso, 2002.

Brenner, Robert. *Merchants and Revolution: Commercial Change, Political Conflict, and London's Overseas Traders, 1550–1653*. Princeton, NJ: Princeton University Press, 1993.

Brenner, Robert. "New Boom or New Bubble?" *New Left Review* I/25 (Jan/Feb 2004): 57–100.

Brenner, Robert. "Structure Vs Conjuncture: The 2006 Elections and the Rightward Shift." *New Left Review* II/43 (January/February 2007): 33–59.

Brenner, Robert. "Uneven Development and the Long Downturn: The Advanced Capitalist Economies from Boom to Stagnation, 1950–1998." *New Left Review* I/229 (May/June 1998): 1–267.

Brenner, Robert. "What Is, and What Is Not, Imperialism?" *Historical Materialism* 14, no. 4 (2006): 79–105.

Brett, E. A. *International Money and Capitalist Crisis: The Anatomy of Global Disintegration*. London: Heinemann, 1983.

Brett, E. A. *The World Economy Since the War: The Politics of Uneven Development*. London: Palgrave, 1985.

Bryson, Bill. *Notes from a Small Island*. London: Black Swan, 1996.

Bryson, Gladys. *Man and Society: The Scottish Inquiry of the Eighteenth Century*. Princeton, NJ: Princeton University Press, 1945.

Brzezinski, Zbigniew. *The Grand Chessboard: American Primacy and Its Geostrategic Imperatives*. New York: Basic Books, 1997.

Bukharin, Nikolai. *Economic Theory of the Leisure Class*. New York: Monthly Review Press, 1972 [1914].

Bukharin, Nikolai. "The Economics of the Transition Period." In *The Politics and Economics of the Transition Period*, edited by Kenneth J. Tarbuck. London: Routledge & Kegan Paul, 1979 [1920].

Bull, Malcolm. "States of Failure." *New Left Review* II/40 (July/Aug 2006): 5–25.

Bunting, Madeleine. *Willing Slaves: How the Overwork Culture Is Ruling Our Lives*. London: Harper Perennial, 2005.

Burawoy, Michael. *The Politics of Production: Factory Regimes Under Capitalism and Socialism*. London: Verso, 1985.

Burawoy, Michael. "Two Methods in Search of Science: Skocpol versus Trotsky." *Theory and Society* 18, no. 6 (Nov 1989): 759–805.

Burbach, Roger. "For A Zapatista Style Postmodernist Perspective." *Monthly Review* 47, no. 10 (March 1996): 31–41.

Burbach, Roger. *Globalization and Postmodern Politics: From Zapatistas to High-Tech Robber Barons*. London: Pluto Press, 2001.

Burbach, Roger. "Roots of the Postmodern Rebellion in Chiapas." *New Left Review* I/205 (May/June 1994): 113–124.

Burke, Peter. *History and Social Theory*. Cambridge, UK: Polity, 1992.

Callinicos, Alex. "Against the New Dialectic." *Historical Materialism* 13, no. 2 (2005): 41–59.

Callinicos, Alex. "David Harvey and Marxism." In *David Harvey: A Critical Reader*, edited by Noel Castree and Derek Gregory. Oxford: Blackwell, 2006.

Callinicos, Alex. "Does Capitalism Need the State System?" *Cambridge Review of International Affairs* 20, no. 4 (Dec 2007): 533–549.

Callinicos, Alex. *Is There a Future for Marxism?* London: Macmillan, 1982.

Callinicos, Alex. *The New Mandarins of American Power*. Cambridge, UK: Polity, 2003.

Callinicos, Alex. "The 'New Middle Class' and Socialist Politics." In *The Changing Working Class: Essays on Class Structure Today*, Alex Callinicos and Chris Harman. London: Bookmarks, 1987 [1983].

Callinicos Alex. "Periodizing Capitalism and Analyzing Imperialism: Classical Marxism and Capitalist Evolution." In *Phases of Capitalist Development: Booms, Crises and Globalizations*, edited by Robert Albritton, Makato

Itoh, Richard Westra, and Alan Zuege. Houndmills, UK: Palgrave, 2001.

Callinicos Alex. "Plumbing the Depths: Marxism and the Holocaust." *Yale Journal of Criticism* 14, no. 2 (2001): 385–414.

Callinicos, Alex. *Theories and Narratives: Reflections on the Philosophy of History*. Cambridge, UK: Polity, 1995.

Callinicos, Alex. *Trotskyism*. Milton Keynes, UK: Open University Press, 1990.

Callinicos, Alex, and Justin Rosenberg. "Uneven and Combined Development: the Social-Relational Substratum of 'the International'? An Exchange of Letters." In *Marxism and World Politics: Contesting Global Capitalism*, edited by Alexander Anievas. London: Routledge, 2010.

Cameron, David. "We Need a Massive, Radical Redistribution of Power." *Guardian* (May 25, 2009).

Cammack, Paul. "Forget the Transnational State." *Papers in the Politics of Global Competitiveness*, No. 3. Institute for Global Studies, Manchester: Manchester Metropolitan University, 2007.

Cannadine, David. "The Context, Performance and Meaning of Ritual: The British Monarchy and the 'Invention of Tradition', c. 1820–1977." In *The Invention of Tradition*, edited by Eric Hobsbawm and Terence Ranger. Cambridge, UK: Cambridge University Press, 1983.

Carchedi, Guglielmo. *For Another Europe: A Class Analysis of European Economic Integration*. London: Verso, 2001.

Carrigan, Ana. "Afterword: Chiapas, the First Postmodern Revolution." In Subcomandante Marcos, *Our Word is Our Weapon*. Seven Stories, 2002.

Castells, Manuel. *The Information Age: Economy, Society and Culture, Volume II, The Power of Identity*. Oxford: Blackwell, 1997.

Castoriadis, Cornelius. "The Problem of the USSR and the Possibility of a Third Historical Solution." In *Political and Social Writings Volume 1, 1946–1955: From the Critique of Bureaucracy to the Positive Content of Socialism*, edited by David Ames Curtis. Minneapolis: University of Minnesota Press, 1988 [1946].

Castoriadis, Cornelius. "Socialism or Barbarism." In *Political and Social Writings, Volume 1*. Minneapolis: University of Minnesota Press, 1988 [1949].

Chang, Ha-Joon. *23 Things They Don't Tell You about Capitalism*. Harmondsworth, UK: Penguin, 2011.

Chernyshevsky, Nikolai. "Selected Writings." In *Late Marx and the Russian Road: Marx and "the Peripheries of Capitalism"*, edited by Teodor Shanin. London: Routledge & Kegan Paul, 1983 [1859].

Chibber, Vivek. "Capital Outbound." *New Left Review* 36 (Nov/Dec 2005): 151–158.

Chua, Amy. *World on Fire: How Exporting Free Market Democracy Breeds Ethnic Hatred and Global Instability*. London: Heinemann, 2003.

Church, Jenny. "Income." In *Focus on Social Inequalities*, edited by Penny Babb, Jean Martin, and Paul Haezewindt. London: Office for National Statistics, 2004.

Clarke, John, and Janet Newman, *The Managerial State: Power, Politics and Ideology in the Remaking of Social Welfare*. London: Sage, 1997.

Clegg, Nick. Interviewed by Fraser Nelson. "Nick Clegg Takes to the Stage." *Spectator* (March 11, 2010).

Cliff, Tony. "Deflected Permanent Revolution." In *Marxist Theory After Trotsky, Selected Writings*, Volume 3. London: Bookmarks, 2003 [1963].

Cliff, Tony. "The Nature of Stalinist Russia." In *Marxist Theory After Trotsky, Selected Writings* Volume 3. London: Bookmarks, 2003 [1948].

Cliff, Tony. *Trotsky*, vol. 1, *Towards October, 1879–1917*. London: Bookmarks, 1989.

Cockburn, Patrick. *The Occupation: War and Resistance in Iraq*. London: Verso, 2007.

Comaroff, Jean, and John L. Comaroff, "Millennial Capitalism: First Thoughts on a Second Coming." In *Millennial Capitalism and the Culture of Neoliberalism*, edited by Jean Comaroff and John L. Comaroff. Durham, NC: Duke University Press, 2001.

Comte, Auguste. *The Positive Philosophy of Auguste Comte, Vol. II*. London: Chapman, 1853.

Condorcet, Marquis de (Marie Jean Antoine Nicolas de Caritat). "Réflexions sur le commerce des bléds." In *Oeuvres de Condorcet*, Vol. 11, edited by François Arago and Arthur O'Connor. Paris: Didot, 1849 [1776].

Condorcet, Marquis de (Marie Jean Antoine Nicolas de Caritat). *Sketch for a Historical Picture of the Progress of the Human Mind*. London: Weidenfeld and Nicolson, 1955 [1794].

Cooper, Robert. *The Breaking of Nations: Order and Chaos in the Twenty-First Century*. London: Atlantic, 2003.

Craig, Carol, in conversation with Tom Devine. "Scotland's 'Velvet Revolution.'" In *Scotland 2020: Hopeful Stories for a Northern Nation*, edited by Gerry Hassan, Eddie Gibb, and Lydia Howland. London: Demos, 2005.

Critser, Greg. *Fat Land: How Americans Became the Fattest People in the World*. Harmondsworth: Penguin, 2004.

Crossman, Richard H. S. "Towards a Philosophy of Socialism." In *New Fabian Essays*, edited by R. S. H. Crossman. London: Turnstile, 1952.

Curtice, John. "Public Attitudes." In *Nations and Regions: The Dynamics of Devolution*. Quarterly Monitoring Programme Quarterly Report. Stirling: University of Stirling, February 2001.

Curtin, Philip D. *The World and the West: The European Challenge and the Overseas Response in the Age of Empire*. Cambridge, UK: Cambridge University Press, 2000.

Dalrymple, William. "After the Blackout." *New Statesman* (October 12–18, 2012): 22–29.

Davidson, Neil. "Enlightenment and Anti-Capitalism." *International Socialism*, second series, 110 (Spring 2006): 85–112.

Davidson, Neil. *How Revolutionary Were the Bourgeois Revolutions?* Chicago: Haymarket, 2012.

Davidson, Neil. "How Revolutionary Were the Bourgeois Revolutions? Continued." *Historical Materialism* 13, no. 4 (2005): 3–54.

Davidson, Neil. "Marx and Engels on the Scottish Highlands." *Science & Society* 65, no. 3 (Fall 2001): 286–326.

Davidson, Neil. *The Origins of Scottish Nationhood*. London: Pluto, 2000.

Davidson, Neil. "Reimagined Communities." *International Socialism* 2, no. 117 (Winter 2008): 143–163.

Davidson, Neil. "Stalinism, 'Nation Theory' and Scottish History: A Reply to John Foster." *Historical Materialism* 10, no. 3 (Jan 1, 2002): 195–222.

Davidson, Neil, Patricia McCafferty, and David Miller, eds. *Neoliberal Scotland: Class and Society in a Stateless Nation*. Newcastle: Cambridge Scholars Press, 2010.

Davis, Mike. "The Barren Marriage of American Labour and the Democratic Party." In Davis, *Prisoners of the American Dream: Politics and Economy in the History of the U.S. Working Class*. London: Verso, 2000.

Davis, Mike. *City of Quartz: Excavating the Future in Los Angeles*. London: Verso, 1990.

Davis, Mike. "Cosmic Dancers on History's Stage?" In *Dead Cities: And Other Tales*. New York: New Press, 2002 [1996].

Davis, Mike. "Nuclear Imperialism and Extended Deterrence." In *Exterminism and Cold War*, edited by New Left Review. London: Verso, 1982.

Davis, Mike. "Occupied America." In *In Praise of Barbarians: Essays against Empire*. Chicago: Haymarket, 2007 [2003].

Davis, Mike. "Planet of Slums." *New Left Review* II/26 (Mar/Apr 2004): 5–34.

Davis, Mike. *Planet of Slums*. London: Verso, 2006.

Davis, Mike. *Prisoners of the American Dream: Politics and Economy in the History of the U.S. Working Class*. London: Verso, 1986.

D'Costa, Anthony P. "Uneven and Combined Development: Understanding India's Software Exports." *World Development* 31, no. 1 (January 2003): 211–226.

Debray, Régis. "A Modest Contribution to the Rites and Ceremonies of the Tenth Anniversary." *New Left Review* I/115 (May/June 1979): 45–65.

Defoe, Daniel. "The True-Born Englishman: An Explanatory Preface." In *The Novels and Selected Writings of Daniel Defoe, Volume 13: The Shortest Way with Dissenters, and Other Pamphlets*. Oxford: Shakespeare Head Press, 1927 [1701].

Desai, Meghnad. *Marx's Revenge: The Resurgence of Capitalism and the Death of Statist Socialism*. London: Verso, 2002.

Deutscher, Isaac. "Four Decades of the Revolution." In *Ironies of History: Essays on Contemporary Communism*. Berkeley: Ramparts Press, 1971 [1957].

Deutscher, Isaac. *The Prophet Armed: Trotsky, 1879–1921*. London: Verso, 2003 [1954].

Devine, T. M. *Scotland's Empire, 1600–1815*. London: Allen Lane, 2003.

Diski, Jenny. *The Sixties: Big Ideas, Small Books*. London: Profile, 2009.

Dore, Ronald. *British Factory – Japanese Factory*. Berkeley: University of California Press, 1973.

Dougary, Ginny. "The Voice of Experience." Interview with Martin Amis. *The Times* (London): (September 9, 2006).

Drabble, Margaret. *The Ice Age*. London: Penguin, 1978.

Draper, John William. *History of the Intellectual Development of Europe*, Volumes I and II, revised edition. London: G. Bell, 1985.

Dukes, Paul. "Introductory Essay." In *The Trotsky Reappraisal*, edited by Terry Brotherstone and Paul Dukes. Edinburgh: Edinburgh University Press, 1992.

Duménil, Gérard, and Dominique Lévy. *Capitalism Resurgent: Roots of the Neoliberal Revolution*. Cambridge, MA: Harvard University Press, 2004.

Dunn, Bill. *Global Political Economy: A Marxist Critique*. London: Pluto Press, 2009.

Durkheim, Emile. *The Division of Labour in Society*. Houndmills: Macmillan, 1984 [1893].

Eagleton, Terry. *After Theory*. London: Allen Lane, 2003.

Eagleton, Terry. "The Crisis of Contemporary Culture." *New Left Review* I/196 (Nov/Dec 1992): 29–41.

Easterly, William. "The Lost Decades: Developing Countries' Stagnation in Spite of Policy Reform 1980–1998." *Journal of Economic Growth* 6, no. 2 (June 2001): 135–157.

Economist. "Capitalism at Bay" October 16, 2008.

Edgar, David. "Bitter Harvest." *New Socialist* 13 (September/October 1983): 19–24.

Edgar, David. "The Free or the Good." In *The Ideology of the New Right*, edited by Ruth Levitas. Cambridge, UK: Polity, 1986.

Eichengreen, Barry. *Exorbitant Privilege: the Rise and Fall of the Dollar and the Future of the International Monetary System*. Oxford: Oxford University Press, 2012.

Eldredge, Niles, and Stephen Jay Gould. "Punctuated Equilibria: An Alternative to Phyletic Gradualism." In *Models in Paleobiology*, edited by Thomas M. Schopf. San Francisco: Freeman, Cooper, 1972.

Eliot, T. S. "Burnt Norton." In *The Complete Poems & Plays, T. S. Eliot*. London: Faber and Faber, 1969.

Elliot, Gilbert. "An Account of a Scheme for Enlarging and Improving the City of Edinburgh, and for Adorning It With Certain Public Buildings, and Other Useful Works." *The Scots Magazine* 14 (August 1752): 369–380.

Elliott, Larry, and Dan Atkinson. *Fantasy Island: Waking Up to the Incredible Economic, Political and Social Illusions of the Blair Legacy*. London: Constable, 2007.

Elliott, Larry, and Dan Atkinson. *The Gods that Failed: How Blind Faith in Markets Has Cost Us Our Future*. London: Bodley Head, 2008.

Emmott, Bill. *20:21 Vision: Twentieth-Century Lessons for the Twenty-First Century*. London: Penguin, 2003.

Engels, Frederick. "Engels to Schmidt, March 12, 1895." *Marx & Engels Collected Works*, vol. 50, *Letters 1892–95*. London: Lawrence & Wishart, 2005 [1895].

Estler, Jon. "The Theory of Combined and Uneven Development: A Critique." In *Analytical Marxism*, edited by John Roemer. Cambridge, UK: Cambridge University Press, 1986.

Evans, Richard J. *The Coming of the Third Reich*. London: Allen Lane, 2003.

Faulkner, Neil. *Apocalypse: the Great Jewish Revolt against Rome AD 66–73*. Stroud, UK: Tempus, 2002.

Fekete, Liz. *A Suitable Enemy: Racism, Migration and Islamophobia in Europe*. London: Pluto Press, 2009.

Ferguson, Iain. "An Attitude Problem? Confidence and Well-being in Scotland." In Davidson, McCafferty, and Miller, *Neoliberal Scotland*.

Ferguson, Niall. *Empire: How Britain Made the Modern World*. London: Allen Lane, 2003.

Ferguson, Niall. *Colossus: The Rise and Fall of the American Empire*. London: Allen Lane, 2004.

Finch, Julia. "In India, It's Service with a Compulsory Smile." *Guardian* (November 17, 2003).

Finch, Julia. "Road to Ruin 2: Twenty-five People at the Heart of the Meltdown . . ." *Guardian* (January 26, 2009).

Fisk, Robert. "For Centuries, We've Been 'Liberating' the Middle East. Why Do We Never Learn?" *Independent* (March 6, 2003).

Florida, Richard. *The Rise of the Creative Class: . . . and How It's Transforming Work, Leisure, Community, and Everyday Life*. New York: Basic Books, 2002.

Forbes, Margaret. *Beattie and His Friends*. Altrincham, UK: J. Martin Stafford, 1990 [1904].

Foster, John. "Review of *The Origins of Scottish Nationhood*." *Historical Materialism* 10, no. 1 (2002): 258–271.

Foster, John Bellamy, and Fred Magdoff. *The Great Financial Crisis: Causes and Consequences*. New York: Monthly Review Press, 2009.

Foster, Stephen. *From Working Class Hero to Absolute Disgrace: An 80s Memoir*. London: Short Books, 2008.

Frank, Robert. *Richistan: A Journey through the 21st Century Wealth Boom and the Lives of the New Rich*. London: Piatkus, 2008.

Frank, Thomas. *What's the Matter with America? The Resistible Rise of the American Right*. London: Secker & Warburg, 2004.

Frank, Thomas. *The Wrecking Crew: The American Right and the Lust for Power*. London: Harvill Secker, 2008.

Fraser, Nancy. "Feminism, Capitalism and the Cunning of History." *New Left Review* II/56 (March/April 2009): 97–117.

Fraser, Steve. "The Great Silence: Their Gilded Age and Ours." In *The Great Credit Crash*, edited by Martijn Konings. London: Verso, 2010.

Freedland, Jonathan. "Discard the Mythology of 'the Israeli Lobby,' the Reality Is Bad Enough." *Guardian* (March 18, 2009).

Freeman, Alan. "The Inequality of Nations." In *The Politics of Empire*, Freeman and Kagarlitsky.

Freeman, Alan, and Boris Kagarlitsky, eds.*The Politics of Empire: Globalisation in Crisis*. London: Pluto, in association with Transnational Institute, 2004.

Friedman, Milton. *Capitalism and Freedom*. Chicago: University of Chicago Press, 1962.

Friedman, Thomas L. *The Lexus and the Olive Tree*. London: HarperCollins, 2000.

Fukuyama, Francis. *The End of History and the Last Man*. New York: Free Press, 1992.

Garten, Jeffrey. "The Unsettling Zeitgeist of State Capitalism." *Financial Times* (January 14, 2008).

Gellner, Ernest. *Nationalism*. London: Weidenfeld & Nicolson, 1997.

Gellner, Ernest. *Nations and Nationalism*. Oxford: Basil Blackwell, 1983.

Gentleman, Amelia. "Life on the Edge." *Guardian*, G2 (March 31, 2010).

George, Susan. *Hijacking America: How the Religious and Secular Right Changed What Americans Think*. Cambridge, UK: Polity, 2008.

Gerschenkron, Alexander. *Economic Backwardness in Historical Perspective*. Cambridge, MS: Harvard University Press, 1962.

Gilly, Adolfo. *The Mexican Revolution*. London: Verso, 1983 [1971].

Glassman, Ronald M. *The New Middle Class and Democracy in Global Perspective*. Houndmills: Macmillan, 1997.

Glotzer, Albert. *Trotsky: Memoir and Critique*. New York: Prometheus Books, 1989.

Gobineau, Joseph-Arthur de. "Essay on the Inequality of Human Races." In *Gobineau: Selected Political Writings*, edited by Michael D. Biddiss. London: Harper & Row, 1970 [1853–55].

Gould, Stephen Jay. *The Structure of Evolutionary Theory*. Cambridge, MA: Belknap, 2002.

Gould, Stephen Jay, and Niles Eldredge. "Punctuated Equilibrium Comes of Age." *Nature* 366, no. 6452 (November 18, 1993): 223–227.

Gow, David. "Car Sales Down 27%—but Porsche Quadruples Its Profits." *Guardian* (April 1, 2009).

Gowan, Peter. "British Euro-Solipsism." In *The Question of Europe*, edited by Peter Gowan and Perry Anderson. London: Verso, 1997.

Gowan, Peter. "Crisis in the Heartland: Consequences of the New Wall Street System." *New Left Review* II/55 (Jan/Feb 2009): 5–29.

Gowan, Peter. "The Gulf War, Iraq and Western Liberalism." In *The Global Gamble: Washington's Faustian Bid for World Dominance*. London: Verso, 1999 [1991].

Graeber, David. "Against Kamikaze Capitalism." In Graeber, *Revolutions in Reverse: Essays on Politics, Violence, Art & the Imagination*. London: Minor Compositions, 2011.

Graeber, David. "Army of Altruists." In Graeber, *Revolutions in Reverse*.

Graeber, David. *Revolutions in Reverse: Essays on Politics, Violence, Art & the Imagination*. London: Minor Compositions, 2011.

Graham, Andrew. "If China Spends Its Trillions, Recession Could Be Averted." *Guardian* (October 15, 2008).

Graham, Stephen. *Cities Under Siege: The New Military Urbanism.* London: Verso, 2010.

Gramsci, Antonio. "The Intellectuals." In Gramsci, *Selections from the Prison Notebooks.*

Gramsci, Antonio. *Selections from the Prison Notebooks.* Edited by Quintin Hoare and Geoffrey Nowell Smith. London: Lawrence & Wishart, 1971.

Granta. "The State of Europe: Christmas Eve 1989," "George Steiner." *Granta 30: New Europe!* (Spring 1990): 129–132.

Gray, John. *Al Qaeda and What It Means to Be Modern.* London: Faber and Faber, 2003.

Gray, John. *False Dawn: The Delusions of Global Capitalism.* London: Granta, 1998.

Gray, John. "Maggie's Gift to Gordon." *New Statesman* (September 24, 2007): 46–49.

Gray, Neil. "Glasgow's *Merchant City*: An Artist Led Property Strategy." *Variant* 34 (Spring 2009): 14–19.

Green, Jonathon. *Days in the Life: Voices from the English Underground, 1961–1971.* London: Minerva, 1989.

Greenberg, Clement. "Interview Conducted by Lily Leino." In *The Collected Essays and Criticism*, Volume 4: *Modernism with a Vengeance, 1957–1969*, edited by John O'Brian. Chicago: University of Chicago Press, 1993 [1969].

Greenfeld, Liah. *The Spirit of Capitalism: Nationalism and Economic Growth.* Cambridge, MA: Harvard University Press, 2001.

Grossman, Henryk. "The Evolutionist Revolt against Classical Economics: II. In England—James Steuart, Richard Jones, Karl Marx." *Journal of Political Economy* 51, no. 6, (December 1943): 506–522.

Gueullette, Agota. "Trotsky's Conceptions Concerning Foreign Economic Relations." In *The Trotsky Reappraisal*, edited by Terry Brotherstone and Paul Dukes. Edinburgh: Edinburgh University Press, 1992.

Guevara, Che. "On Our Common Aspiration—the Death of Imperialism and the Birth of a Moral World." In *Venceremos!: The Speeches and Writings of Che Guevara*, edited by John Gerassi. London: Panther Books, 1969 [1964].

Guibernau, Montserrat. *Nationalisms: The Nation-State and Nationalism in the Twentieth Century.* Cambridge, UK: Polity, 1996.

Guldin, Gregory Eliyu. *What's a Peasant to Do? Village Becoming Town in Southern China.* Boulder, CO: Westview Press, 2001.

Hall, Stuart, Chas Critcher, Tony Jefferson, John Clarke, and Brian Roberts. *Policing the Crisis: Mugging, the State, and Law and Order.* London: Macmillan, 1978.

Hallas, Duncan. "Fourth International in Decline: From Trotskyism to Pabloism 1944–1953." *International Socialism*, first series, no. 60 (July 1973): 17–23.

Hallas, Duncan. *Trotsky's Marxism.* London: Pluto Press, 1979.

Halliday, Fred. "The Great Anomaly." *Review of International Studies* 27, no. 4

(October 2001): 701–704.

Halliday, Fred. *Rethinking International Relations*. London: Macmillan, 1994.

Halliday, Fred. *Revolution and World Politics: The Rise and Fall of the Sixth Great Power*. London: Macmillan, 1999.

Halliday, Fred. *Two Hours That Shook the World: September 11, 2001: Causes & Consequences*. London: Saqi Books, 2002.

Hansard Parliamentary Debates 2008 (February 18, 2008).

Hansard Parliamentary Debates 2009 (March 25, 2009).

Harding, Luke. "Energy Conflicts Could Bring Military Clashes, Russian Security Strategy Warns." *Guardian* (May 14, 2009).

Hardt, Michael. "An Interview with Michael Hardt." *Historical Materialism* 11, no. 3 (2003): 121–152.

Hardt, Michael, and Antonio Negri. *Empire*. London: Harvard University Press, 2000.

Harman. Chris. "China's Economy and Europe's Crisis." *International Socialism*, second series, no. 109 (Winter 2006): 69–90.

Harman, Chris. "The Rate of Profit and the World Today." *International Socialism*, second series, no. 115 (Summer 2007): 141–161.

Harman, Chris. "The State and Capitalism Today." *International Socialism* 2, no. 51 (Summer 1991): 3–54.

Harris, Nigel. *The Return of Cosmopolitan Capital: Globalisation, the State and War*. London: I. B. Taurus, 2003.

Hartley, Victoria. "Northern Rock Criticised over 'Aggressive Repossessions.'" *Guardian* (October 17, 2008).

Hartz, Louis. *The Liberal Tradition in America: An Interpretation of American Political Thought Since the Revolution*. New York: Harcourt, Brace, 1955.

Harvey, David. "The Geopolitics of Capitalism." In Harvey, *Spaces of Capital: Towards a Critical Geography*. Edinburgh: Edinburgh University Press, 2001 [1985].

Harvey, David. *The Limits to Capital*. London: Verso, 2006 [1982].

Harvey, David. *The New Imperialism*. Oxford: Oxford University Press, 2003.

Harvey, David. "Reclaiming the City for Anti-Capitalist Struggle." In *Rebel Cities: From the Right to the City to the Urban Revolution*. London: Verso, 2012.

Harvey, David. "Reinventing Geography: An Interview with the Editors of *New Left Review*." In Harvey, *Spaces of Capital*.

Harvey, David. *Spaces of Capital: Towards a Critical Geography*. Edinburgh: Edinburgh University Press, 2001 [1985].

Hayek, Friedrich. *Individualism: True and False*. Dublin and Oxford: Hodges, Figgis and H. Blackwell, 1946.

Heartfield, James. *Unpatriotic History of the Second World War*. Winchester, UK: Zero Books, 2012.

Hegel, Georg. *The Philosophy of History*. New York: Dover Publications, 1956 [1830–1831].

Heider, Ulrike. *Anarchism: Left, Right, and Green*. San Francisco: City Lights, 1994.

Hellman, Judith Adler. "Real and Virtual Chiapas: Magic Realism and the Left." In *The Socialist Register 2000: Necessary and Unnecessary Utopias*, edited by Leo Panitch and Colin Leys. London: Merlin, 2000.

Henwood, Doug. "The "Business Community."" In *The Socialist Register 2006*, edited by Leo Panitch and Colin Leys. London: Merlin, 2006.

Herder, Johann von. "Letters Concerning the Progress of Humanity (1792) [Excerpts on European Politics]." In *Philosophical Writings*, edited by Michael Forster. Cambridge, UK: Cambridge University Press, 2002 [1792].

Herder, Johann von. "Letters for the Advancement of Humanity (1793–1797) – Tenth Collection: Letter 115." In Herder, *Philosophical Writings* [1797].

Hirsch, Joachim. "The State Apparatus and Social Reproduction: Elements of a Theory of the Bourgeois State." In Holloway and Picciotto, *State and Capital* [1974].

Hirschman, Albert O. *The Passions and the Interests: Political Arguments for Capitalism Before Its Triumph*, Twentieth anniversary edition, Princeton: Princeton University Press, 1996 [1976].

Hirst, Paul. "Anderson's Balance Sheet." In *Marxism and Historical Writing*. London: Routledge & Kegan Paul, 1985.

Hobsbawm, Eric. *The Age of Empire, 1875–1914*. London: Weidenfeld & Nicolson, 1987.

Hobsbawm, Eric. *Globalisation, Democracy and Terrorism*. London: Little, Brown, 2007.

Hobsbawm, Eric. *Nations and Nationalism since 1780: Programme, Myth, Reality*. Cambridge, UK: Cambridge University Press, 1990.

Hobsbawm, Eric. *The New Century: In Conversation with Antonio Polito*. London: Abacus, 2000.

Hobsbawm, Eric. *Primitive Rebels: Studies in Archaic Forms of Social Movement in the 19th and 20th Centuries*. Manchester: Manchester University Press, 1971 [1959].

Holloway, John, and Sol Picciotto, eds. *State and Capital: A Marxist Debate*, London: Edward Arnold, 1978.

Houellebecq, Michel. *Atomised*. London: Vintage, 2001.

Hughes, Christopher R. *Chinese Nationalism in the Global Era*. London: Routledge, 2006.

Hughey, Michael W. "The New Conservatism: Political Ideology and Class Structure in America." In *The New Middle Classes: Life-styles, Status Claims and Political Orientations*, edited by Arthur J. Vidich. Houndmills: Macmillan, 1995 [1982].

Hume, David. "Of National Characters." In *Hume: Political Essays*, edited by Knud Haakonssen. Cambridge, UK: Cambridge University Press, 1994 [1748/53].

Hume, David. "Of the Populousness of Ancient Nations." In *Essays: Moral, Political, and Literary*, edited by Eugene F. Miller. Indianapolis: Liberty Fund, 1987 [1758].

Huntington, Samuel P. *The Clash of Civilizations and the Remaking of World Order.* London: Simon and Schuster, 1998.

Hurd, Douglas. *An End to Promises: Sketch of a Government, 1970–74.* London: Collins, 1979.

Huws, Ursula. "The Making of a Cybertariat: Virtual Work in a Real World." In *The Making of a Cybertariat: Virtual Work in a Real World.* New York: Monthly Review Press, 2003.

Iles, Anthony, and Tom Roberts. *All Knees and Elbows of Susceptibility and Refusal: Reading History from Below.* London: Strickland Distribution with Transmission Gallery and Mute Books, 2012.

Immerwahr, John. "Hume's Revised Racism." *Journal of the History of Ideas* 53, no. 3 (July–Sept 1992): 481–486.

Irvin, George. *Super Rich: The Rise of Inequality in Britain and the United States.* Cambridge, UK: Polity, 2008.

Israel, Jonathan. *The Dutch Republic: Its Rise, Greatness, and Fall, 1477–1806.* Oxford: Clarendon Press, 1998.

Israel, Jonathan I. *Radical Enlightenment: Philosophy and the Making of Modernity, 1650–1750.* Oxford: Oxford University Press, 2001.

Jacoby, Susan. *The Age of American Unreason.* New York: Pantheon Books, 2008.

James, C. L. R. *Notes on Dialectics: Hegel, Marx, Lenin.* London: Alison & Busby, 1980 [1948].

James, Oliver. *Affluenza: How to Be Successful and Stay Sane.* London: Vermilion, 2007.

Jenkins, Simon. "The End of Capitalism? No, Just Another Burst Bubble." *Guardian* (October 15, 2008).

Jenkins, Simon. "The State Is Utterly Clueless on the Public-Private Divide." *Guardian* (February 20, 2008).

Jenkins, Simon, and Tony Travers. "Cameron's Best Hope: Delegate the Axe." *Guardian* (August 14, 2009).

Jha, Prem Shankar. *The Twilight of the Nation State: Globalisation, Chaos and War.* London: Pluto, 2006.

Johnson, Chalmers. *Blowback: the Costs and Consequences of American Empire,* second edition. New York: Henry Holt, 2002.

Johnson, Chalmers. "No Longer the 'Lone' Superpower." In *The World according to TomDispatch: America in the New Age of Empire,* edited by Tom Engelhardt. London: Verso, 2008.

Judt, Tony. *Postwar: A History of Europe since 1945.* London: Allen Lane, 2006.

Kagan, Robert. *The Return of History and the End of Dreams.* London: Atlantic Books, 2008.

Kagarlitsky, Boris. "From Global Crisis to Neo-Imperialism: The Case for a Radical Alternative." In Freeman and Kagarlitsky, *The Politics of Empire.*

Kames, Lord (Henry Home). *Essay on the Origin of Men and of Languages and Their Progress with Regard to Food and Population.* Glasgow: W. Falconer, 1814 [1778].

Kames, Lord (Henry Home). *Sketches of the History of Man*, vol. 1. Edinburgh: Creech, Strahan, and Cadell, 1778.

Kant, Immanuel. "Idea for a Universal History with a Cosmopolitan Aim." In *Kant: Political Writings*, edited by H. S. Reiss. Cambridge, UK: Cambridge University Press, 1991 [1784].

Kant, Immanuel. "Perpetual Peace: A Philosophical Sketch." In *Kant: Political Writings* [1795].

Kapur, Ajay, Niall Macleod, and Narendra Singh. "Plutonomy: Buying Luxury, Explaining Global Imbalances." Citigroup Equity Strategy Industry Note (October 16, 2005).

Kautsky, Karl. "Ultra-imperialism." In *Lenin's Struggle for a Revolutionary International: Documents, 1907–1916*, edited by John Riddell. New York: Pathfinder, 1984 [1914].

Kelly, Brian. "Materialism and the Persistence of Race in the Jim Crow South." *Historical Materialism* 12, no. 2 (Jan 2004): 3–19.

Kemp, Tom. *Historical Patterns of Industrialisation*. Harlow, UK: Longman, 1978.

Kennedy, Helena. "Foreword." In Power, "Power to the People: The report of Power: An Independent Inquiry into Britain's Democracy." The POWER Inquiry, 2006.

Kershaw, Ian. *Fateful Choices: Ten Decisions That Changed the World, 1940–1941*. London: Allen Lane, 2007.

Kershaw, Ian. *Hitler, 1936–1945: Nemesis*. London: Allen Lane, 2000.

Khaldun, Ibn. *The Muqaddimah: An Introduction to History*, edited by N. J. Dawood. London: Routledge and Kegan Paul, 1967 [1377].

Kidron, Michael "The Injured Self." *The Socialist Register 2002: A World of Contradictions*, edited by Leo Panitch and Colin Leys. London: Merlin, 2002: 229–44.

Kidron, Michael. "Maginot Marxism: Mandel's Economics." In *Capitalism and Theory*. London: Pluto, 1974 [1969].

Klein, Naomi. *No Logo: Standing Up to the Brand Bullies*. London: HarperCollins, 2000.

Kliman, Andrew. "A Crisis for the Centre of the System." *International Socialism*, second series, no. 120 (Autumn 2008): 61–76.

Knei-Paz, Baruch. *The Social and Political Thought of Leon Trotsky*. Oxford: Clarendon Press, 1978.

Koselleck, Reinhardt. *Futures Past: On the Semantics of Historical Time*, revised edition. New York: Columbia University Press, 2004 [1985].

Kracauer, Siegfried. *History: The Last Things Before the Last*. New York: Oxford University Press, 1969 [1966].

Kristol, Irving. *Two Cheers for Capitalism*. New York: Basic Books, 1978.

Krugman, Paul. "State of Paralysis." *New York Times* (May 24, 2009).

Kumar, Krishan. *Prophecy and Progress: The Sociology of Industrial and Post-Industrial Society*. Harmondsworth: Penguin, 1978.

Kundnani, Hans. "Rich Get Even Richer in Third World." *Guardian* (June 21, 2006).

Kuusinen, Otto, ed. *Fundamentals of Marxism-Leninism*. London: Lawrence & Wishart, 1961.

Labour Research. "'What Do We Have to Lose?'" *Labour Research* 98, no. 8 (August 2009): 9–11.

Lacher, Hannes. *Beyond Globalization: Capitalism, Territoriality and the Internal Relations of Modernity*. London: Routledge, 2006.

Lacher, Hannes. "International Transformation and the Persistence of Territoriality: Toward a New Political Geography of Capitalism." *Review of International Political Economy* 12, no. 1 (Feb 2005): 26–52.

Lansley, Stewart. *Rich Britain: The Rise and Rise of the New Super-Wealthy*. London: Politicos, 2006.

Lasch, Christopher. *The Revolt of the Elites and the Betrayal of Democracy*. New York: W. W. Norton, 1996.

Latour, Bruno. *We Have Never Been Modern*. Cambridge, MA: Harvard University Press, 1993 [1991].

Law, Alex. "Hatred and Respect: The Class Shame of Ned 'Humour.'" *Variant* 25, no. 2 (Spring 2006): 28–30.

Law, Alex, and Gerry Mooney. "Financialisation and Proletarianisation: Changing Landscapes of Neoliberal Scotland." In Davidson, McCafferty, and Miller, *Neoliberal Scotland*.

Leadbeater, Charles. *Living on Thin Air: The New Economy*. Harmondsworth: Penguin, 2000.

Lecourt, Dominique. "Appendix: Dissidence or Revolution?" In *The Mediocracy: French Philosophy since 1968*. London: Verso, 2001 [1978].

Lefebvre, Henri. *Critique of Everyday Life Volume 3: From Modernity to Modernism (Towards a Metaphilosophy of Daily Life)*. London: Verso, 2005.

Leibniz, Gottfried von. "Discourse on the Natural Theology of the Chinese." In *Writings on China*, edited and translated by Daniel J. Cook and Henry Rosemont Jr. Chicago: Open Court, 1994 [1716].

Leibniz, Gottfried von. "Monadology." In *Philosophical Texts*, translated and edited by R. S. Woolhouse and Richard Francks. Oxford: Oxford University Press, 1998 [1714].

Leibniz, Gottfried von. *New Essays on Human Understanding*, edited by Peter Rennant and Jonathan Bennett. Cambridge, UK: Cambridge University Press, 1981 [1704].

Leibniz, Gottfried von. "On an Academy of Arts and Science." In *Selections*, edited by Phillip Wiener. New York: Scribner, 1951 [1712].

Leibniz, Gottfried von. "Preface to the *Novissima Sinica*." In *Writings on China* [1697/1699].

Lenin, Vladimir. "The Awakening of Asia." In *Collected Works, vol. 19*. Moscow: Foreign Languages Publishing House, 1963 [1913].

Lenin, Vladimir. "Conspectus of Hegel's Book *The Science of Logic*." In *Collected Works*, vol. 38: *Philosophical Notebooks*. Moscow: Foreign Languages Publishing House, 1960 [1914–16].

Lenin, Vladimir. "The Fall of Port Arthur." In *Collected Works, vol. 8*. Moscow: Foreign Languages Publishing House, 1962 [1905].

Lenin, Vladimir. "Imperialism, the Highest Stage of Capitalism: A Popular Outline." In *Collected Works*, vol. 22. Moscow: Foreign Languages Publishing House, 1964 [1916].

Lenin, Vladimir. "Introduction." In Nikolai Bukharin, *Imperialism and World Economy*. London: Merlin, 1972 [1915].

Leys, Colin "The Rise & Fall of Development Theory." In *The Rise and Fall of Development Theory*. Nairobi, Bloomington, IN, and Oxford: EAEP, Indiana University Press, and James Currey, 1996.

Lilla, Mark. "The Tea Party Jacobins." *New York Review of Books* (May 27, 2010).

Lipovetsky, Gilles. "May '68, or the Rise of Transpolitical Individualism." In *New French Thought: Political Philosophy*, edited by Mark Lilla. Princeton, NJ: Princeton University Press, 1994 [1986].

Lipsitz, George. *Dangerous Crossroads: Popular Music, Postmodernism and the Poetics of Place*. London: Verso, 1994.

List, Frederick. *The National System of Political Economy*, new edition. London: Longmans, Green, 1904 [1840].

Locke, John. "An Essay Concerning the True Original Extent and End of Civil Government." In *Two Treatises of Government*, edited by Peter Laslett. Cambridge, UK: Cambridge University Press, 1999 [1679–1683, 1689].

Lodge, David. *Nice Work*. Harmondsworth, UK: Penguin, 1989.

Lomnitz, Larissa. "The Social and Economic Organization of a Mexican Shanty Town." In *Cities in the Developing World: Issues, Theory, and Policy*, edited by Josef Gugler. Oxford: Oxford University Press, 1997.

Looker, Robert, and David Coates. "The State and the Working Class." In *The Rise of the Modern State*, edited by James Anderson. Brighton, UK: Harvester, 1986.

Lott, Tim. *The Scent of Dried Roses*. Harmondsworth: Penguin, 1997.

Löwy, Michael. "From the 'Logic' of Hegel to the Finland Station in Petrograd." *Critique* 6, no. 1 (Spring 1976): 5–15.

Löwy, Michael. *Fire Alarm: Reading Walter Benjamin's "On the Concept of History."* London: Verso, 2005.

Löwy, Michael. *The Politics of Combined and Uneven Development: The Theory of Permanent Revolution*. London: Verso, 1981.

Lucretius. *On the Nature of Things*. Bloomington, IN: Indiana University Press, 2001 [1st century BCE].

Lukács, Georg. *History and Class Consciousness: Studies in Marxist Dialectics*. London: Merlin, 1971 [1923].

Lukács, Georg. "Moses Hess and the Problem of Idealist Dialectics." In *Tactics and Ethics: Political Writings, 1919–1929*, edited by Rodney Livingstone. London: New Left Books, 1972 [1926].

Lukács, Georg. "Reification and the Consciousness of the Proletariat." In Lukács, *History and Class Consciousness* [1923].

Lukács, Georg. "What Is Orthodox Marxism?" In Lukács, *History and Class Consciousness* [1923].

Luttwak, Edward. *Turbo Capitalism: Winners and Losers in the Global Economy.* London: Weidenfeld & Nicholson, 1996.

Macalister, Terry. "Global Trend for Sit-Ins and Occupations as Mass Redundancies Continue." *Guardian* (July 24, 2009).

Macaulay, Thomas Babington. "Government of India." In *Speeches on Politics and Literature by Lord Macaulay.* London: J. M. Dent & Sons, 1909 [1833].

MacDonald, Ian. *Revolution in the Head: the Beatles' Records and the Sixties.* London: Fourth Estate, 1994.

MacIntyre, Alasdair. *Alasdair MacIntyre's Engagement with Marxism: Selected Writings, 1953–1974,* edited and introduced by Paul Blackledge and Neil Davidson. Lieden: E. J. Brill, 2008.

MacIntyre, Alasdair. "Notes from the Moral Wilderness." In MacIntyre, *Alasdair MacIntyre's Engagement with Marxism* [1958–59].

Maclean, John. "The Coming War with America." In *In the Rapids of Revolution: Essays, Articles and Letters, 1902–1903,* edited by Nan Milton. London: Alison and Busby, 1977 [1919].

Macwhirter, Iain. "Rising from the Ashes . . . How to Rebuild the World." *Sunday Herald* (Glasgow) (October 19, 2008).

Maine, Henry. *Ancient Law: Its Connection with the Early History of Society and in Relation to Modern Ideas.* London: Murray, 1906 [1861].

Malraux André. *Man's Estate.* London: Hamish Hamilton, 1968 [1933].

Malthus, Thomas. *An Essay on the Principle of Population,* edited by Antony Flew. Harmondsworth: Penguin, 1970 [1798/1826].

Mandel, Ernest. *Late Capitalism.* London: New Left Books, 1975.

Mandel, Ernest. *Revolutionary Marxism Today,* edited by Jon Rothschild. London: New Left Books, 1979.

Mandel, Ernest . *Trotsky: A Study in the Dynamic of His Thought.* London: New Left Books, 1979.

Mandel, Ernest. *Trotsky as Alternative.* London and New York: Verso, 1995.

Mann, Michael. "The Autonomous Power of the State: Its Origins, Mechanisms and Results." In *States in History,* edited by John A. Hall. Oxford: Basil Blackwell, 1986.

Mann, Michael. *The Dark Side of Democracy: Explaining Ethnic Cleansing.* Cambridge, UK: Cambridge University Press, 2005.

Mann, Michael. *Incoherent Empire.* London: Verso, 2003.

Marcos, Subcomandante. *Our Word Is Our Weapon: Selected Writings,* edited by Juana Ponce de León. London: Serpent's Tail, 2001.

Marcos, Subcomandante. "The Punch Card and the Hourglass." *New Left Review* II/9 (May/June 2001): 69–79.

Marcus, Greil. *Mystery Train: Images of America in Rock 'n' Roll Music.* London: Omnibus Press, 1977.

Marshall, Tyler. "Bush's Foreign Policy Shifting." *Los Angeles Times* (June 5, 2005).

Marx, Karl. *Capital: A Critique of Political Economy*, vol. 3. Harmondsworth, UK: Penguin, 1981 [1894].

Marx, Karl. "Critique of Hegel's Philosophy of Right. Introduction." In *Early Writings*. Harmondsworth, UK: Penguin, 1975 [1843–44].

Marx, Karl. "Draft of an Article on Frederick List's Book, *Das Nationale System der Politischen Oekonomie*." In *Marx & Engels Collected Works*, Volume 4, 1975 [1844].

Marx, Karl. "Marx to Engels, 16 January 1858." In *Marx & Engels Collected Works*, Volume 40, 1983 [1858].

Marx, Karl. "Preface to 'A Contribution to the Critique of Political Economy.'" In *Early Writings* [1859].

Marx, Karl, and Frederick Engels. "The German Ideology: Critique of Modern German Philosophy According to Its Representatives Feuerbach, B. Bauer and Stirner, and of German Socialism According to Its Various Prophets." In *Marx & Engels* Collected Works, Volume 5, 1975 [1845–46].

Mason, Tim. "Internal Crisis and War of Aggression, 1938–1939." In Mason, *Nazism, Fascism and the Working Class*, edited by Jane Caplan. Cambridge, UK: Cambridge University Press, 1995 [1975].

Mason, Tim. *Nazism, Fascism and the Working Class*.

Mason, Tim. "The Primacy of Politics: Politics and Economics in Nationalist Socialist Germany." In Mason, *Nazism, Fascism and the Working Class* [1968].

Massey, Doreen. *Spatial Divisions of Labour: Social Structures and the Geography of Production*, second edition. London: Macmillan, 1995.

Massey, Doreen. *World City*. Cambridge, UK: Polity, 2007.

Maxwell, Robert, ed. *Select Transactions of the Honourable the Society of the Improvers in the Knowledge of Agriculture in Scotland*. Edinburgh: Sands, Brymer, Murray, and Cochran, 1743.

McAllister, Carol. "The Uneven and Combined Character of Third World Development: Lessons from Women's Everyday Forms of Resistance in Negeri Sembilan, Malaysia." Working Paper No. 9. Amsterdam: International Institute for Research and Education, 1990.

McDaniel, Tim. *Autocracy, Capitalism, and Revolution in Russia*. Berkeley, CA: University of California Press, 1988.

McKibbin, Ross. "Anything but Benevolent." *London Review of Books* 35, no. 8 (April 25, 2013): 3–5.

McKibbin, Ross. "Mondeo Man in the Driving Seat." *London Review of Books* 21, no. 19 (September 30, 1999): 8–10.

McMurtry, John. *The Cancer Stage of Capitalism: From Crisis to Cure*. London: Pluto, 1999.

McNally, David. "From Financial Crisis to World-Slump: Accumulation, Financialisation, and the Global Slowdown." *Historical Materialism* 17, no. 2 (2009): 35–83.

Mearsheimer, John J. *The Tragedy of Great Power Politics*. London: Norton, 2001.

Mearsheimer, John J., and Stephen M. Walt. *The Israel Lobby and U.S. Foreign*

Policy. New York: Farrar, Straus and Giroux, 2007.

Meek, James. "Human Revenue." *London Review of Books* 34, no. 7 (April 5, 2012): 8.

Mészáros, István. "The Rise and Fall of Historical Temporality." In *History, Economic History and the Future of Marxism: Essays in Memory of Tom Kemp (1921–1933)*, edited by Terry Brotherstone and Geoff Pilling. London: Porcupine Press, 1996.

Metcalf, Thomas R. *Ideologies of the Raj*, volume 3, part 4 of *The New Cambridge History of India*. Cambridge, UK: Cambridge University Press, 1994.

Michaels, Walter Benn. *The Trouble with Diversity: How We Learned to Love Identity and Ignore Inequality*. New York: Metropolitan/Henry Holt, 2006.

Miéville, China. *Between Equal Rights: A Marxist Theory of International Law*. Leiden: E. J. Brill, 2005.

Milanović, Branko. "The Two Faces of Globalization: Against Globalization as We Know It." *World Development* 31, no. 4 (2003): 667–83.

Mill, John Stuart. "On Liberty." In *On Liberty and Other Essays*, edited by John Gray. Oxford: Oxford University Press, 1998 [1859].

Millar, John. "The Origin of the Distinction of Ranks." In *John Millar of Glasgow, 1735–1801: His Life and Thought and His Contributions to Sociological Analysis*, William Lehmann. London: Cambridge University Press, 1960 [1771].

Mises, Ludwig von. *Nation, State, and Economy: Contributions to the Politics and History of Our Time*. Indianapolis: Liberty Fund, 2006 [1919].

Mitchell, Timothy. "Dreamland." In *Evil Paradises: Deamworlds of Neoliberalism*, edited by Mike Davis and Daniel Bertrand Monk. New York: New Press, 2007.

Mitropoulos, Angela. "Precari-Us?" *Mute* 1, no. 29, *Precarious Issue* (January 2005).

Moellendorf, Darrel. "Racism and Rationality in Hegel's Philosophy of Subjective Spirit." *History of Political Thought* 13, no. 2 (February 1992): 243–55.

Molyneux, John. *Leon Trotsky's Theory of Revolution*. Brighton, UK: Harvester, 1981.

Monbiot, George. *Captive State: The Corporate Takeover of Britain*. London: Macmillan, 2000.

Montesquieu, Charles-Louis de Secondat. *Montesquieu: The Spirit of the Laws*, edited by Anne M. Cohler, Basia Carolyn Miller, and Harold Samuel Stone. Cambridge, UK: Cambridge University Press, 1989 [1748].

Montesquieu, Charles-Louis de Secondat. *Persian Letters*. Harmondsworth, UK: Penguin, 1993 [1721].

Moseley, K. P. "In Defense of the Primitive." In *Rethinking the Third World: Contributions Toward a New Conceptualization*, edited by Rosemary E. Galli. New York: Crane Russak, 1992.

Murray, Kate. "'We Are Trying to Reinvent Public Services.'" *Guardian (Society)* (November 21, 2012).

Muthu, Sankar. *Enlightenment against Empire*. Princeton, NJ: Princeton University Press, 2003.

Myrdal, Gunnar. *Economic Theory and Under-Developed Regions*. London: Gerald Duckworth, 1957.

Nairn, Tom. "Scotland and Europe." In Nairn, *The Break-Up of Britain: Crisis and Neo-Nationalism*, second Edition. London: Verso, 1981 [1974].

Nairn, Tom. "Terrorism and the Opening of Black Pluto's Door." In *Global Matrix: Nationalism, Globalism and State-Terrorism*, Tom Nairn and Paul James. London: Pluto, 2005.

Nairn, Tom. "The Twilight of the British State." In *The Break-Up of Britain* [1977].

Napoleoni, Loretta. *Rogue Economics*. New York: Seven Stories, 2008.

National Security Council. "NCS-68: A Report to the National Security Council." *Naval War College Review* 28, no. 3 (May–June 1975 [1950]): 51–108.

Neilson, Brett, and Ned Rossiter. "Precarity as a Political Concept, or, Fordism as Exception." *Theory, Culture and Society* 25, no. 7–8 (2008): 51–72.

Norberg, Johan. *In Defense of Global Capitalism*. Stockholm: Cato Institute, 2001.

Notes from Nowhere. "Emergence: An Irresistible Global Uprising." In *We Are Everywhere: The Irresistible Rise of Global Anticapitalism*, edited by Notes from Nowhere. London: Verso, 2003.

Novack, George. "Uneven and Combined Development in World History." In *Understanding History: Marxist Essays*. New York: Pathfinder, 1980 [1957].

Novick, Peter. *The Holocaust and Collective Memory: The American Experience*. London: Bloomsbury, 1999.

O'Connor, James. "Uneven and Combined Development and Ecological Crisis: A Theoretical Introduction." *Race & Class* 30, no. 3 (January 1989): 1–11.

Offer, Alvin. "Costs and Benefits, Prosperity and Security, 1870–1914." In *The Oxford History of the British Empire*, vol. 3: *The Nineteenth Century*, edited by Andrew Porter. Oxford: Oxford University Press, 1999.

Oliveira, Francisco de. "The Duckbilled Platypus." *New Left Review* II/24 (Nov–Dec 2003): 40–57.

Ollman, Bertell. "Marxism and Political Science: Prolegomenon to a Debate on Marx's Method." In *Dance of the Dialectic: Steps in Marx's Method*. Urbana, IL: University of Illinois Press, 2003 [1973].

Olssen, Mark. "In Defence of the Welfare State and Publicly Provided Education: A New Zealand Perspective." *Journal of Educational Policy* 11, no. 3 (1996): 337–62.

Otte, T. G. "The Great Carnage." *New Statesman* (December 14–20, 2012): 19–21.

Panitch, Leo, and Sam Gindin. "Global Capitalism and American Empire." In *The Socialist Register 2004: The New Imperial Challenge*, edited by Leo Panitch and Colin Leys. London: Merlin, 2004 (1–42).

Pashukanis, Evgeny. *Law and Marxism: A General Theory. Towards a Critique of the Fundamental Juridical Concepts*, edited by Chris Arthur. London: Ink Links, 1978 [1924].

Pascal, Blaise. "Preface to the Treatise on Vacuum." In *The Provincial Letters; and Pensees; and Scientific Treatises*, Chicago: Chicago University Press, 1952 [1647].

Paterson, Lindsay, Frank Bechhofer, and David McCrone. *Living in Scotland: Social and Economic Change since 1980*. Edinburgh: Edinburgh University

Press, 2004.

Phillips, Kevin. *American Theocracy: The Peril and Politics of Radical Religion, Oil, and Borrowed Money in the 21ˢᵗCentury.* New York: Viking Penguin, 2006.

Pieterse, Jan Nederveen. "Globalization North and South: Representations of Uneven Development and the Interaction of Modernities." *Theory, Culture & Society* 17, no. 1 (February 2000): 129–137.

Pilkington, Ed. "The Grim Reality of Life under Alabama's Brutal Immigration Law." *Guardian* (October 15, 2011).

Pollin, Robert. "Resurrection of the Rentier." *New Left Review* II/46 (July/Aug 2007): 140–153.

Pollard, Sidney. *The Wasting of the British Economy: British Economic Policy 1945 to the Present,* third edition. London: Croom Helm, 1992 [1981].

Porter, Bernard. *Empire and Superempire: Britain, America and the World.* New Haven, CT: Yale University Press, 2006.

Post, Ken, and Phil Wright. *Socialism and Underdevelopment.* London: Routledge, 1989.

Poulantzas, Nicos. *Political Power and Social Classes.* London: Verso, 1973 [1978].

Power. "Power to the People: The report of Power: An Independent Inquiry into Britain's Democracy." The POWER Inquiry, 2006.

Pozo-Martin, Gonzalo. "Autonomous or Materialist Geopolitics?" *Cambridge Review of International Affairs* 20, no. 4 (December 2007): 551–563.

Priestland, David. *Merchant, Soldier, Sage: A New History of Power.* London: Allen Lane, 2012.

Pritchett, Lant. "Divergence, Big Time." *Journal of Economic Perspectives* 11, no. 3 (Summer 1997): 3–17.

Rand, Ayn. *The Virtue of Selfishness.* New York: Signet, 1964.

Randall, Vicky. "Using and Abusing the Concept of the Third World." *Third World Quarterly* 25, no. 1 (2004): 41–53.

Rees, John. *The Algebra of Revolution: The Dialectic and the Classical Marxist Tradition.* London: Routledge, 1998.

Retort. *Afflicted Powers: Capital and Spectacle in a New Age of War.* London: Verso, 2005.

Rist, Gilbert. *The History of Development: From Western Origins to Global Faith,* new edition, revised and expanded. London: Zed Books, 2002.

Robinson, William I. "The Pitfalls of Realist Analysis of Global Capitalism: A Critique of Ellen Meiksins Wood's *Empire of Capital.*" *Historical Materialism* 15, no. 3 (2007): 71–93.

Robinson, William I. *A Theory of Global Capitalism: Production, Class, and State in a Transnational World.* Baltimore, MD: Johns Hopkins University Press, 2004.

Romagnolo, David J. "The So-Called 'Law' of Uneven and Combined Development." *Latin American Perspectives* 2, no. 1 (Spring 1975): 7–31.

Rosdolsky, Roman. *The Making of Marx's 'Capital'.* London: Pluto, 1977 [1967].

Rosenberg, Justin. *The Empire of Civil Society*. London: Verso, 1994.

Rosenberg, Justin. "Globalization Theory: A Post Mortem." *International Politics* 42, no. 1 (2005): 2–74.

Rosenberg, Justin. "International Relations—The 'Higher Bullshit': A Reply to the Globalization Theory Debate." *International Politics* 44, no. 4 (July 2007): 450–482.

Rosenberg, Justin. "Isaac Deutscher and the Lost History of International Relations." *New Left Review* I/215 (Jan/Feb 1996): 3–15.

Rosenberg, Justin. "Why Is There No International Historical Sociology?" *European Journal of International Relations* 12, no. 3 (Sept 2006): 307–40.

Roy, Arundhati. *The Algebra of Infinite Justice*. London: Flamingo, 2002.

Russett, Bruce. *Grasping the Democratic Peace: Principles for a Post–Cold War World*, with the collaboration of William Antholis, Carol R. Ember, Melvin Ember, and Zeev Maoz. Princeton, NJ: Princeton University Press, 1993.

Saad-Filho, Alfredo. "Marxian and Keynesian Critiques of Neoliberalism." In *The Socialist Register 2008: Global Flashpoints. Reactions to Imperialism and Neoliberalism*, edited by Leo Panitch and Colin Leys. London: Merlin, 2007 (337–345).

Saint-Simon, Henri. "From Feudalism to Industrialism: The Role of the Lawyers and Metaphysicians." In Saint-Simon, *Selected Writings on Science, Industry and Social Organisation*, edited by Keith Taylor. London: Croom Helm, 1975 [1821].

Saint-Simon, Henri. "On the Intermediate (Bourgeois) Class." In Saint-Simon, *Selected Writings on Science* [1823].

Saint-Simon, Henri. *Selected Writings on Science*.

Saville, John. "The Communist Experience: A Personal Appraisal." In *The Socialist Register 1991*, edited by Ralph Miliband and Leo Panitch. London: Merlin, 1991.

Saville, John. *The Consolidation of the Capitalist State, 1800–1850*. London: Pluto Press, 1994.

Say, Jean-Baptiste. "Essai historique sur l'origine, les progrès et les résultats probables de la souverainete des anglais aux Indes." In *An Economist in Troubled Times*, edited by R. R. Palmer. Princeton, NJ: Princeton University Press, 1997 [1824].

Say, Jean-Baptiste. "Revue encyclopédique, vol. 27." In *An Economist in Troubled Times* [1828].

Sayer, Derek. *Marx's Method: Ideology, Science and Critique in Capital*. Brighton, UK: Harvester, 1979.

Schumpeter, Joseph A. *Capitalism, Socialism and Democracy*. London: Routledge, 1994 [1942].

Schwartz, Herman. *States versus Markets: The Emergence of a Global Economy*, second edition. London: Palgrave Macmillan, 2000 [1994].

Scott, Walter. *Waverley, or 'Tis Been Sixty Years Hence*, edited by Andrew Hook. Harmondsworth, UK: Penguin, 1972.

Scruton, Roger. *The West and the Rest: Globalisation and the Terrorist Threat.* London: Continuum, 2002.

Seabrook, Jeremy. "Progress on Hold." *Guardian* (October 23, 2003).

Serge, Victor. *Memoirs of a Revolutionary.* New York: New York Review Books, 2012 [1951].

Serge, Victor, and Natalia Sedova Trotsky. *The Life and Death of Leon Trotsky.* New York: Basic Books, 1975.

Service, Elman. "The Law of Evolutionary Potential." In *Evolution and Culture,* edited by Marshall D. Sahlins and Elman R. Service. Ann Arbor, MI: University of Michigan Press, 1960.

Seymour, Richard. *The Liberal Defence of Murder.* London: Verso, 2008.

Sharzer, Greg. *No Local: Why Small-Scale Alternatives Won't Change the World.* Winchester, UK: Zero Books, 2012.

Shaw, Margaret. "Work." In *Focus on Social Inequalities.*

Silver, Beverly J. *Forces of Labor: Workers' Movements and Globalization since 1870.* Cambridge, UK: Cambridge University Press, 2003.

Skinner, Quentin. *The Foundations of Modern Political Thought, Volume 1: The Renaissance.* Cambridge, UK: Cambridge University Press, 1978.

Sklair Leslie. *The Transnational Capitalist Class.* Oxford: Blackwell, 2001.

Smith, Adam. *An Inquiry into the Nature and Causes of the Wealth of Nations,* edited by Edwin Cannan. Chicago: University of Chicago Press, 1976 [1776].

Smith, Neil. *American Empire: Roosevelt's Geographer and the Prelude to Globalization.* Berkeley: University of California Press, 2003.

Smith, Neil. *The Endgame of Globalization.* New York: Routledge, 2005.

Smith, Neil. *Uneven Development: Nature, Capital, and the Production of Space.* Oxford: Blackwell, 1990 [1984].

Sorrell, Martin. "After a Week of Turmoil, Has the World Changed?" Interview with Emily Butselaar. *Guardian* (September 20, 2008).

Southwood, Ivor. *Non-Stop Inertia.* Winchester, UK: Zero Books, 2011.

Spencer, Herbert. *Principles of Sociology,* edited by Stanislav Andreski. London: Macmillan, 1969 [1874–1896].

Spencer, Herbert. "Progress: Its Law and Cause." In *Essays: Scientific, Political and Speculative.* London: Williams and Norgate, 1891 [1857].

Stallabrass, Julian. *Art Incorporated: The Story of Contemporary Art.* Oxford: Oxford University Press, 2004.

Stedman Jones, Gareth. "The Mid-Century Crisis and the 1848 Revolutions: A Critical Comment." *Theory and Society* 12, no. 4 (July 1983): 505–19.

Stewart, Heather. "Pay Cuts, Recruit Freezes, Unpaid Leave: Recession Prompts a Working Revolution." *Guardian* (June 23, 2009).

Stiglitz, Joseph E. *Globalization and Its Discontents.* New York: W. W. Norton, 2002.

Stinchcombe, Arthur L. *Theoretical Methods in Social History.* New York: Academic Press, 1978.

Stokes, Eric. *The English Utilitarians and India.* New Delhi: Oxford University Press, 1959.

Stone, Norman. *World War One: A Short History*. London: Allen Lane, 2007.

Tacitus, Gaius Cornelius. "The Germania." In *The Agricola and the Germania*. Harmondsworth, UK: Penguin, 1970 [c. 98].

Teschke, Benno. *The Myth of 1648: Class, Geopolitics and the Making of Modern International Relations*. London: Verso, 2003.

Teschke, Benno, and Hannes Lacher. "The Changing 'Logics' of Capitalist Competition." *Cambridge Review of International Affairs* 20, no. 4 (Dec 2007): 565–80.

Thatcher, Ian D. *Trotsky*. London: Routledge, 2003.

Thatcher, Ian D. "Uneven and Combined Development." *Revolutionary Russia* 4, no. 2 (Dec 1991): 235–58.

Thatcher, Margaret. Interviewed by Douglas Keay. "AIDS, Education and the Year 2000!" *Woman's Own* (October 31, 1987).

Therborn, Göran. *What Does the Ruling Class Do When It Rules?: State Apparatuses and State Power under Feudalism, Capitalism and Socialism*. London: New Left Books, 1978.

Thucydides. "From Book 1 of *The Peloponnesian War*." In *The Portable Greek Historians: The Essence of Herodotus, Thucydides, Xenophon, Polybius*, edited by M. I. Finley, New York: Viking Press, 1960 [5th century BCE].

Ticktin, Hillel and Michael Cox. "The Ideas of Leon Trotsky." In *The Ideas of Leon Trotsky*, edited by Hillel Ticktin and Michael Cox. London: Porcupine, 1995.

Tilly, Charles. *European Revolutions, 1492–1992*. Oxford: Blackwell, 1996.

Tilly, Charles. "Reflections on the History of European State-Making." In *The Formation of National States in Western Europe*, edited by Charles Tilly. Princeton, NJ: Princeton University Press, 1975.

Time. "We Are All Keynesians Now." December 31, 1965.

Todd, Emmanuel. *After the Empire: The Breakdown of the American Order*. London: Constable, 2004.

Toíbín, Colm. "'Looking at Ireland, I Don't Know Whether to Laugh or Cry.'" *Guardian* (November 20, 2010).

Tönnies, Ferdinand. *Community and Society*, edited by Charles Loomis. East Lansing, MI: Michigan State University Press, 1957 [1887].

Toynbee, Polly, and David Walker. *Unjust Rewards: Exposing Greed and Inequality in Britain Today*. London: Granta Books, 2008.

Travis, Alan, and Matt Wells. "Nationalise Railtrack, Says Public." *Guardian* (October 26, 1999).

Trevor-Roper, Hugh. "The Scottish Enlightenment." In *Studies on Voltaire and the Eighteenth Century* 58 (1967): 1635–58.

Trotsky, Leon. *1905*. Harmondsworth: Penguin Books, 1972 [1908–1909/1922].

Trotsky, Leon. "Attention to Theory!" In *Problems of Everyday Life: Creating the Foundations for a New Society in Revolutionary Russia*. New York: Pathfinder, 1973 [1922].

Trotsky, Leon. "Can a Counter-Revolution or a Revolution Be Made on Schedule?" In *The First Five Years of the Communist International*, vol. 2. London: New Park, 1974 [1923].

Trotsky, Leon. "The Chinese Revolution and the Theses of Comrade Stalin." In *Leon Trotsky on China*, edited by Les Evans and Russell Block. New York: Monad, 1976 [1927].

Trotsky, Leon. "Class Relations in the Chinese Revolution." In *Leon Trotsky on China* [1927]. Trotsky, Leon. "The Death Agony of Capitalism and the Tasks of the Fourth International." In *The Transitional Program for Socialist Revolution*, edited by George Breitman and Fred Stanton. New York: Pathfinder, 1973 [1938].

Trotsky, Leon. "In Defense of the Russian Revolution." In *Leon Trotsky Speaks*. New York: Pathfinder, 1972 [1932].

Trotsky, Leon. "The Draft Programme of the Communist International—A Criticism of Fundamentals." In *The Third International after Lenin*. London: New Park, 1974 [1928].

Trotsky, Leon.. "Flood-Tide." In *The First Five Years of the Communist International*, vol. 2 [1921],.

Trotsky, Leon. *The History of the Russian Revolution*. London: Pluto, 1977 [1932].

Trotsky, Leon. "In a Backward Country." In *The Balkan Wars, 1912–1913*, edited by George Weissman and Duncan Williams. New York: Monad, 1980 [1912].

Trotsky, Leon. "Introduction to *Ferdinand Lassalle's Speech to the Jury*." In *Witnesses to Permanent Revolution: The Documentary Record*, edited by Richard B. Day and Daniel Gaido. Leiden: E. J. Brill, 2009 [1905].

Trotsky, Leon. "Introduction to the First (Russian) Edition (Published in Berlin)." In *The Permanent Revolution and Results and Prospects*, third edition. New York: Pathfinder Press, 1969 [1929].

Trotsky, Leon. "Introduction to the German Edition." In *The Permanent Revolution* and *Results and Prospects* [1930].

Trotsky, Leon. "The Italo-Ethiopian Conflict." In *Writings of Leon Trotsky [1935–36]*, edited by Naomi Allen and George Breitman. New York: Pathfinder, 1970 [1935].

Trotsky, Leon. "Japan Heads for Disaster." In *Writings of Leon Trotsky [1932–33]*, edited by George Breitman and Sarah Lovell. New York: Pathfinder, 1972 [1933].

Trotsky, Leon. "Karl Kautsky." In *Portraits, Personal and Political*, edited by George Breitman and George Saunders. New York: Pathfinder, 1977 [1919].

Trotsky, Leon. "Karl Marx." In *Leon Trotsky Presents the Living Thoughts of Karl Marx*. London: Cassell, 1940.

Trotsky, Leon. "The Lessons of October." In *The Challenge of the Left Opposition (1923–25)*, edited by Naomi Allen. New York: Pathfinder, 1975 [1923].

Trotsky, Leon. "The Lessons of Spain: The Last Warning." In *The Spanish Revolution (1931–1939)*, edited by Naomi Allen and George Breitman. New York: Pathfinder, 1973 [1937].

Trotsky, Leon. "The Letter of Comrade Trotsky to the Plenum of the Central Committee of the Russian Communist Party." In *The Challenge of the Left Opposition (1923-25)*, 304–8 [1925].

Trotsky, Leon. "Marxism and the Relation between Proletarian and Peasant Revolution." In *The Challenge of the Left Opposition (1928-29)*, edited by Naomi Allen and George Saunders. New York: Pathfinder, 1981 [1928].

Trotsky, Leon. *My Life: An Attempt at an Autobiography*. Harmondsworth, UK: Penguin, 1975 [1930].

Trotsky, Leon. "The Negro Question in America." In *Leon Trotsky on Black Nationalism and Self-Determination*, edited by George Breitman. New York: Pathfinder, 1978 [1933].

Trotsky, Leon. "The New Course." In *The Challenge of the Left Opposition (1923-25)* [1923].

Trotsky, Leon. "New Opportunities for the Chinese Revolution, New Tasks, and New Mistakes." In *Leon Trotsky on China* [1927].

Trotsky, Leon. "The New Turkey." In *The Balkan Wars, 1912–1913* [1909].

Trotsky, Leon. "Ninety Years of the *Communist Manifesto*." In *Writings of Leon Trotsky [1937-38]*, edited by Naomi Allen and George Breitman, second edition. New York: Pathfinder, 1976 [1937].

Trotsky, Leon. "Not a Workers' State and Not a Bourgeois State?" In *Writings of Leon Trotsky [1937-38]*, second edition [1937].

Trotsky, Leon. "The Notebooks in Translation." In *Trotsky's Notebooks, 1933–1935: Writings on Lenin, Dialectics, and Evolutionism*. New York: Columbia University Press, 1986 [1933–5].

Trotsky, Leon. "On the Slogan of Soviets in China." In *Leon Trotsky on China* [1927].Trotsky, Leon. *Our Political Tasks*. London: New Park, 1983 [1904].

Trotsky, Leon.. "Peasant War in China and the Proletariat." In *Leon Trotsky on China* [1932].

Trotsky, Leon. *The Permanent Revolution*. In *The Permanent Revolution and Results and Prospects* [1929].

Trotsky, Leon. "Perspectives of World Development." In *Europe and America: Two Speeches on Imperialism*. New York: Pathfinder, 1971 [1924].

Trotsky, Leon. "Preface to the Re-Issue of This Work Published in Moscow in 1919." In *The Permanent Revolution* and *Results and Prospects* [1919].

Trotsky, Leon. "Prospects and Tasks in the East." In *Leon Trotsky Speaks*, 198–208 [1924].

Trotsky, Leon. "Radio, Science, Technology, and Society." In *Problems of Everyday Life* [1926].

Trotsky, Leon. "Report on the World Economic Crisis and the New Tasks of the Communist International." In *The First Five Years of the Communist International*, vol. 1. London: New Park, 1974 [1921].

Trotsky, Leon. "Report on the Fourth World Congress." In *The First Five Years of the Communist International*, vol. 2 [1922].

Trotsky, Leon. *Results and Prospects.* In *Permanent Revolution and Results and Prospects* [1906].

Trotsky, Leon. "Revolution and War in China." In *Leon Trotsky on China* [1938].

Trotsky, Leon. *The Revolution Betrayed: What Is the Soviet Union and Where Is It Going?* New York: Pathfinder, 1937.

Trotsky, Leon. "The Revolution in Spain." In *Spanish Revolution(1931–1939),* [1931].

Trotsky, Leon. "A Serious Work on Russian Revolutionary History." In *Writings of Leon Trotsky Supplement (1934–40),* edited by George Breitman. New York: Pathfinder, 1979 [1940].

Trotsky, Leon. "Social Democracy and Revolution." In *Witnesses to Permanent Revolution* [1905].

Trotsky, Leon.. "The Spanish Revolution and the Dangers Threatening It." In *Spanish Revolution (1931–39)* [1931].

Trotsky, Leon. "Speech to the Seventh (Enlarged) Plenum of the ECCI." In *The Challenge of the Left Opposition (1926–27),* edited by Naomi Allen and George Saunders. New York: Pathfinder, 1980 [1926].

Trotsky, Leon. "Stojan Novakovic." In *Balkan Wars, 1912–1913* [1913].

Trotsky, Leon. "Summary and Perspectives of the Chinese Revolution: Its Lessons for the Countries of the Orient and for the Whole of the Comintern." In *Leon Trotsky on China,* [1928].

Trotsky, Leon. *Terrorism and Communism: A Reply to Karl Kautsky.* London: New Park, 1975 [1920].

Trotsky, Leon. "Three Conceptions of the Russian Revolution." In *Writings of Leon Trotsky [1939–40],* edited by Naomi Allen and George Breitman, second edition. New York: Pathfinder, 1973 [1939], 55–73.

Trotsky, Leon. "Trade Unions in the Epoch of Imperialist Decay." *Fourth International* 2, no. 2 (Feb 1941 [1940]): 40–43.

Trotsky, Leon. "Trotsky to the Central Committee of the Russian Communist Party, August 5, 1919." In *The Trotsky Papers, 1917–1922,* vol. 1, *1917–1919,* edited by Jan M. Meijer. The Hague: Mouton, 1964 [1919].

Trotsky, Leon. "Trotsky to Ol'minskij, December 6, 1921." In *The Trotsky Papers, 1917–1922,* vol. 2, *1920–1922,* edited by Jan M. Meijer. The Hague: Mouton,1971 [1921].

Trotsky, Leon. "Trotsky to the People's Commissariat of Foreign Affairs, June 4, 1920." In *Trotsky Papers, 1917–1922,* vol. 2, *1920–1922,* [1920].

Trotsky, Leon. *Trotsky's Diary in Exile 1935.* London: Faber and Faber, 1958 [1935].

Trotsky, Leon. "Trotsky's Letter to Ispart, August 25, 1921." *Revolutionary History* 9, 1.

Trotsky, Leon. *The Russian Revolution of 1905: Change through Struggle* (2005 [1921]): 117–19.

Trotsky, Leon. "The Turkish Revolution and the Tasks of the Proletariat." In *Balkan Wars, 1912–1913* [1908], 3–7.

Trotsky, Leon. "Uneven and Combined Development and the Role of American Imperialism: Minutes of a Discussion." In *Writings of Leon Trotsky [1932–33]* [1933].

Trotsky, Leon. "Up to the Ninth of January." In *Witnesses to Permanent Revolution* [1905], 273–332.

Trotsky, Leon. "The USSR in War." In *In Defense of Marxism (Against the Petty-Bourgeois Opposition)*. London: New Park, 1966 [1939].

Trotsky, Leon. "What Is National Socialism?" In *The Struggle against Fascism in Germany*. Harmondsworth, UK: Penguin, 1975 [1933].

Trotsky, Leon. "Where Is Britain Going?" In *Collected Writings and Speeches on Britain*, vol. 2, edited by R. Chappell and Alan Clinton. London: New Park, 1974 [1925].

Tuchman, Barbara. *A Distant Mirror: The Calamitous 14th Century*. Harmondsworth, UK: Penguin, 1979.

Tuckman, Jo. "Zapatistas Go Back to the Grassroots to Start Again." *Guardian* (December 27, 2003).

Turgot, Anne-Robert. "A Philosophical Review of the Successive Advances of the Human Mind." In *Turgot on Progress, Sociology and Economics*. Cambridge, UK: Cambridge University Press, 1973 [1750].

Tylor, Edward. *Primitive Culture: Researches into the Development of Mythology, Philosophy, Religion, Art, and Custom*. London: John Murray, 1871.

United Nations Human Development Programme 2003. "Human Development Report 2003: Millennium Development Goals: A Compact among Nations to End Human Poverty." New York: United Nations, 2003.

United Nations Human Settlement Programme 2003. "The Challenge of Slums: Global Report on Human Settlements 2003." London: UN-Habitat, 2003.

Van der Pijl, Kees. "Historicising the International: Modes of Foreign Relations and Political Economy." *Historical Materialism* 18, no. 2 (2010): 3–34.

Veblen, Thorstein. *The Theory of the Leisure Class: An Economic Study of Institutions*, new edition. London: George Allen & Unwin, 1924.

Vico, Giambattista. *New Science: Principles of the New Science Concerning the Common Nature of Nations*. Harmondsworth, UK: Penguin, 1999 [1725].

Vidal, John, and Owen Bowcott, "Scramble for the Seabed: Or How Rockall Could Be the Key to a British Oil Bonanza." *Guardian* (September 22, 2007).

Volney, Constantin-François. *The Ruins, or, A Survey of the Revolutions of Empires*, facsimile of the 1811 edition. Otley, UK: Woodstock, 2000 [1791].

Vulliamy, Ed. *Amexica: War along the Borderline*. London: Vintage, 2011.

Wacquant, Loïc. "Territorial Stigmatization in the Age of Advanced Marginality." *Thesis Eleven* 91, no. 1 (November 2007): 66–7.

Wade, Robert. "Financial Regime Change?" *New Left Review* II/53 (Sept/Oct 2008): 5–21.

Walicki, Andrzej. *The Controversy over Capitalism: Studies in the Social Philosophy of the Russian Populists*. Oxford: Clarendon, 1969.

Wallace, George. *System of the Principles of the Law of Scotland*, vol. 1. Edinburgh: printed for A. Millar, 1760.

Wallace, Robert. *Characteristics of the Present Political State of Great Britain*, second edition. Edinburgh: printed for A. Millar, 1758.

Wallerstein, Immanuel. "The Curve of American Power." *New Left Review* II/40 (July/Aug 2006): 77–94.

Wasserstein, Bernard. *Barbarism and Civilization: A History of Europe in Our Time*. Oxford: Oxford University Press, 2007.

Watson, Ben. *Art, Class & Cleavage: Quantulumcunque Concerning Materialist Esthetix*. London: Quartet, 1998.

Webb, Tim. "Industrial Inaction: Workers Fall into Line as Recession Leaves us Fearing for our Jobs." *Guardian* (July 4, 2009).

Weber, Max. *General Economic History*. London: George Allen & Unwin, 1923 [1919–20].

Weber, Max. "The Profession and Vocation of Politics." In *Political Writings*, edited by Peter Lassman and Ronald Speirs. Cambridge, UK: Cambridge University Press, 1994 [1919].

Weeks, John. "Globalize, Globa-lize, Global Lies: Myths of the World Economy During the 1990s." In *Phases of Capitalist Development*.

Weight, Richard. *Patriots: National Identity in Britain, 1940–2000*. London: Macmillan, 2002.

Weiss, Gary. *Ayn Rand Nation: The Hidden Struggle for America's Soul*. New York: St. Martin's Press, 2012.

Wendt, Alexander. "Why a World State Is Inevitable." *European Journal of International Relations* 9, no. 4 (Dec 2003): 491–542.

Wertheim, W. F. *Evolution and Revolution: The Rising Waves of Emancipation*. Harmondsworth: Penguin, 1974.

Wilkinson, Richard. *The Impact of Inequality: How to Make Sick Societies Healthier*. New York: New Press, 2005.

Wilkinson, Richard, and Kate Pickett. *The Spirit Level: Why More Equal Societies Almost Always Do Better*. London: Allen Lane, 2009.

Williams, Hywel. *Britain's Power Elites: The Rebirth of a Ruling Class*. London: Constable, 2006.

Williams, Raymond. *Politics and Letters: Interviews with New Left Review*. London: New Left Books, 1979.

Williams, Raymond. *Towards 2000*. Harmondsworth, UK: Penguin, 1983.

Wilson, Ben. *What Price Liberty? How Freedom Was Won and Is Being Lost*. London: Faber and Faber, 2009.

Wintour, Patrick. "Labour Should Focus on Value for Money, Says Rising Star of Party." *Guardian* (August 15, 2012).

Wokler, Robert. "Apes and Races in the Scottish Enlightenment: Monboddo and Kames on the Nature of Man." In *Philosophy and Science in the Scottish Enlightenment*, edited by Peter Jones. Edinburgh: John Donald, 1988.

Wolf, Martin. "The World Wakes from the Wish-Dream of Decoupling." *Financial*

Times (October 21, 2008).

Wolfe, Tom. "The 'Me' Decade and the Third Great Awakening." In *Mauve Gloves & Madmen, Clutter & Vine*. New York: Bantam Books, 1977.

Wollen, Peter. "Our-Post Communism: The Legacy of Karl Kautsky." *New Left Review* I/202 (Nov/Dec 1993): 85–93.

Wood, Ellen Meiksins. *Empire of Capital*. London: Verso, 2003.

Wood, Ellen Meiksins. "Logics of Power: A Conversation with David Harvey." *Historical Materialism* 14, no. 4 (Jan 2006): 9–34.

Wood, Ellen Meiksins. *The Pristine Culture of Capitalism: A Historical Essay on Old Regimes and Modern States*. London: Verso, 1991.

Wood, Ellen Meiksins. "A Reply to Critics." *Historical Materialism* 15, no. 3 (Jan 2007), 143–170.

Woodhouse, A. S. P., ed. *Puritanism and Liberty: Being the Army Debates (1647–49) from the Clarke Manuscripts*. London: J. M. Dent and Sons, 1974.

Wright, Patrick. *A Journey through Ruins: The Last Days of London*, revised edition. Oxford: Oxford University Press, 2009 [1991].

Yates, Robert. "What the £140m Penthouse Tells Us about the Lives of London's Super Rich." *Guardian* (January 23, 2011).

World Bank. "World Development Report 1995: Workers in an Integrated World." Oxford: Oxford University Press for the World Bank, 1995.

Ziegler, Phillip. *The Black Death*. Harmondsworth, UK: Penguin, 1970.

Žižek, Slavoj. *The Year of Dreaming Dangerously*. London: Verso, 2012.

Žižek, Slavoj. "Afterword: Lenin's Choice." In V. I. Lenin, *Revolution at the Gates: A Selection of Writings from February to October 1917*, edited and with an introduction and afterword by Slavoj Žižek. London and New York: Verso, 2002.

NOTES

Introduction: The End of Neoliberalism?

1. Georg W. F. Hegel, "Preface," in *The Philosophy of Right* (Oxford: Oxford University Press, 1953 [1821]), 3.

2. Antonio Gramsci, "Problems of Marxism," in *Selections from the Prison Notebooks,* Q7§24.

3. Eric J. Hobsbawm, *Age of Extremes: The Short Twentieth Century, 1914–1991* (London: Allen Lane, 1994), 412–413; "The End of Neo-liberalism," *Marxism Today* (Nov/Dec 1998, special issue), 4; *Interesting Times: A Twentieth-Century Life* (London: Allen Lane, 2002), 277.

4. Iain Macwhirter, "The Prophets of Greed," *Sunday Herald* (Glasgow), (September 21, 2008).

5. David J. Blacker, *The Falling Rate of Learning and the Neoliberal Endgame* (Winchester, UK: Zero Books, 2013), 22.

6. Iain Sinclair, "Diary: Thatcher in Gravesend," *London Review of Books* 35, no. 9 (May 9, 2013), 39.

7. Fareed Zakaria, "The Capitalist Manifesto: Greed Is Good (To a Point)," *Newsweek* (June 22, 2009), 40.

8. Barry Eichengreen, "The Last Temptation of Risk," *National Interest* 101 (May/June 2009), 8.

9. Colin Crouch, "What Will follow the Demise of Privatised Keynesianism?," *Political Quarterly* 79, no. 4 (Oct–Dec 2008); *The Strange Non-Death of Neoliberalism* (Cambridge, UK: Polity, 2011), chapter 5.

10. Kean Birch and Vlad Mykhnenko, "Conclusion: The End of an Economic Order?," in *The Rise and Fall of Neoliberalism: The Collapse of an Economic Order?*, Kean Birch and Vlad Mykhnenko, eds. (London: Zed Books, 2010), 255.

11. Even those prepared to use this over-hastily concocted neologism were understandably tentative about what it might actually mean. See, for example, Ulrich Brand and Nicola Sekler, "Postneoliberalism: Catch-All Word or Valuable Analytical and Political Concept?—Aims of a Beginning Debate," *Development Dialogue* 51 (January 2009), 6–7.

12. Gérard Duménil and Dominique Lévy, *The Crisis of Neoliberalism* (Cambridge, MA: Harvard University Press, 2013), 33–42.

13. Alfredo Saad-Filho, "Crisis *in* Neoliberalism or Crisis *of* Neoliberalism?," in *The Socialist Register 2011: The Crisis This Time*, Leo Panitch, Greg Albo, and

Vivek Chibber, eds. (London: Merlin Books, 2010), 242, 249.

14. Richard Dienst, *The Bonds of Debt: Borrowing Against the Common Good* (London: Verso, 2011), 12.

15. Crouch, *Strange Non-Death of Neoliberalism*, 118–119.

16. Eric J. Hobsbawm, "Socialism Has Failed. Now Capitalism Is Bankrupt. So What Comes Next?," *Guardian*, (April 10, 2009).

17. Robert Peston, *Who Runs Britain? How Britain's New Elite Are Changing Our Lives* (London: Hodder and Stoughton, 2008), 342.

18. Martin Wolf, "Tackling Britain's Fiscal Debacle," *Financial Times* (May 7, 2009).

19. Karl Marx, "The Eighteenth Brumaire of Louis Bonaparte," in *Surveys from Exile*, vol. 2, *Political Writings*, David Fernbach, ed. (Harmondsworth, UK: Penguin Books/New Left Review, 1973 [1852]), 146. According to Hayden White, the four "modes of emplotment" are comedy, romance, satire, and tragedy. See Hayden White, *Metahistory: The Historical Imagination in Nineteenth-Century Europe* (Baltimore: John Hopkins University Press, 1973), x.

20. Aditya Chakrabortty, "Welcome to Austeria—A Nation Robbing Its Poor to Pay for the Next Big Crash," *Guardian* (November 24, 2015).

21. Carl Schmitt, *Political Theology: Four Chapters on the Concept of Sovereignty* (Chicago: University of Chicago Press, 2006 [1922]), 5.

22. Enzo Traverso, *Fire and Blood: The European Civil War, 1914–1945* (London: Verso 2016 [2007]), 236–45; see also Giorgio Agamben, *State of Exception* (Chicago: University of Chicago Press, 2005), 56.

23. Walter Benjamin, "On the Concept of History," in *Selected Writings*, vol. 4, *1938–1940*, Howard Eiland and Michael W. Jennings, eds. (Cambridge, MA: Belknap Press of Harvard University Press, 2003 [1940]), 392.

24. Löwy, *Fire Alarm*, 57–60.

25. Chris Harman, "Theorising Neoliberalism," *International Socialism*, second series, no. 117 (Winter 2008).

26. David Marquand, *Mammon's Kingdom: An Essay on Britain, Now* (London: Allen Lane, 2014), 74–76.

27. Pierre Dardot and Christian Laval, *The New Way of the World: On Neoliberal Society* (London: Verso: 2013 [2009]), 148–150.

28. Joshua Clover, *Riot, Strike, Riot: The New Era of Uprisings* (London: Verso, 2016), 131–32.

29. Ha-Joon Chang, *Economics: The User's Guide* (London: Penguin, 2014), 87–106.

30. Manfred B. Steger and Ravi K. Roy, *Neoliberalism: A Very Short Introduction* (Oxford: Oxford University Press, 2010), 11.

31. Luke Cooper and Simon Hardy, *Beyond Capitalism? The Future of Radical Politics* (Winchester, UK: Zero Books, 2012), 66–67.

32. Ben Fine and Laurence Harris, *Rereading* Capital (London: Macmillan, 1979), 112–70.

33. Fredric Jameson, "The Cultural Logic of Late Capitalism," in *Postmodernism, or, The Cultural Logic of Late Capitalism* (London: Verso, 1991 [1984]), 35.

Jameson's periodization is actually considerably clearer than that of Mandel himself, who focuses far more on the changing nature of technology across the different stages. However, Jameson misrepresents Mandel in two respects. First, the latter identifies four periods in the history of capitalism, down to the early 1970s, not three, each characterized by different forms of technology. See Mandel, *Late Capitalism*, 120–21. Second, Mandel regarded the period which Jameson sees as starting in the postwar years as definitively ending with the crisis which opened in 1974–5, rather than, as Jameson does, continuing into the present—a point with which I am in agreement. See Mike Davis, "Urban Renaissance and the Spirit of Postmodernism," *New Left Review* I/151 (May/June 1985), 107–108.

34. Mandel, *Late Capitalism*, 120–21; Paul Mason, *Postcapitalism: A Guide to Our Future* (London: Allen Lane, 2015), 35–48.

35. Michael Kidron, *Western Capitalism Since the War* (Harmondsworth, UK: Pelican, 1970), 47.

36. R. H. Tawney, *Religion and the Rise of Capitalism* (New York: Harcourt, 1928), viii)

37. Duménil and Lévy, *Crisis of Neoliberalism*, 2.

38. Alex Law, *Social Theory for Today: Making Sense of Social Worlds* (London: Sage, 2015), 13, and 13–29 more generally. Compare with John Holloway: "This implies a rejection of two distinct understandings of crisis. First, it rejects the traditional concept of the crisis as an *opportunity* for revolution. This is a concept shared by Marxists of many different perspectives. The argument is that when the big crisis of capitalism comes, this will be the moment in which revolution becomes possible: economic crisis will lead to an intensification of class struggle, and this, if guided by effective revolutionary organisation, can lead to revolution. This approach understands crisis as economic crisis, as something distinct from class struggle, rather than as being itself class struggle, a turning point in class struggle, the point at which the mutual repulsion of capital and anti-labour (humanity) obliges capital to restructure its command or lose control.

"Second, this approach rejects the view that the crisis of capital can be equated with its restructuring. This view sees crisis as being functional for capital, a 'creative destruction' (to use Schumpeter's phrase) which destroys inefficient capitals and imposes discipline on the workers. The crisis of one economic model or paradigm of rule leads automatically, in this view, to the establishment of a new one. The argument here is that a crisis is essentially open. Crisis may indeed lead to a restructuring of capital and to the establishment of a new pattern of rule, but it may not. To identify crisis with restructuring is to close the possibility of the world, to rule out the definitive rupture of capital. To identify crisis with restructuring is also to be blind to the whole world of struggle that capital's transition from its crisis to its restructuring has always involved.

"Crisis is, rather, the falling apart of the social relations of capitalism. It can never be assumed in advance that capital will succeed in recomposing them. Crisis involves a *salto mortale* for capital, with no guarantee of a safe landing. Our struggle is against capital's restructuring, our struggle is to intensify the disintegration of capitalism." John Holloway, *Change the World Without Taking Power: The Meaning of Revolution Today*, second edition (London: Pluto Press, 2010 [2002]), 204.

39. Antonio Gramsci, "Modern Prince," 184, Q13§17.

40. For a survey of these positions and those subsequent to Cliff, from a position hostile to all of them, see Marcel van der Linden, *Western Marxism and the Soviet Union: A Survey of Critical Theories and Debates since 1917* (Leiden: E. J. Brill, 2007), 49–63, 91–93, 107–26, 160–61, 180–93, 258–80, 310–13. The first use of the concept, if not the actual term, appears in Friedrich Engels, *Anti-Dühring: Herr Eugen Dühring's Revolution in Science*, in *Collected Works*, vol. 25 (London: Lawrence & Wishart, 1987 [1877]), 266.

41. One of these writers, Andrew Kliman, helpfully gives references to the authors who take this view, including Carchedi, Desai, Freeman, Harman, Mattick, Roberts, Onishi, and Potts. See *The Failure of Capitalist Production: Underlying Causes of the Great Recession* (London: Pluto Press, 2012), 7–8. To these names we can also add: Joseph Choonara, "Once More (with Feeling) on Marxist Accounts of the Crisis," *International Socialism* 132 (Autumn 2011), and "A Reply to David McNally," *International Socialism* 135 (Summer 2012); and—specifically in relation to the United States—Dimitris Paitardis and Lefteris Tsoulfidis, "The Growth of Unproductive Activities, the Rate of Profit, and the Phase-Change of the U.S. Economy," *Review of Radical Political Economy* 44, no. 2 (2012), and Murray E. G. Smith and Jonah Butovsky, "Profitability and the Roots of the Global Crisis: Marx's 'Law of the Tendency of the Rate of Profit to Fall' and the US Economy, 1950–2007," *Historical Materialism*, 20, no. 4 (Jan 2012).

42. See, for example, Robert Brenner and Mark Glick, "The Regulation Approach: History and Theory," *New Left Review* I/188 (Jul/Aug 1991).

43. Chris Harman, *Explaining the Crisis: A Marxist Re-Appraisal* (London: Bookmarks, 1984 [1981–2]), 52–99.

44. Andrew Rawnsley, *Servants of the People: The Inside Story of New Labour*, revised edition (Harmondsworth, UK: Penguin Books, 2001), 309.

45. Eric J. Hobsbawm, "The Forward March of Labour Halted?," in *The Forward March of Labour Halted?*, Martin Jacques and Francis Mulhern, eds. (London: Verso, 1981 [1978]); Stuart Hall and Martin Jacques, "Introduction," in *The Politics of Thatcherism*, Stuart Hall and Martin Jacques, eds. (London: Lawrence & Wishart/Marxism Today, 1983), 14–16.

46. Michael Hardt and Antonio Negri, *Multitude: War and Democracy in the Age of Empire* (Harmondsworth, UK: Penguin Books, 2004), 99–138.

47. Guy Standing, *The Precariat: The New Dangerous Class* (London: Bloomsbury, 2011), 25, 147–54.

48. Ian Birchall, *Tony Cliff: A Revolutionary for His Times* (London: Bookmarks,

2011), 449.

49. Tony Cliff, *Trotskyism after Trotsky: The Origins of the International Socialists* (London: Bookmarks, 1999), 81–82; Trotsky, "The Death Agony of Capitalism."

50. Harman, *Explaining the Crisis*, 121.

51. Harman, "Rate of Profit," 157, note 48, 159.

52. Fredrick Engels, "Introduction [to Karl Marx's *The Class Struggles in France, 1848 to 1850*]," in *Marx & Engels Collected Works*, vol. 27 (London: Lawrence & Wishart, 1990 [1895]), 510.

53. Loïc Wacquant, *Punishing the Poor: The Neoliberal Government of Social Insecurity* (Durham, NC: Duke University Press, 2009), 306.

54. It will become obvious that, while I find these categories useful and broadly agree with the territorial distribution which Jessop ascribes to them, my conception of their content differs from his in several respects. In particular, I entirely reject the view that the Stalinist regimes ruled over "state socialist" societies.

55. Bob Jessop, "From Hegemony to Crisis? The Continuing Ecological Dominance of Neoliberalism," in Birch and Mykhnenko, *Rise and Fall of Neoliberalism*, 172–74.

56. Which is why Perry Anderson's decision to omit Britain, "whose history since the fall of Thatcher has been of little moment," from his study of the European Union is mistaken. Blair's variant on the neoliberal regime has been far more insidiously influential than that of Thatcher. See Anderson, "Foreword," *The New Old World* (London: Verso, 2009), xii–xiii.

57. Karl Marx, *Grundrisse: Foundations of the Critique of Political Economy (Rough Draft)* (Harmondsworth, UK: Penguin Books/New Left Review 1973 [1857–8]), 105. See also Karl Marx, *Capital: A Critique of Political Economy*, vol. 1 (Harmondsworth, UK: Penguin Books/New Left Review, 1976 [1867]), 90.

Chapter 1: False Intellectual Antecedents and True Material Origins

1. Hugo Young, *One of Us: A Biography of Margaret Thatcher* (London: Macmillan, 1989), 528.

2. Margaret Thatcher, *The Downing Street Years* (London: HarperCollins, 1993), 618. See also David Torrance, *"We in Scotland": Thatcherism in a Cold Climate* (Edinburgh: Birlinn, 2009), 25, 57, 161, 165.

3. Quoted in Daniel Stedman Jones, *Masters of the Universe: Hayek, Friedman, and the Birth of Neoliberal Politics* (Princeton, NJ: Princeton University Press, 2012), 102. Not all proto-neoliberals were as ahistorical as this. As was quite often the case, Mises was more realistic: "Nobody should believe that he will find in Smith's inquiry information about present-day economics or about present-day problems of economic policy.... Neither will the reader find in the *Wealth of Nations* a refutation of the teachings of Marx, Veblen, Keynes,

and their followers." See Ludwig von Mises, "Introduction," in Adam Smith, *An Inquiry into the Nature and Causes of the Wealth of Nations* (Washington DC: Henry Regnery, 1952), 3.

4. Dennis MacLeod and Michael Russell, *Grasping the Thistle: How Scotland Must React to the Three Key Challenges of the Twenty First Century* (Glendaruel, UK: Argyll Publishing, 2006), 95–96.

5. Elmar Altvater, "The Roots of Neoliberalism," in *The Socialist Register 2008*, 346.

6. James D. Young, *The Herald* (Glasgow) (March 21, 2007).

7. Dimitris Milonakis and Ben Fine, *From Political Economy to Economics: Method, the Social and the Historical in the Evolution of Economic Theory* (Abingdon, UK: Routledge, 2009), 48.

8. Smith, *An Inquiry into the Nature and Causes of the Wealth of Nations*, Book I (Chicago: University of Chicago Press), 144, 277–78.

9. Emma Rothschild, *Economic Sentiments: Adam Smith, Condorcet, and the Enlightenment* (Cambridge, MA: Harvard University Press, 2001), 65.

10. Compare Smith, *The Wealth of Nations*, Book I, 7–16, with ibid, Book IV, 302–303.

11. James Buchan, *Adam Smith and the Pursuit of Perfect Liberty* (London: Profile Books, 2006), 5–7, 9; Neal Curtis, *Idiotism: Capitalism and the Privatisation of Life* (London: Pluto, 2013), 29–34; Neil Davidson, "The Scottish Path to Capitalist Agriculture 3: The Enlightenment as the Theory and Practice of Improvement," *Journal of Agrarian Change* 5, no. 1 (Jan 2005), 47–53, 62–64; Dogen Göçmen, *The Adam Smith Problem: Human Nature and Society in* The Theory of Moral Sentiments *and* Wealth of Nations (London: I. B. Tauris, 2007), 114–18; Lisa Hill, "Adam Smith, Adam Ferguson and Karl Marx on the Division of Labour," *Journal of Classical Sociology* 7, no. 3 (Nov 2007); Stedman Jones, *Masters of the Universe*, 100–10.

12. Stanley Aronowitz, *The Death and Life of American Labor: Toward a New Workers' Movement* (New York: Verso, 2014), 43–44.

13. Milonakis and Fine, *From Political Economy to Economics*, 12, 93.

14. Davidson, "Scottish Path," 56–59; Saville, *Consolidation of the Capitalist State*, 33–36.

15. Milonakis and Fine, *From Political Economy to Economics*, 94–95, 102–103.

16. Fredrick von Hayek, "The Complexity of Problems of Human Interaction," in *The Fatal Conceit: The Errors of Socialism*, W. W. Bartley III ed. (London: Routledge, 1988), 148.

17. Andrew Gamble, *Hayek: The Iron Cage of Liberty* (Boulder, CO: Westfield Press 1996), 31–36.

18. Davidson, "Scottish Path," 18. Indeed, in 1883 Menger explicitly criticized Smith for his "one-sided rationalistic liberalism," his "effort to do away with what exists," which Menger claimed "inexorably leads to socialism." See Rothschild, *Economic Sentiments*, 65.

19. David Graeber, "Introduction: The Iron Law of Liberalism and the Era of

Total Bureaucratization," in *The Utopia of Rules: On Technology, Stupidity, and the Secret Joys of Bureaucracy* (New York: Melville House, 2015), 8.

20. Karl Polanyi, *The Great Transformation: The Political and Economic Origins of Our Time* (Boston: Beacon Press, 1957 [1944]), 149.

21. Carl J. Friedrich, "The Political Thought of Neo-liberalism," *American Political Science Review* 49, no. 2 (June 1955); Anthony Nicholls, "The Other Germany—The 'Neo-Liberals,'" in *Ideas into Politics: Aspects of European History, 1880–1950*, R. J. Bullen, H. Pogge von Strandmann, and A. B. Polonsky, eds. (London: Croom Helm, 1984). The term "free economy, strong state" was revived by Andrew Gamble to describe the politics of Thatcherism, but it can be applied to neoliberalism more generally. See Andrew Gamble, "The Free Economy and the Strong State," in *The Socialist Register 1979*, edited by Ralph Miliband and John Saville (London: Merlin, 1979), and *The Free Economy and the Strong State: The Politics of Thatcherism* (Houndmills, UK: Macmillan, 1988).

22. Joseph A. Schumpeter [1919], "The Sociology of Imperialism," in *Imperialism and Social Classes*, Paul M. Sweezy, ed. (Oxford: Blackwell, 1951), 84–97, and Fredrick von Hayek, *The Road to Serfdom* (London: George Routledge, 1944), chapter 12. Having defined socialism in this way, it is unsurprising that Hayek and his co-thinkers could then detect it throughout history. See Fredrick von Hayek, "The Present State of the Debate," in *Collectivist Economic Planning*, Frederick von Hayek, ed. (London: George Routledge, 1935), 17. In a book first published in 1928 and introduced by von Mises (*A Socialist Empire*), the French economist Louis Baudin claimed that the collective nature of property in pre-Columbian Peru meant that Inca society represented a form of socialist dictatorship. See Louis Baudin, *A Socialist Empire: the Incas of Peru*, Princeton, NJ: D. Van Nostrand, 1961 [1928]. Looking even further back in time, Hayek himself claimed the decline of Rome from the second century AD was due to the advance of "state socialism" following the supposed abandonment of free market economics and the rule of law. See Fredrick von Hayek, *The Constitution of Liberty* (London: Routledge and Kegan Paul, 1969), 167. Whatever their other disagreements, Max Weber shared with Hayek a belief in "the achievements of ancient capitalism" supposedly displayed by the early Roman Empire. See Max Weber, *The Agrarian Sociology of Ancient Civilizations* (London: Verso, 1998 [1908]), 355.

23. Bukharin, *Imperialism and World Economy*, 104–109, 122–29; Jan Romein, *The Watershed of Two Eras: Europe in 1900* (Middletown, CT: Wesleyan University Press, 1978), 271–95.

24. A. J. P. Taylor, *English History, 1914–1945* (Oxford: Clarendon Press, 1965), 1–2.

25. Sidney Webb, *Socialism in England* (London: Swan Sonnenschein, 1890), 116–17.

26. Graeber, "Introduction: The Iron Law," 9.

27. Hayek, *Road to Serfdom*, 5, 16–17, 34–35, 124–49.

28. Keith Tribe, "Liberalism and Neoliberalism in Britain, 1930–1980," in *The Road from Mont Pèlerin: The Making of the Neoliberal Thought Collective*, Philip Mirowski and Dieter Plehwe, eds. (Cambridge, MA: Harvard University Press, 2009), 74.

29. Max Weber, *The Protestant Ethic and the Spirit of Capitalism* (London: George Allen & Unwin, 1976 [1904–1905]), 181.

30. Max Weber, "Socialism," in Lassman and Speirs, *Political Writings*, 279 [1918].

31. David Graeber, "The Utopia of Rules, or Why We Really Love Bureaucracy after All," and "Introduction," in *Utopia of Rules*, 153, 154.

32. Nicholas Wapshott, *Keynes Hayek: The Clash that Defined Modern Economics* (New York: W. W. Morton, 2012), 165.

33. Costas Lapavitsas, "Mainstream Economics in the Neoliberal Era," in *Neoliberalism: A Critical Reader*, Alfredo Saad-Filho and Deborah Johnston, eds. (London: Pluto, 2005), 31–32.

34. Polanyi, *The Great Transformation*, 73. For examples of how this passage has been used in more recent debates see: David Harvey, *A Brief History of Neoliberalism* (Oxford: Oxford University Press, 2005), 167; Chris Hedges, *Empire of Illusion: The End of Literacy and the Triumph of Spectacle* (New York: Nation Books, 2009), 184–85; Colin Leys, *Market-Driven Politics: Neoliberal Democracy and the Public Interest* (London: Verso, 2001), 6; and Emmanuel Todd, *Who Is Charlie? Xenophobia and the New Middle Class* (Cambridge, UK: Polity, 2015), 97. For a useful extended discussion of Polanyi's work and legacy, see Gareth Dale, *Karl Polanyi: the Limits of the Market* (Cambridge, UK: Polity, 2010).

35. Andy Beckett, *When the Lights Went Out: Britain in the Seventies* (London: Faber & Faber, 2009), 272.

36. Kidron, *Western Capitalism Since the War*, 11 [1968].

37. Angus Maddison, "Economic Policy and Performance in Europe, 1913–1970," in *The Fontana Economic History of Europe*, vol. 6, the *Twentieth Century*, part two, Carlo M. Cipolla, ed. (Glasgow: Collins/Fontana Books, 1976), 477.

38. David Hare, *The Blue Touch Paper: A Memoir* (London: Faber & Faber, 2015), 205.

39. Wapshott, *Keynes Hayek*, 256, 268.

40. Andrew Gamble, *The Free Economy and the Strong State* (Hounsmills: Palgrave, 1988), 43.

41. John Maynard Keynes, "From Keynes to Roosevelt: Our Recovery Plan Assayed," *New York Times* (December 31, 1933).

42. Chris Harman, *Zombie Capitalism: Global Crisis and the Relevance of Marx* (London: Bookmarks, 2009), 149–50, 162.

43. Kidron, *Western Capitalism Since the War*, chapter 3; Harman, *Explaining the Crisis*, 78–84.

44. Mike Davis, "The Political Economy of Late Imperial America," in *Prisoners of the American Dream*, 195–201. As Davis has suggested elsewhere, the theo-

ries of the permanent arms economy a la Kidron and the Regulation School a la Aglietta complete each other: "each holds a different part of the elephant of contemporary capitalism, mistaking it for the whole." See Mike Davis, "'Fordism,'" in "Crisis: A Review of Michel Aglietta's *Régulation et Crises: L'experience des Etats-Unis*," *Review* 2, no. 2 (Fall 1978), 251.

45. For one outstanding national case study of his process, see Paul Ginsborg, *A History of Contemporary Italy: Society and Politics, 1943-1988* (Harmondsworth, UK: Penguin, 1990), 210-235.

46. Maddison, "Economic Policy and Performance in Europe," 491; Göran Therborn, *European Modernity and Beyond The Trajectory of European Societies, 1945-2000* (London: Sage, 1995), 131-46.

47. Harvey, *Brief History of Neoliberalism*, 19.

48. David Miller, "How Neoliberalism Got where it is: Elite Planning, Corporate Lobbying and the Release of the Free Market," in Birch and Mykhnenko, *Rise and Fall of Neoliberalism*, 39.

49. Hobsbawm, *Age of Extremes*, 403–16. Although, as Perry Anderson rightly remarks, the period since 1973 has seen dramatic, if uneven, improvements in the living conditions of millions in the Global South who were excluded from the prosperity of the Long Boom. See Perry Anderson, "The Vanquished Left: Eric Hobsbawm," in *Spectrum: from Right to Left in the World of Ideas* (London: Verso, 2005 [2002]), 301.

50. Tony Judt, "Introduthen: The World We Have Lost," in *Reappraisals: Reflections on the Forgotten Twentieth Century* (London: William Heinemann, 2008), 10.

51. Francis Beckett, *What Did the Baby Boomers Ever Do for Us? Why the Children of the Sixties Lived the Dream and Failed the Future* (London: Biteback, 2010), 154–55.

52. Kidron, *Western Capitalism Since the War*, 20–21.

53. Anthony Howard, "'We Are the Masters Now,'" in *Age of Austerity, 1945–1951*, Michael Sissons and Philip French, eds. (Harmondsworth, UK: Penguin, 1964), 33.

54. David Kynaston, *Austerity Britain, 1945–51* (London: Bloomsbury, 2007), 376–77; and *Family Britain, 1951-57* (London: Bloomsbury, 2009), 97–99, 331–34, 391–92.

55. Elizabeth Wilson, *Only Halfway to Paradise: Women in Postwar Britain, 1945–1968* (London: Tavistock, 1980), 6.

56. Mike Davis, "The Fall of the House of Labour," in *Prisoners of the American Dream*, 116.

57. Sidney Blumenthal, *The Rise of the Counter-Establishment: From Conservative Ideology to Political Power* (New York: Harper and Row, 1986), 110; Robert Brenner, "The Paradox of Social Democracy: The American Case," in *The Year Left: An American Socialist Yearbook, 1985*, Mike Davis, Fred Pfeil, and Michael Sprinkler, eds. (London: Verso, 1985), 55–59; Frances Fox Piven, *The War at Home: The Domestic Costs of Bush's Militarism* (New York: New Press,

2004), 66–67; Judith Stein, "Conflict, Change, and Economic Policy in the Long 1970s," in *Rebel Rank and File: Labor Militancy and Revolt from Below During the Long 1970s*, Aaron Brenner, Robert Brenner, and Cal Winslow, eds. (London: Verso, 2010), 86.

58. Carl Freedman, *The Age of Nixon: A Study in Cultural Power* (Winchester, UK, Zero Books, 2012), 144–47. Freedman makes an interesting case for regarding Nixon, rather than Kennedy, as the more liberal of the two candidates in the 1960 presidential election. See ibid, 162–70.

59. Jeremy Engels, *The Politics of Resentment: A Genealogy* (University Park, PA: Penn State University Press, 2015), 74 and 75–96.

60. For the use of these terms see, respectively, Harvey, *Brief History of Neoliberalism*, 10, and Leys, *Market-Driven Politics*, 40.

61. Richard Hoggart, *The Uses of Literacy: Aspects of Working-Class Life with Special Reference to Publications and Entertainments* (Harmondsworth, UK: Penguin Books, 1958), 13.

62. Lynsey Hanley, *Respectable: The Experience of Class* (London: Allen Lane, 2016), 12.

63. Edward P. Thompson, "An Open Letter to Leszek Kolakowski," in *The Socialist Register 1973*, Ralph Miliband and John Saville, eds. (London: Merlin Books, 1973), 53.

64. Hilde Eileen Nafstad et al., "Ideology and Power: The Influence of Current Neo-Liberalism in Society," *Journal of Community and Applied Social Psychology* 17, no. 4 (July 2007), 314.

65. Blond, *Red Tory*, 15.

66. Steve Fraser, *The Age of Acquiescence: The Life and Death of American Resistance to Organized Wealth and Power* (New York: Little, Brown & Company, 2015), 197.

67. Paul Mattick, *Marx and Keynes: The Limits of the Mixed Economy* (London: Merlin, 1971), 279–80.

68. Nigel Harris, *The End of the Third World: Newly Industrialising Countries and the Decline of an Ideology* (Harmondsworth, UK: Penguin, 1986), 42.

69. Mattick, *Marx and Keynes*, 284.

70. Michael Haynes, *Russia: Class and Power, 1917–2000* (London: Bookmarks 2002), 210–14.

71. Klein has acknowledged her debt to Harvey. See Naomi Klein, *The Shock Doctrine: The Rise of Disaster Capitalism* (London: Allen Lane, 2007), 190, 532; and Naomi Klein and Neil Smith, "*The Shock Doctrine*: A Discussion," *Environment and Planning D: Society and Space* 26, no. 4 (Aug 2008), 583.

72. Klein, *Shock Doctrine*, 6–7, 140–41.

73. Peter Hennessey, *Having It So Good: Britain in the Fifties* (London: Allen Lane, 2006), 199–217; Kynaston, *Family Britain*, 74–5.

74. See, for example, Andrew Marr, *A History of Modern Britain* (London: Macmillan, 2007), 131.

75. Kynaston, *Family Britain*, 75–76.

76. Klein, *Shock Doctrine*, 67–70.

77. Alan Greenspan, *The Age of Turbulence: Adventures in a New World* (London: Penguin, 2008), 275. See also Marttheolf, *Why Globalization Works: The Case for the Global Market Economy* (New Haven, CT: Yale University Press, 2004), 72, 291.

78. Karin Fischer, "The Influence of Neoliberals in Chile before, during, and after Pinochet," in Mirowski and Plehwe, *Road from Mont Pèlerin*, 317.

79. Klein, *Shock Doctrine*, 88, 165–68.

80. Atilio Boron, *State, Capitalism, and Democracy in Latin America* (Boulder, CO: Lynne Rienner, 1999), chapter 7.

81. Harris, *End of the Third World*, 54–60; John Lanchester, *Whoops! Why Everyone Owes Everyone and No One Can Pay* (London: Allen Lane, 2010), 6–7.

82. Richard Cockett, *Thinking the Unthinkable: Think-Tanks and the Economic Counter-Revolution, 1931–1983* (London: Fontana, 1995), 281–82; David Miller and William Dinan, *A Century of Spin: How Public Relations Became the Cutting Edge of Corporate Power* (London: Pluto, 2008), 73–77.

83. Klein, *Shock Doctrine*, 57.

84. Richard Vinen, *A History in Fragments: Europe in the Twentieth Century* (London: Abacus, 2002), 331.

85. David Vogel, "Why Businessmen Distrust Their State: The Political Consciousness of American Corporate Executives," *British Journal of Political Science* 8, no. 1 (Jan 1978), 78 and 74–78 more generally.

86. Theodore Levitt, "The Johnson Treatment," *Harvard Business Review* 45 (1967).

87. Blumenthal, *Rise of the Counter-Establishment*, 75–76.

88. Quoted in Leonard Silk and David Vogel, *Ethics and Politics: The Crisis in Confidence in American Business* (New York: Simon and Schuster, 1976), 219.

89. Anthony Seldon, "The Heath Government in History," in *The Heath Government, 1970–1974: A Reappraisal*, Stuart Ball and Anthony Seldon, eds. (London: Longman, 1996), 14–15.

90. Stein, "Conflict, Change, and Economic Policy," 86, 87–88.

91. Jamie Peck, "Remaking Laissez-faire," *Progress in Human Geography* 32, no. 1 (2008), 18–22.

92. Vinen, *History in Fragments*, 333.

93. Elmar Altvater et al., "On the Analysis of Imperialism in the Metropolitan Countries: the West German Example," *Bulletin of the Conference of Socialist Economists* (Spring 1974), 20; Will Hutton, *The State We're In* (London: Jonathan Cape, 1995), 262–68; Stedman Jones, *Masters of the Universe*, 121–26.

94. Wolfgang Streeck, "Citizens as Customers: Considerations on the New Politics of Consumption," *New Left Review* II/76 (July/Aug 2012), 29.

95. See, for example, Elliott and Atkinson, *The Gods That Failed*, pp. 75–80, or Neal Lawson, *All Consuming: How Shopping Got Us Into This Mess and How We Can Find Our Way Out* (Harmondsworth, UK: Penguin, 2009), 105.

96. Debray, "A Modest Contribution," 48, 58.

97. Francis Beckett, *What Did the Baby Boomers Ever Do for Us?*, xii.

98. Polly Toynbee, "Did We Baby Boomers Bring About a Revolution in the 60s or Just Usher In Neoliberalism?" *Guardian* website (September 8, 2016).

99. Lipovetsky, "May '68," 216.

100. Ed Howker and Shiv Malik, *Jilted Generation: How Britain Has Bankrupted Its Youth* (London: Icon, 2010), 171 and 170–72 more generally.

101. Damian Thompson, *Counterknowledge: How We Surrendered to Conspiracy Theories, Quack Medicine, Bogus Science, and Fake History* (London: Atlantic, 2008), 123–24.

102. Dick Pountain and David Robins, *Cool Rules: Anatomy of an Attitude* (London: Reaktion, 2000), 85.

103. Pountain and Robins, *Cool Rules*, 105.

104. Perry Anderson, "The Vanquished Left: Eric Hobsbawm," in *Spectrum: from Right to Left in the World of Ideas* (London: Verso, 2005 [2002]) 251.

105. Hobsbawm, *Age of Extremes*, 334.

106. Tony Judt, "The Social Question Redivivus," in *Ill Fares the Land* (London: Allen Lane, 2010), 89. And as he rightly points out, while individualism was fine at home, Chinese workers and peasants were expected to act in uniformity with the wishes of Mao Tse-tung.

107. Owen Hatherley, *The Ministry of Nostalgia* (London: Verso, 2016), 11.

108. Tony Judt, "The Wrecking Ball of Innovation," in *When the Facts Change: Essays, 1995–2010,* Jennifer Homans, ed. (London: Vintage, 2015 [2007]), 315.

109. Tony Judt, "What Is Living and What Is Dead in Social Democracy?" in Homans, *When the Facts Change*, 324 [2009].

110. See, for example, Diski, *The Sixties*, 8–9, 88–89, 114–15, 135–39.

111. Green, *Days in the Life*, 341.

112. Arthur Marwick, *The Sixties: Cultural Revolution in Britain, France, Italy, and the United States, c. 1958–c. 1974* (Oxford: Oxford University Press, 1998), 13.

113. Marwick, *The Sixties*, 802.

114. Ballard, *Miracles of Life*, 226.

115. Wolfe, "The 'Me' Decade," 144.

116. MacDonald, *Revolution in the Head*, 29–30.

117. Richard Goldstein, *Another Little Piece of My Heart: My Life of Rock and Revolution in the '60s* (London: Bloomsbury Circus, 2015), 95.

118. Mark Lilla, "A Tale of Two Reactions," *New York Review of Books* (May 14, 1998).

119. Graeber, "Introduction," in *Utopia of Rules*, 19.

120. Ron Jacobs, *Daydream Sunset: The 60s Counterculture in the 70s* (Petrolia, CA: Counterpunch, 2015), 91–92.

121. David Hepworth, *1971: Never a Dull Moment* (London: Bantam, 2016), 150.

122. Selina Todd, *The People: The Rise and Fall of the Working Class, 1910–2010* (London: John Murray, 2014), 307–308.

123. Marie Cerna et al., "Revolutions," in *Europe's 1968: Voices of Revolt*, Robert Gildea, James Mark, and Anette Warring, eds. (Oxford: Oxford University Press, 2013), 118.

124. Hare, *Blue Touch Paper*, 95.

125. Stephen Eric Bronner, "Reconstructing the Experiment: Political Culture and the American New Left," in *Moments of Decision: Political History and the Crises of Radicalism* (New York: Routledge, 1992 [1983/4]), 113.

126. Jacoby, *Age of American Unreason*, 163.

127. Hall et al., *Policing the Crisis*, 254.

128. Standing, *Precariat*, 66–67.

129. Jann Wenner, "John Lennon: The Rolling Stone Interview," *Rolling Stone*, February 4, 1971, 11–12.

130. Hare, *Blue Touch Paper*, 240–41.

131. Marcus, *Mystery Train*, 103, 104.

132. Jackson Browne, "The Pretender," from *The Pretender*, Electra Records, 1976.

133. Nile Rodgers, *Le Freak: An Upside Down Story of Family, Disco, and Destiny* (London: Sphere, 2011), 115–16.

134. Jeremy Gilbert, "The Real Abstraction of Michael Jackson," in *The Resistible Demise of Michael Jackson*, Mark Fisher, ed. (Winchester, UK: Zero Books, 2010), 148–49.

135. Lecourt, "Appendix," 205, 206.

136. Including in this context Anthony Charles Lynton Blair: "It would be too simplistic to say that the left has won the battle over values and the right has won the battle over policy direction, but it is a little like that." Tony Blair, *A Journey* (London: Arrow, 2011), xxi.

137. John Maynard Keynes, *The General Theory of Employment, Interest and Money*, in *Collected Writings*, vol. 7 (London: Macmillan and Cambridge University Press for the Royal Economic Society, 1974 [1936]), 383, 384.

138. Hayek, *Road to Serfdom*, 2.

139. Miller and Dinan, *Century of Spin*, chapter 5.

140. Philip Mirowski, "Postface: Defining Neoliberalism," in Mirowski and Plehwe, *Road from Mont Pèlerin*, 432.

141. Lawson, *All Consuming*, 92.

142. Keith Joseph, "Letter," *Economist* (September 28, 1974).

143. Ruth Levitas, "Introduction: Ideology and the New Right," in Levitas, *Ideology of the New Right*, 15. See also Richard Vinen, *Thatcher's Britain: The Politics and Social Upheaval of the 1980s* (London: Simon and Schuster, 2009), 7.

144. Stedman Jones, *Masters of the Universe*, 258.

145. Stuart Hall, "Gramsci and Us," *Marxism Today* (June 1987), 19.

146. Michael C. Howard and John E. King, *The Rise of Neoliberalism in Advanced Capitalist Economies: A Materialist Analysis* (Houndmills, UK: Palgrave Macmillan, 2008), 7, 9.

147. William Davies, *The Happiness Industry: How the Government and Big Business Sold Us Well-Being* (London: Verso, 2015), 160–61.

148. Milton Friedman and Rose Friedman, *Two Lucky People: Memoirs* (Chicago: University of Chicago Press, 1998), 583–84.

149. Damien Cahill, "Ideas-Centred Explanations of the Rise of Neoliberalism: A Critique," *Australian Journal of Political Science* 48, no. 1 (2013), 81.

150. Peter Fleming, *The Mythology of Work: How Capitalism Persists Despite Itself* (London: Pluto, 2015), 45.

151. John Kenneth Galbraith, *American Capitalism: The Concept of Countervailing Power* (Harmondsworth, UK: Penguin, 1963 [1952]), 122–67.

152. David McNally, *Another World Is Possible: Globalisation and Anti-Capitalism*, revised expanded edition (Winnipeg: Arbeiter Ring, 2006), 39.

153. Jacques Rancière, *Hatred of Democracy* (London: Verso, 2006), 82.

154. Morris Berman, *Dark Ages America: The Final Phase of Empire* (New York: W. W. Norton, 2007), 54.

155. Thomas Friedman, "Read My Lips," *New York Times* (June 11, 2003).

156. Peter Oborne, "Land of the Bung," *New Statesman* (June 5–11, 2015), 45.

157. Wolf, *Why Globalization Works*, 19.

158. For data on the increasing frequency with which the term "globalization" was used, see Doug Henwood, *After the New Economy: The Binge . . . And the Hangover that Won't Go Away* (New York: New Press, 2003), 145–55.

159. See, for example, Alfredo Saad-Filho and Deborah Johnson, "Introduction," in Saad-Filho and Johnson, *Neoliberalism: A Critical Reader*, 2.

160. Karl Marx and Fredrick Engels, "Manifesto of the Communist Party," in *Political Writings*, vol. 1, *The Revolutions of 1848*, David Fernbach, ed. (Harmondsworth, UK: Penguin Books/New Left Review, 1973 [1848]), 68–73.

161. Robert J. Holton, *Making Globalization* (Houndmills: Palgrave Macmillan, 2005), 14–15.

162. Leslie Sklair, "The Emancipatory Potential of Generic Globalization," *Globalizations* 6, no. 4 (Dec 2009), 529–34.

163. David Kotz, "The State, Globalisation and Phases of Capitalist Development," in Robert Albritton et al., *Phases of Capitalist Development*, 104.

164. Wolfgang Streeck, *Buying Time: The Delayed Crisis of Democratic Capitalism* (London: Verso, 2014), 20–21.

165. Michael Mann, *The Sources of Social Power*, vol. 4, *Globalizations, 1945–2011* (Cambridge, UK: Cambridge University Press, 2013), 146.

166. Ashley Lavelle, "Explanations for the NeoLiberal Direction of Social Democracy: Germany, Sweden and Australia Compared," in *In Search of Social Democracy: Responses to Crisis and Modernisation*, John Callaghan et al., eds. (Manchester, UK: Manchester University Press, 2009), 23.

167. Chris Harman, *Explaining the Crisis*, 99–102; Robert Brenner, *The Economics of Global Turbulence: The Advanced Capitalist Economies from Long Boom to Long Downturn, 1945–2005* (London: Verso, 2006 [1998]), 99–101. Harman argues that an increase in the organic composition of capital (as a result of declining effectiveness of the permanent arms economy as a countervailing tendency) was the reason for the falling rate of profit. Brenner rejects this explanation (see Brenner, *Economics of Global Turbulence*, 14–15, note 1), but both he and Harman agree that the falling rate of profit is nevertheless central to the crisis.

168. Al Campbell, "The Birth of Neoliberalism in the United States: a Reorgani-

zation of Capitalism," in Saad-Filho and Johnston, *Neoliberalism: A Critical Reader*, 189.

169. Robert Reich, *Supercapitalism: The Battle for Democracy in an Age of Big Business*, second edition (London: Icon, 2009), 12.

170. Wolf, *Why Globalization Works*, 132.

171. Andrew Gamble, "Neo-liberalism," *Capital and Class* 75 (Autumn 2001), 133.

172. G. A. Cohen, "Back to Socialist Basics," in *On the Currency of Egalitarian Justice, and Other Essays in Political Philosophy*, Michael Otsuka, ed. (Princeton: Princeton University Press, 2011 [1994]), 212–13.

173. Guillermo Levy, "Considerations on the Connections between Race, Politics, Economics, and Genocide," *Journal of Genocide Research* 8, no. 2 (2006), 142.

174. Andrew Glyn and Bob Sutcliffe, *British Capitalism, Workers and the Profits Squeeze* (Harmondsworth, UK: Penguin, 1972), 50–102.

175. Harman, *Explaining the Crisis*, appendix 1; Brenner, *Economics of Global Turbulence*, chapter 1.

176. Anthony Burgess, *1985* (London: Hutchison, 1978), 130. In several remarkable passages. Burgess anticipated what was to be the successor moral panic of the neoliberal epoch: Islam. In his dystopia, Britain ("Tucland") is kept going by infusions of Arab oil money: "To remind Britain that Islam was not just a faith for the rich, plenty of hard-working Pakistanis and East African Muslims flowed in without hindrance, for the adjustment of immigration laws (which had too-stringent quota clauses) in favour of the Islamic peoples was a necessary political consequence of Arab financial patronage" (Burgess, *1985*, 121).

177. Michal Kalecki, "Political Aspects of Full Employment," *Political Quarterly* 14, no. 4 (1943), 327.

178. John Carson-Parker, "The Options Ahead for the Debt Economy," *Businessweek* (October 12, 1974), 120–21.

179. Bruce Springsteen, "Independence Day," Columbia, 1980.

Chapter 2: Vanguard Neoliberalism

1. Harold Wilson, *The Labour Government, 1964–70: A Personal Record* (London: Weidenfeld and Nicolson and Michael Joseph, 1971), 64–66.

2. Andy Beckett, *When the Lights Went Out*, 355–57.

3. James Petras and Morris Morley, *Latin America in the Time of Cholera: Electoral Politics, Market Economics, and Permanent Crisis* (New York: Routledge, 1992), 165–66.

4. Antonio Gramsci, "State and Civil Society," in *Selections from the Prison Notebooks*, 211 [1929–1934].

5. Samuel Brittan, "Breaking the Mould," in *The Role and Limits of Government: Essays in Political Economy* (London: Temple Smith, 1983), 239–40.

6. Andy Beckett, *When the Lights Went Out*, 322–23, 335–39; Leo Panitch and Colin Leys, *The End of Parliamentary Socialism: From New Left to New Labour*

(London: Verso, 1997), 110–18.

7. Paul du Gay and Alan Scott, "State Transformation or Regime Shift? Addressing Some Confusions in the Theory and Sociology of the State," *Sociologica* 2 (2010).

8. Bernard Donoughue, *Prime Minister: The Conduct of Policy under Harold Wilson and James Callaghan* (London: Jonathan Cape, 1987), 191. In fact, as Donoughue's subsequently published diaries show, Callaghan was far from convinced that such a sea change had actually occurred and instead thought that Labour couldn't win "unless" it had. See Bernard Donoughue, *Downing Street Diary*, vol. 2, *with James Callaghan in No. 10* (London: Jonathan Cape, 2008), 483–84. The contrast between these two passages is highlighted in Dominic Sandbrook, *Seasons in the Sun: The Battle for Britain, 1974–1979* (London: Allen Lane, 2012), 601.

9. Gamble, *Free Economy*, 194–97, 224–27.

10. See, for example, Trotsky, "Lessons of October," 249–53.

11. Thatcher, *Downing Street Years*, 306.

12. Alasdair MacIntyre, "Trotsky in Exile," in *Alasdair MacIntyre's Engagement with Marxism*, 275 [1963]. MacIntyre is here summarizing and defending the argument in Trotsky, *History of the Russian Revolution*, 343–44.

13. John Gray, "Misunderstanding the Present: Ed Miliband Wants to Govern a Country that Doesn't Exist," *New Statesman* (February 13–19, 2015), 34.

14. Andy Beckett, *When the Lights Went Out*, 5, 282, 463. For further reflections on "the accidental quality of her ascendancy," by a repentant former Thatcherite, see John Gray, *Black Mass: Apocalyptic Religion and the Death of Utopia* (Harmondsworth, UK: Penguin, 2007), 109–10.

15. Colin Hay, "Chronicles of a Death Foretold: The Winter of Discontent and Construction of the Crisis of British Keynesianism," *Parliamentary Affairs* 63, no. 3 (July 2010), 464–66.

16. James Kelman, "Fighting for Survival: The Steel Industry in Scotland," in *"And the Judges Said . . .": Essays* (London: Secker & Warburg, 2002), 122.

17. Antonio Gramsci, *Prison Notebooks*, vol. 3, Joseph A. Buttigieg, ed. (New York: Columbia University Press, 2007 [1930–1932]), 324–25, Q8§158.

18. Christopher Harvie, *Fool's Gold: The Story of North Sea Oil* (London: Hamish Hamilton, 1994), chapter 10; Young, *One of Us*, 298.

19. Andy Beckett, *Promised You a Miracle: UK80–82* (London: Allen Lane, 2015), 74–75.

20. John Hoskyns, *Just in Time: Inside the Thatcher Revolution* (London: Aurum, 2000), 147.

21. David Sanders et al., "Government Popularity and the Falklands War: A Reassessment," *British Journal of Political Science* 17, no. 3 (July 1987); Vinen, *Thatcher's Britain*, 143–46, 150–53.

22. Georg Lukács, *Lenin: A Study on the Unity of his Thought* (London: New Left, 1970 [1924]), chapter 5.

23. Thatcher, *Downing Street Years*, 686.

24. Blumenthal, *Rise of the Counter-Establishment*, chapter 9; Sheldon S. Wolin, *Democracy Incorporated: Managed Democracy and the Specter of Inverted Totalitarianism* (Princeton, NJ: Princeton University Press, 2008), 271–72.

25. Andy Beckett, *Promised You a Miracle*, 227.

26. Adam Curtis, "The Economists' New Clothes," Adam Curtis blog, February 23, 2010; Adam Curtis *Pandora's Box Part 3: The League of Gentlemen*, BBC 2 11 June 1992.

27. Vinen, *Thatcher's Britain*, 132–33.

28. Kevin Doogan, *New Capitalism? The Transformation of Work* (Cambridge, UK: Polity Press, 2009), 192.

29. Keith Aitken, *The Bairns O' Adam: The Story of the STUC* (Edinburgh: Polygon, 1997), 267.

30. Christopher Harvie, "Scotland after 1978: From Referendum to Millennium," in *The New Penguin History of Scotland: From the Earliest Times to the Present Day*, R. A. Houston and W. W. J. Knox, eds. (London: Allen Lane, 2001), 502.

31. Aitken, *Bairns O' Adam*, 269.

32. Former NUM President Arthur Scargill has repeatedly drawn attention to how near the Thatcher government came to a settlement on several occasions. See, for example, Arthur Scargill, "'We Could Surrender—or Stand and Fight,'" *Guardian* (March 7, 2009). The vulnerability of the government, even as late as the beginning of 1985, is supported by two historians otherwise unremittingly hostile to Scargill's leadership of the strike. See Francis Beckett and David Henke, *Marching to the Faultline: The 1984 Miners' Strike and the Death of Industrial Britain* (London: Constable, 2009), 146–55, 186–87, 198–201.

33. John MacInnes, "The Deindustrialisation of Glasgow," *Scottish Affairs* 11 (Spring 1995), 73, 74, 87.

34. Ian Jack, "Finished with Engines," in *Before the Oil Ran Out: Britain, 1977–87* (London: Flamingo, 1988), 2–3.

35. Thomas M. Devine, *The Scottish Nation: 1700–2007*, second edition, (Harmondsworth, UK: Penguin Books, 2008 [1999]), 597–98; David Newlands, "The Oil Economy", in *Aberdeen, 1800–2000: A New History*, W. Hamish Fraser and Clive H. Lee, eds. (East Linton, UK: Tuckwell, 2000), 174–82; Peter L. Payne, "The Economy," in *Scotland in the 20th Century*, T. M. Devine and R. J. Finlay, eds. (Edinburgh: Edinburgh University Press, 1996), 24–25; John Scott, "Declining Autonomy: Recent Trends in the Scottish Economy," in *Scottish Government Yearbook 1983*, David McCrone, eds. (Edinburgh: Edinburgh University Press, 1983),172.

36. Andy Beckett, *When the Lights Went Out*, 206–208; Newlands, "The Oil Economy," 143–45, 152.

37. Beatrice Campbell, "New Times Towns," in *New Times: The Changing Face of Politics in the 1990s*, Stuart Hall and Martin Jacques, eds. (London: Lawrence and Wishart, 1990), 281–86; John Gapper, "New Town Looks to Young and Unskilled," *Financial Times* (January 8, 1988).

38. John Leopold, "Trade Unions in Scotland—Forward to the 1990s?," in *The Scottish Government Yearbook 1989*, Alice Brown and David McCrone, eds. (Edinburgh: Edinburgh University Press, 1989), 78.

39. Harvie, "Scotland after 1978," 500.

40. MacInnes, "The Deindustrialisation of Glasgow," 74, 80–85; Massey, *Spatial Divisions of Labour*, 281–86; Kim Moody, *US Labor in Trouble and Transition: The Failure of Reform from Above, the Promise of Revival from Below* (London: Verso, 2007), 43–47.

41. Graham Turner, *The Credit Crunch: Housing Bubbles, Globalisation and the Worldwide Economic Crisis* (London: Pluto, 2008), 10.

42. Doogan, *New Capitalism?*, 78–82.

43. Hanley, *Respectable*, 82.

44. Edmund White, *City Boy: My Life in New York During the 1960s and '70s* (London: Bloomsbury, 2009), 9, 11, 138.

45. John McIlroy, "A Brief History of British Trade Unions and Neoliberalism: From the Earliest Days to the Birth of New Labour," in *Trade Unions in a Neoliberal World: British Trade Unions under New Labour*, Gary Daniels and John McIlroy, eds. (London: Routledge, 2009), 27, 37.

46. Mirowski, "Postface: Defining Neoliberalism," 431.

47. Harman, "Theorising Neoliberalism," 118.

48. Daniel T. Rodgers, *Age of Fracture* (Cambridge, MA: Belknap Press of Harvard University Press, 2011), 55.

49. Aditya Chakrabortty, "The De-industrial Revolution," *Soundings* 50 (Spring 2012), 75.

50. See, for example, Glyn Jones and Michael Barnes, *Britain on Borrowed Time* (Harmondsworth, UK: Penguin Books, 1967), chapter 3. Ironically, as Theo Nichols pointed out, during the recession of 1979–82, "the Thatcherites actually presided over what was in all probability the highest level of 'overmanning' in British manufacturing in living memory—an overmanning induced by the inability of employers to shed labour fast enough to match their falling order books." See Theo Nichols, *The British Worker Question: A New Look at Workers and Productivity in Manufacturing* (London: Routledge and Kegan Paul, 1986), 186.

51. Thatcher, *Downing Street Years*, 676–87.

52. Ursula Huws, "Crisis as Capitalist Opportunity: The New Accumulation through Public Service," in *Labor in the Global Digital Economy; The Cybertariat Comes of Age* (New York: Monthly Review, 2015 [2012]), 133–34.

53. Leys, *Market-Driven Politics*, 53–54.

54. Harman, "Theorizing Neoliberalism,"104–108; Leys, *Market-Driven Politics*, 83–84.

55. Göran Therborn, *From Marxism to Post-Marxism?* (London: Verso, 2008), 18.

56. Mann, *Sources of Social Power*, vol. 4, 153.

57. Perry Anderson, "The Figures of Descent," in *English Questions* (London: Verso, 1992 [1987]), 180–81; Cockett, *Thinking the Unthinkable*, 201, 215–16,

267; Gamble, *The Free Economy and the Strong State*, 103–104, 124; Vinen, *Thatcher's Britain*, 192–99; Young, *One of Us*, 358–59.

58. In the UK, 'council housing' refers to public housing developments owned by local authorities ('councils') and leased to tenants at subsidized rates – at least until the policies adopted by the Thatcher government described in this paragraph.

59. Gamble, *The Free Economy and the Strong State*, 124–25, 138; Andrew Glyn, *Capitalism Unleashed: Finance, Globalization, and Welfare* (Oxford: Oxford University Press, 2006), 37–42; Simon Jenkins, *Thatcher & Sons: A Revolution in Three Acts* (London: Allen Lane, 2006), 91–92; Stedman Jones, *Masters of the Universe*, 308–15; Vinen, *Thatcher's Britain*, 199–200.

60. Anthony Heath, Roger Jowell, and John Curtice, *How Britain Votes* (Oxford: Pergamon, 1985), 49.

61. Todd, *The People*, 318.

62. Howker and Malik, *Jilted Generation*, 34.

63. Andy Beckett, *Promised You a Miracle*, 218–27.

64. Alan Bissett, in *Unstated: Writers on Scottish Independence*, Scott Hames, ed. (Edinburgh: Word Power, 2012), 33.

65. Francis Fukuyama, "The End of History?," *National Interest* 16 (Summer 1989).

66. John Williamson, "What Washington Means by Policy Reform," in *Latin American Adjustment: How Much Has Happened?*, John Williamson, ed. (Washington DC: Institute for International Economics, 1990).

67. John Williamson, "A Short History of the Washington Consensus," paper commissioned by Fundación CIDOB for a conference, "From the Washington Consensus towards a New Global Governance," Barcelona (September 24–25, 2004).

68. Bob Jessop et al., *Thatcherism: A Tale of Two Nations*, (Cambridge, UK: Polity, 1988), 37.

69. Lanchester, *Whoops!*, 8–9.

70. See, for example, Seumas Milne, "Communism May Be Dead, but Clearly Not Dead Enough," *Guardian* (February 16, 2006).

71. Alex Callinicos, *Against the Third Way: An Anti-Capitalist Critique* (Cambridge, UK: Polity, 2001), 7.

72. Alain Badiou, *The Meaning of Sarkozy* (London: Verso, 2008), 28–29.

Chapter 3: Social Neoliberalism

1. Alan Hollinghurst, *The Line of Beauty* (London: Picador, 2004), 393.

2. Huws, "Introduction," in *Labor in the Global Digital Economy*, 19–22.

3. John Micklethwait and Adrian Wooldridge, *The Right Nation: Why America Is Different* (Harmondsworth, UK: Penguin Books, 2005), 97.

4. Thomas Frank, *Listen, Liberal: Or, What Ever Happened to the Party of the People?* (New York: Metropolitan Books, 2016), 86.

5. Adam Przeworski, *Capitalism and Social Democracy* (Cambridge, UK: Cambridge University Press, 1985), 220.

6. Fredric Jameson has claimed that Marxists have much in common with neoliberals, in that neither have a political philosophy as such and both believe that certain kinds of political arrangement will emerge once economic life has been reorganized. See Fredric Jameson, "Postmodernism and the Market," in *Postmodernism*, 265. In fact, Marxism argues that the revolutionary overthrow of the existing state—a sociopolitical process—has to precede the reorganization of economic life, which will then be carried out under new forms of collective democratic organization. This is the complete opposite of neoliberal theory—although, as we have seen, in practice neoliberals do believe in using the existing state to reorganize the economy. There are, however, more general points of agreement between Marxists and the more serious neoclassical and neoliberal thinkers like Hayek and Schumpeter about the nature of capitalism, above all in their recognition of the inevitability of economic crisis. See, for example, Andrew Gamble, *The Spectre at the Feast: Capitalist Crisis and the Politics of Recession* (London: Palgrave Macmillan, 2009), 46–49. Some of the more perceptive among the Austrians were even prepared to accept that social roles were what ultimately determined human behavior: "It is in vain to advocate a bureaucratic reform through the appointment of businessmen as heads of various departments. The quality of being an entrepreneur is not inherent in the personality of the entrepreneur; it is inherent in the position which he occupies in the framework of market society. A former entrepreneur who is given charge of a government bureau is in this capacity no longer a business man but a bureaucrat. His objective can no longer be profit, but compliance with the rules and regulations." See Ludwig von Mises, *Bureaucracy* (New Haven: Yale University Press, 1944), 49.

7. Streeck, *Buying Time*, 87.

8. Hayek, *Road to Serfdom*, 52–53; and "Letter from F. Hayek to The Times," *The Times* (London), (August 3, 1978).

9. Fredrick von Hayek, "The Economic Conditions of Interstate Federalism," *New Commonwealth Quarterly* 5, no. 2 (1939). See the discussion in Streeck, *Buying Time*, 97–103.

10. Ellen Meiksins Wood, "Democracy as Ideology of Empire," in *The New Imperialists: Ideologies of Empire*, Colin Mooers, ed. (Oxford: Oneworld Publications, 2006), p. 21.

11. Philip Bobbitt, *The Shield of Achilles: War, Peace and the Course of History* (London: Allen Lane, 2002), 234.

12. Przeworski, *Capitalism and Social Democracy*, 220–21.

13. Perry Anderson, "US Elections: Testing Formula Two," *New Left Review* II/8 (Mar/Apr 2001), 7.

14. Andrew Gamble, *Between Europe and America: The Future of British Politics* (Houndmills, UK: Palgrave Macmillan, 2003), 181–82.

15. Anthony Giddens, *The Third Way: The Renewal of Social Democracy* (Cam-

bridge, UK: Polity, 1998), chapter 1.

16. Alex Law and Gerry Mooney, "Beyond New Labour: Work and Resistance in the 'New' Welfare State," in *New Labour/Hard Labour? Restructuring and Resistance inside the Welfare Industry,* Gerry Mooney and Alex Law, eds. (Bristol: Policy Press, 2007), 264–65.

17. Ian Bullock, "The Rise and Fall of New Labour? A Social Democracy for 21st Century Britain?," *Labour/Le Travail* 64 (Fall 2009), 176.

18. Harvey, *Brief History of Neoliberalism,* 14–15; David Miller, "How Neoliberalism Got Where It Is: Elite Planning, Corporate Lobbying and the Release of the Free Market," in Birch and Mykhnenko, *Rise and Fall of Neoliberalism,* 28–29; Miller and Dinan, *Century of Spin,* 67.

19. Jonathan Crary, *24/7: Late Capitalism and the Ends of Sleep* (London: Verso, 2013), 111.

20. Todd, *The People,* 285–86.

21. Todd, *The People,* 307.

22. Alex Callinicos, *Against Postmodernism: A Marxist Critique* (London: Polity, 1989), 165–69; Ranciere, *Hatred of Democracy,* 87–88. For an outstanding critique of attempts to recuperate "1968," with specific reference to France, see Kristin Ross, *May '68 and Its Afterlives* (Chicago: University of Chicago Press, 2002), 182–95.

23. One might argue that the first indications of what would eventually be regarded as neoliberalism in the Third World actually emerged in Egypt, in less obviously dramatic circumstances than Chile, following Anwar Sadat's shift in allegiance from Russia to the USA and the policy of *infitah* or "opening" to private and international capital from 1976. But this process was partially halted by the "bread riots" of January 1977 against reductions in long-standing subsidies on food and fuel. More generally, worker and peasant resistance helped block the progress of neoliberalism, although government spending and public-sector employment continued to be cut from the mid-1980s: the real imposition of neoliberalism dates from the aftermath of the Gulf War in 1991. See Rabab El-Mahdi and Philip Marfleet, eds. *Egypt: The Moment of Change* (London: Zed Books, 2009), 2–4; and Karen Pfeifer, "Economic Reform and Privatization in Egypt," in *The Journey to Tahrir: Revolution, Protest, and Social Change in Egypt,* Jeannie Sowers and Chris Toensing, eds. (London: Verso, 2012), 205–208.

24. Quoted in J. A. G. Griffith, *The Politics of the Judiciary* (Glasgow: Fontana, 1977), 144.

25. Alan Sinfield, "The Politics and Cultures of Discord (1997)," in *Literature, Politics and Culture in Postwar Britain,* third edition (London: Continuum, 2004 [1997]), 337.

26. Marwick, *The Sixties,* 4.

27. Vinen, *Thatcher's Britain,* 7, 30–31, 292–95.

28. Jeffrey C. Goldfarb, *The Cynical Society: The Culture of Politics and the Politics of Culture in American Life* (Chicago: University of Chicago Press, 1991), 49.

29. Owen Hatherley, *A Guide to the New Ruins of Great Britain* (London: Verso, 2010), xiii–xiv.

30. Jamie Peck and Adam Tickell, "Neoliberalizing Space," *Antipode* 34, no. 3 (2002), 40–45; Alex Law, "'The Callous Credit Nexus': Ideology and Compulsion in the Crisis of Neoliberalism," *Sociological Research Online* 14, no. 4 (Aug 2009), paragraphs 2.2, 2.4–2.6). The latter text draws explicitly on Gramsci. For the original discussion, see Antonio Gramsci, "State and Civil Society," in *Selections from the Prison Notebooks*, 229–39.

31. Andrew Gamble, "The Lady's Not for Turning: Thatcherism Mark III," *Marxism Today* (June 1984), 9.

32. Gamble, "Neo-liberalism,"134; and *Spectre at the Feast*, 88.

33. Martin Kettle, "Iraq Must Not Blind Us to Blair's Skill and Seriousness," *Guardian* (February 28, 2013).

34. Gregory Elliott, *Labourism and the English Genius: The Strange Death of Labour England?* (London: Verso, 1993), 1–17.

35. Judt, "Social Question Redivivus," 142–43.

36. Sinfield, "Politics and Cultures of Discord,", xxx–xxxiv.

37. Gerassimos Moschanos, *In the Name of Social Democracy: The Great Transformation: 1945 to the Present* (London: Verso 2002), 200–202. Italics in the original.

38. Bruce Jesson, "The Disintegration of a Labour Tradition: New Zealand Politics in the 1980s," *New Left Review* I/192 (Mar/Apr 1992).

39. Pat Devine, "The 1970s and After: The Political Economy of Inflation and the Crisis of Social Democracy," *Soundings* 32 (Mar 2006), 158.

40. Blair, *A Journey*, 99.

41. Andrew Rawnsley, *The End of the Party: The Rise and Fall of New Labour* (London: Viking, 2010), 477.

42. David Lammy, *Out of the Ashes: Britain after the Riots,* (London: Guardian Books, 2011), 17–19.

43. Howker and Malik, *Jilted Generation*, 220–21.

44. Edward Luttwak, "Central Bankism," in *The Question of Europe*.

45. Glyn, *Capitalism Unleashed*, 32.

46. Michael R. King, Distributional Politics and Central Bank Independence: New Labour's Reform of the Bank of England (LSE, March 2003 Draft), [15].

47. Paul Anderson and Nyta Mann, *Safety First: The Making of New Labour* (London: Granta Books, 1997), 107–11; Rawnsley, *Servants of the People*, 31–38, 41–44.

48. Paul Mason, *Meltdown: The End of the Age of Greed* (London: Verso, 2009), 135.

49. Wolf, *Why Globalization Works*, 133.

50. Klein, *Shock Doctrine*, 191–217.

51. See, for example, Geoffrey Howe interviewed in John Harris, "We've Been Here Before," *Guardian*(January 17, 2009).

52. Jenkins, *Thatcher & Sons*, 4; Ferdinand Mount, "Britain and the Intellectuals: In Thrall to Bad Old Days," *National Interest* 64 (Summer 2001), 86.

53. Merril Stevenson, "Britannia Redux: A Special Report on Britain," *Economist* (February 3, 2007), 15.

54. John McIlroy and Richard Croucher " Skills and training: A Strategic Role for Trade Unions or the Limits of Neoliberalism" in Gary Daniels and John McIlroy, ed. *Trade Unions in a Neoliberal World: British Trade Unions under New Labour* (Routledge, London 2009) 283–316.

55. John Redwood, *Singing the Blues: The Once and Future Conservatives* (London: Methuen, 2004), 63.

56. Anderson, "Figures of Descent," 181.

57. Antonio Polito, Cool Britannia: Gli inglesi (e gli italiani) visti da Londra (Rome: Donzelli, 1998), 17.

58. Peter Burnham, "The Politics of Political Management in the 1990s," *New Political Economy* 4, no. 1 (1999), 47–50.

59. William Burroughs, *The Naked Lunch* (London: Corgi, 1968[1959]), 207.

60. Greenspan, *Age of Turbulence*, 332.

61. Wolin, *Democracy Incorporated*, 66.

62. Gramsci, "Modern Prince," 177–78.

63. Peter Oborne, *The Triumph of the Political Class* (London: Simon & Schuster, 2007), 93.

64. Dan Hind, The Return of the Public: Democracy, Power, and the Case for Media Reform (London: Verso, 2010), 100.

65. Neil O'Brien, "David Cameron Must Make the Conservative Party Look Like the Nation," *Guardian*, April 30, 2012, https://www.theguardian.com/commentisfree/2012/apr/29/cameron-make-conservatives-look-like-nation.

66. Mike Davis, "Can Obama See the Grand Canyon?," in *Be Realistic: Demand the Impossible* (Chicago: Haymarket Books, 2012), 21.

67. Benn Michaels, "Against Diversity," 34. See also, Frank, *Listen, Liberal*, 196.

68. James Bloodworth, The Myth of Meritocracy: Why Working-Class Kids Still Get Working-Class Jobs (London: Biteback, 2016), 111.

69. Fredric Jameson, "The End of Temporality," *Critical Inquiry* 29, no. 4 (Summer 2003), 703.

70. Alex Niven, *Folk Opposition* (Winchester, UK: Zero Books, 2012), 11.

71. James Davis, "At War with the Future: Catastrophism and the Right," in Sasha Lilley et al., *Catastrophism: The Apocalyptic Politics of Collapse and Rebirth* (PM Press: Oakland, CA, 2012), 101.

72. Peter Mair, "Ruling the Void," *New Left Review* II/42 (Nov/Dec 2006), 32–45.

73. Elizabeth Whiting, "Participation," in Babb et al., *Focus on Social Inequalities*(, 91.

74. Mair, "Ruling the Void," 48.

75. Steinar Haugsvær, "Main Conclusions of the Norwegian Study on Power and Democracy" (August 26, 2003), 2, 7, http://www.oecd.org/dataoecd/52/54/33800474.pdf. Even this critique is couched in terms of the market: "the political purchasing power of the voter ballot has been diminished." See p. 1. For similar conclusions in relation to Britain, see "The Myth

of Apathy," in Power, "Power to the People," chapter 1.

76. Streeck, *Buying Time*, 114

Chapter 4: Boom Economies?

1. Stedman Jones, *Masters of the Universe*, 82.
2. Harvey, Brief History of Neoliberalism, p. 19.
3. Harvey, Brief History of Neoliberalism, 19.
4. George Packer, *The Unwinding: An Inner History of the New America* (New York: Farrar, Straus and Giroux, 2013), 381, 382.
5. Streeck, *Buying Time*, 32–46.
6. Brenner, *Economics of Global Turbulence*, 268.
7. Wade, "Financial Regime Change?," 11.
8. McNally, "From Financial Crisis to World-Slump," 45.
9. Harman, *Explaining the Crisis*, 121.
10. Duménil and Lévy, *Crisis of Neoliberalism*, 77.
11. Danny Dorling 2010, 'Indenture': labour for miserable reward, a fifth of all households', *Renewal*, 18(1/2),59-66 157.
12. Brenner, Economics of Global Turbulence, 335.
13. Harvey, *New Imperialism*, 144–61; Harvey, *Brief History of Neoliberalism*, 159–65.
14. Harman, "Theorizing Neoliberalism," 100–108.
15. Marx, *Capital*, pp. 873–940.
16. Brenner, *Economics of Global Turbulence*, 324–27; Gowan, "Crisis in the Heartland," 25; Harman, "China's Economy and Europe's Crisis," 80–83; Turner, *The Credit Crunch*, 10–11, 61–62, 76–78.
17. Arnold, "China's Economic Recovery"; Batson, "China Rises on Power of Stimulus."
18. Arrighi, *Adam Smith in Beijing*, 156–61, 228–34; Harman, "Theorizing Neo-liberalism," 100.
19. Duménil and Levy, *Capitalism Resurgent*, 16, 69, 165.
20. Gowan, "Crisis in the Heartland," 29.
21. Smith, Endgame of Globalization, 22.
22. Campbell, "Birth of Neoliberalism ," 190.
23. Gowan, "Crisis in the Heartland," 209.
24. Law and Mooney, "Financialisation and Proletarianisation," 139–46.
25. Mann, *Sources of Social Power*, vol. 4, 329–31.
26. McNally, "From Financial Crisis to World-Slump," 55.
27. Finch, "Road to Ruin 2."
28. Bunting, *Willing Slaves*, 157. Italics in the original.
29. Irvin, *Super Rich*, 190.
30. Shaw, "Work," 30.
31. Meek, "Human Revenue," 8.

32. Phillips, *American Theocracy*, 327.

33. Phillips, *American Theocracy*, 325.

34. Foster and Magdoff, *The Great Financial Crisis*, 30–31.

35. Turner, *The Credit Crunch*, 26.

36. Southwood, *Non-Stop Inertia*, 10–11.

37. Martijn Konings, *The Emotional Logic of Capitalism: What Progressives Have Missed* (Stanford, CA: Stanford University Press, 2015), 119.

38. Kliman, "Crisis for the Centre of the System," 70. For predictions of the ensuing debacle, from opposing political perspectives, see Phillips, *American Theocracy*, 295, 375–78; and Brenner, "New Boom or New Bubble?," 78–82.

39. Vinen, *Thatcher's Britain*, 9.

40. Pollard, Wasting of the British Economy, 2–3.

41. Duménil and Levy, *Capitalism Resurgent*, 139.

42. Saad-Filho, "Marxian and Keynesian Critiques," 342–43.

43. Milanović, "Two Faces of Globalization," 674.

44. Freeman, "Inequality of Nations," 70–73.

45. Milanović, "Two Faces of Globalization," 674–76; Wade "Financial Regime Change?," 17–19.

46. Berman, *Dark Ages America*, 59.

47. McNally, Another World Is Possible, 54.

48. George, *Hijacking America*, 214.

49. Toynbee and Walker, *Unjust Rewards*, 5.

50. Kapur, Macleod, and Singh, "Plutonomy," 13. See also Frank, *Richistan*, 151.

51. Kapur, Macleod, and Singh, "Plutonomy," 2.

52. Yates, "What the £140m Penthouse Tells Us."

53. Bukharin, Economic Theory of the Leisure Class, 23–33; Veblen, Theory of the Leisure Class, 1–189.

54. Napoleoni, *Rogue Economics*, 45–56. Napoleoni is not alone in invoking Veblen when drawing similarities between the contemporary scene and that of a hundred years ago. See, for example, Frank, *Richistan*, 123.

55. Fraser, "The Great Silence," 317. See also Fraser, *Age of Acquiescence*, 8–9.

56. Crouch, Strange Non-Death of Neoliberalism, 118–19.

57. Graeber, "Against Kamikaze Capitalism," 113.

58. Rand, Virtue of Selfishness, 151.

59. Peck, "Remaking Laissez-faire," 7–8.

60. Curtis, *Idiotism*, 53.

61. Chris Lehmann, *Rich People Things: Real Life Secrets of the Predator Class*, updated edition, (Chicago: Haymarket, 2011), 159–60.

62. Davis, "At War with the Future," , 90–91.

Chapter 5: Broken Societies?

1. Marquand, *Mammon's Kingdom*, 56–57.

2. Elizabeth Wilson, *Bohemians: The Glamorous Outcasts* (New Brunswick, NJ: Rutgers University Press, 2000), 19.

3. Bell, Cultural Contradictions of Capitalism, 145; Kristol, Two Cheers for Capitalism, 67–68.

4. Konings, *Emotional Logic of Capitalism*, 89.

5. Ash, "Epochal Crisis"; Giddens, *Third Way*, 15; Gray, "Maggie's Gift to Gordon," 46.

6. Gray, *Black Mass*, 108.

7. Michael Portillo, "Britain Had to Change, Margaret Thatcher Had the Courage to Make It Happen," posted April 14, 2013, https://www.theguardian.com/commentisfree/2013/apr/14/margaret-thatcher-courage-vision-legacy.

8. Anderson and Mann, *Safety First*, 42. See also Blair, *A Journey*, 90–91.

9. Davies, *Happiness Industry*, 208.

10. Wilkinson and Pickett, *Spirit Level*, 5,

11. Wilkinson and Pickett, *Spirit Level*, 190–91.

12. Judt, "What Is Living and What Is Dead?," 328–30.

13. For the impact of neoliberal managerialism see, in relation to health care, Allyson Pollock, *NHS plc: The Privatisation of our Health Care*, new edition, (London: Verso, 2005 [2004]), 38–41, 106–107, 225–28; and, in relation to higher education, Alex Callinicos, *Universities in a Neoliberal World* (London: Bookmarks, 2006), 16–23; and Alex Law and Hazel Work, "Ambiguities and Resistance: Academic Labour and the Commodification of Higher Education," in *New Labour/Hard Labour?*, 140–150.

14. Wolin, *Democracy Incorporated*, 213.

15. Michael Fielding, "Personalisation, Education and the Market," *Soundings* 38 (Spring 2008), 64.

16. Harman, "Theorising Neoliberalism," 106.

17. Slavoj Žižek, *Violence: Six Sideways Reflections* (London: Profile, 2008), 76.

18. Wilson, *What Price Liberty?*, 314–15.

19. Thatcher, "AIDS, Education and the Year 2000!".

20. Bauman, "Happiness in a Society of Individuals," 23.

21. David Graeber, interviewed in Zoe Williams, "The Metropolitan Elite: Britain's New Pariah Class" *Guardian*, G2, May 21, 2015, https://www.theguardian.com/politics/2015/may/20/metropolitan-elite-britains-new-pariah-class.

22. Wilson, *What Price Liberty?*, 324.

23. Sinfield, "Politics and Cultures of Discord," 349.

24. Ballard, *Kingdom Come*, 11–12.

25. Arendt, *Origins of Totalitarianism*, 437–79.

26. Bourdieu, "Neo-liberalism, the Utopia," 95.

27. Kidron, "Injured Self, " 230. For happiness as a personal responsibility, see Ferguson, "An Attitude Problem?"

28. Goldfarb, *Cynical Society*, 129.

29. David Graeber, The Democracy Project: A History, a Crisis, a Movement

(London: Allen Lane, 2013), 124–25.

30. Bissett, *Unstated*, 32.

31. Blacker, *Falling Rate of Learning*.

32. Crary, 24/7, 56

33. Giovanni Arrighi, Terence K. Hopkins, and Immanuel Wallerstein, *Anti-Systemic Movements* (London: Verso, 1989), 108, 109.

34. Streeck, "Citizens as Customers," 33.

35. Ballard, *Extreme Metaphors*, 244.

36. Stuart Hall et al. , *Policing the Crisis*, 258.

37. Mark Greif, "Afternoon of the Sex Children," in *Against Everything: On Dishonest Times* (New York: Verso, 2016 [2006]), 26–27.

38. Perry Anderson, "Homeland," *New Left Review* II/81 (May/June 2013), 15.

39. George Monbiot, "Labour Can Still Survive, but Only if It Abandons Hope of Governing Alone," *Guardian* (July 5, 2016), https://www.theguardian.com/commentisfree/2016/jul/05/labour-survive-governing-alone-political-alliance-unity-british-left-power.

40. Hall et al., *Policing the Crisis*, 258.

41. Peter Hitchens, *The Cameron Delusion* (London: Continuum, 2010), 122.

42. Viv Albertine, *Clothes Clothes Clothes Music Music Music Boys Boys Boys* (London: Faber and Faber, 2014), 241. The "just want to be on the side that's winning" phrase is a conscious reference to Bob Dylan's "Positively 4th Street," which Albertine earlier recalls defending against Sid Vicious. See Albertine, *Clothes Clothes Clothes*, 132.

43. Lilla, "Tea Party Jacobins.".

44. Gray, *Black Mass*, 109.

45. Perry Anderson, *The Origins of Postmodernity* (London: Verso, 1998), 85–86.

46. Angela Nagle, Kill All Normies: Online Culture Wars from 4Chan and Tumblr to Trump and the Alt-Right (Winchester, UK: Zero Books, 2017), 39, 67.

47. Micklethwait and Woolridge, *Right Nation*, 253.

48. Robert Elms interviewed in Daniel Rachel, Walls Come Tumbling Down: The Music and Politics of Rock Against Racism, 2 Tone and Red Wedge, 1976–1992 (London: Picador, 2016), 371–72, 534.

49. Jefferson Cowie, *Stayin' Alive: The 1970s and the Last Days of the Working Class* (New York: New Press, 2010), 240.

50. Peter York, *Authenticity Is a Con* (London: Biteback, 2014), 30.

51. John Pilger, "Never Forget that Bradley Manning, Not Gay Marriage, Is the Issue," *New Statesman* (May 16, 2012), 20.

52. Jon Savage, "New York: Sylvain Sylvain," in *The England's Dreaming Tapes* (London: Faber and Faber, 2009), 73.

53. Carl Cederström and Peter Fleming, *Dead Man Working* (Winchester, UK: Zero Books, 2012).

54. Dominic Sandbrook, The Great British Dream Factory: The Strange History of Our National Imagination (London: Allen Lane, 2015), 531.

55. Doreen Massey, "The Political Struggle Ahead," in *The Neo-Liberal Crisis: A*

Soundings *Collection*, edited by Sally Davison and Katherine Harris (London: Lawrence and Wishart, 2015 [2010]), 80.

56. Megan Erickson, *Class War: The Privatization of Childhood* (London: Verso, 2015), 63–64.
57. Mark Greif, "What Was the Hipster?," in *Against Everything* [2006], 219.
58. Ian Martin, "The City that Privatised Itself to Death: 'London Is Now a Set of Improbable Sex Toys Poking Gormlessly into the Air," *Guardian* (February 25, 2015).

Chapter 6: Market States?

1. Hayek, *Individualism*, 23.
2. Edgar, "Bitter Harvest," 20--22, 23–24; Edgar, "The Free or the Good," 57–59, 63–76; Gamble, *Free Economy and the Strong State*, 31–37.
3. Smith, Endgame of Globalization, 208.
4. Harvey, Brief History of Neoliberalism, 82.
5. *Granta*, "The State of Europe," 131.
6. Judt, "Introduction: The World we Have Lost ," 424.
7. Duménil and Lévy, *Crisis of Neoliberalism*, 88.
8. Wasserstein, *Barbarism and Civilization*, 757.
9. Harman, "Theorizing Neoliberalism," 97.
10. Dunn, Global Political Economy, 29.
11. Lapavitsas, "Mainstream Economics," 35.
12. Bobbitt, *Shield of Achilles*, 234.
13. Clarke and Newman, *The Managerial State*, 25.
14. Jenkins, "State Is Utterly Clueless."
15. Glyn, *Capitalism Unleashed*, 165–67; Harman, "Theorizing Neoliberalism," 112–16.
16. Clarke and Newman, *Managerial State*, 29.
17. See, for example, Elliott and Atkinson, *Fantasy Island*, 19–21; or Gamble, *Between Europe and America*, 7.
18. Harvey, "Reclaiming the City," 82, 83.
19. Leys, Market-Driven Politics, 27.
20. Massey, *World City*, 11–12, 85–94.
21. Cameron, "We Need a Massive, Radical Redistribution."
22. Howker and Malik, *Jilted Generation*, 212.
23. Wintour, "Labour Should Demand Value."
24. Murray, "'We Are Trying to Reinvent.'"
25. A. Sivanandan, "The Market State vs the Good Society," *Race & Class* 54, no. 3 (Jan–Mar 2013), 5.
26. Sharzer, *No Local*, 119–20.
27. Sharzer, *No Local*, 158–59.
28. Blond, *Red Tory*, 15. Similar position, also seeking legitimation from a read-

ing of E. P. Thompson's account of working-class agency in *The Making of the English Working Class*, can be found in the analogous figures to Blond in the Labour Party, notably "Blue Labour" figures such as Maurice Glasman and MP John Cruddas. See Iles and Roberts, *All Knees and Elbows*, 249–59.

29. Jenkins and Travers, "Cameron's Best Hope."
30. Bobbitt, *Shield of Achilles*, 234.
31. Olssen, "In Defence of the Welfare State," 340.
32. Lefebvre, *Critique of Everyday Life*, 127–28.
33. See, for example, Castells, *Information Age*, 299–303.
34. Jenkins, *Thatcher & Sons*, 4, 5.
35. Gramsci, "Problems of Marxism," 408, Q7§24.
36. David Graeber, "Of Flying Cars and the Declining Rate of Profit," in *Utopia of Rules* [2012], 129.
37. Priestland, *Merchant, Soldier, Sage*, 5–6, 10–11.
38. Priestland, *Merchant, Soldier, Sage*, 248–49.
39. McKibbin, "Anything but Benevolent," 3.
40. David Boyle, *Broke: Who Killed the Middle Classes?* (London: Fourth Estate, 2013), 144–45.
41. Howard and King, *Rise of Neoliberalism*, 226.
42. See chapter 5 in this volume.
43. Polanyi, *Great Transformation*, 73.
44. Dardot and Laval, *New Way of the World*, 182–91.
45. Fred Block, "Beyond Relative Autonomy: State Managers as Historical Subjects," in *Revising State Theory: Essays in Politics and Postindustrialism* (Philadelphia: Temple University Press, 1987), 84, 86–87.
46. William Waldegrave, *The Binding of Leviathan: Conservatism and the Future* (London: Hamish Hamilton, 1978).
47. New Statesman, "The Economic Consequences of Mr. Osborne," *New Statesman* (March 14–20, 2014), 29. See https://www.newstatesman.com/politics/uk-politics/2014/03/leader-economic-consequences-mr-osborne.
48. Will Hutton, "Power Is Fragmenting. But What Is the True Cost to Democracy?," *Observer* (August 25, 2013).
49. Chang, *23 Things*, 190–91.
50. Tamasin Cave and Andy Rowell, A Quiet Word: Lobbying, Crony Capitalism and Broken Politics in Britain (London: Bodley Head, 2014).
51. Žižek, *Year of Dreaming Dangerously*, 11.
52. Henwood, " 'Business Community,'" 71, 73.
53. Victor G. Kiernan, "Modern Capitalism and Its Shepherds," in *Imperialism and Its Contradictions*, edited by Harvey J. Kaye (London: Routledge, 1995 [1990]), 42.
54. Joris Luyendijk, *Swimming with Sharks: My Journey into the World of the Bankers* (London: Guardian Books and Faber and Faber, 2015), 153–54. See also 98–99.
55. Phillip Inman, "Time to Force Companies to Unlock Cash Pils," *Guardian* (November 16, 2015)..

56. Redwood, *Singing the Blues*, 63.

57. Anderson, "Figures of Descent," 181.

58. Polito, *Cool Britannia*, 17.

59. Burnham, "Politics of Political Management,", 47–50.

60. Tóibín, "'Looking at Ireland.'"

61. John Lanchester, How to Speak Money: What the Money People Say—and What It Really Means (London: Faber and Faber, 2014), 5

62. Harry Lambert, "Yanis Varoufakis: My Five Month Battle to Save Greece," *New Statesman* (July 17–23, 2015), 33.

63. Mair, "Ruling the Void," 48.

64. Wolin, *Democracy Incorporated*, 66.

65. Oborne, *Triumph of the Political Class*, 93.

66. Nancy Fraser, "A Triple Movement? Parsing the Politics of Crisis after Polanyi," *New Left Review* II/81 (May/June 2013), 122–23.

67. Monica Prasad, The Politics of Free Markets: The Rise of Neoliberal Economic Policies in Britain, France, Germany, and the United States (Chicago: University of Chicago Press, 2006), 93.

68. Oborne, Triumph of the Political Class, 113–53.

69. Hansard Parliamentary Debates 2009, column 3.

70. Colin Leys, "The Cynical State," in *Total Capitalism: Market Politics, Market State* (Monmouth, UK: Merlin Press, 2008 [2005]), 130..

71. Mair, "Ruling the Void," 32–45.

72. Erik Olin Wright, "The Class Structure of Advanced Capitalist Societies," in *Class, Crisis and the State* (London: Verso, 1978 [1976]), 61–63, 74–87.

73. Andrew Adonis and Stephen Pollard, *A Class Act: The Myth of Britain's Classless Society* (Harmondsworth: Penguin Books, 1998), 106, 112–13; Paul Bagguley, "Middle-Class Radicalism Revisited," in *Social Change and the Middle Classes*, edited by Tim Butler and Mike Savage (London: University College, 1995), 304; Scott Lash and John Urry, *The End of Organized Capitalism* (Madison, WI: University of Wisconsin Press, 1987), 195; Anthony Heath and Mike Savage, "Political Alignments within the Middle Classes, 1972–89," in Butler and Savage, *Social Change and the Middle Classes*, 291–92.

74. Leon D. Trotsky, "The Only Road," in *Struggle against Fascism in Germany* [1932], 271–73.

75. Bagguley, "Middle-Class Radicalism," 308–309.

76. Mike Savage et al., *Property, Bureaucracy and Culture: Middle-Class Formation in Contemporary Britain* (London: Routledge, 1992), 204, 206, 207.

77. Davis, "Political Economy of Late Imperial America," 211, 221–22.

78. John Kenneth Galbraith, *The Culture of Contentment* (Harmondsworth, UK: Penguin Books, 1992), 15.

79. Davis, *City of Quartz*, 153.

80. Galbraith, *Culture of Contentment*, 172–73.

81. Hughey, "New Conservatism," 330–31.

82. Nolan McCarty, Keith T. Poole, and Howard Rosenthal, *Polarized Ameri-*

ca: *The Dance of Ideology and Unequal Riches* (Cambridge, MA: MIT Press, 2006), 193.

83. Prasad, Politics of Free Markets, 39.
84. Hughey, "New Conservatism," 327.
85. Davis: "Political Economy of Late Imperial America," 221–30; *City of Quartz*, chapter 3.
86. Krugman, "State of Paralysis."
87. Anna Minton, Ground Control: Fear and Happiness in the Twenty-First Century City (Harmondsworth, UK: Penguin, 2009), 77.

Conclusion: A New Phase of Capitalist Development or a "Third Period" of Neoliberalism?

1.   John Bellamy Foster, "The End of Rational Capitalism," *Monthly Review* 56, no. 10 (Mar 2005), 13.
2.   Ken MacLeod, *Descent* (London: Orbit, 2014), 129–42.
3.   Damien Cahill, "The Embedded Neoliberal Economy," in *Neoliberalism: Beyond the Free Market*, edited by Damien Cahill, Lindy Edwards, and Frank Stilwell (Cheltenham, UK: Edward Elgar, 2012), 123–24.
4.   Franco Moretti, *The Bourgeois: Between History and Literature* (London: Verso, 2013), 187.
5.   Roula Khalaf, Heba Saleh, and Abeer Allam, "The Economics of the Arab Spring," *Financial Times* (October 9, 2011).
6.   Aronowitz, *Death and Life of American Labor*, 81–82. See also 123.
7.   Engels, *Politics of Resentment*, 110.
8.   Stiglitz, *Globalization and Its Discontents*, 249–50.
9.   Klein, *Shock Doctrine*, 20.
10. Harvey, *Brief History of Neoliberalism*, 183–84, 206.
11. Pollin, "Resurrection of the Rentier," 155.
12. Mason, *Meltdown*, 141.
13. *Hansard Parliamentary Debates* 2008, column 29; Eliot, "Burnt Norton," 172.
14. Hartley, "Northern Rock Criticised."
15. Jenkins, "State Is Utterly Clueless"; Macwhirter, "Rising from the Ashes."
16. Wolf, "World Wakes from the Wish-Dream."
17. Andy Beckett, *When the Lights Went Out*, 521. The phrase was in fact first uttered by Milton Friedman, for whom it did not describe a desirable state of affairs. See *Time*, "We Are All Keynesians Now.".
18. The Economist, "Capitalism at Bay," October 16, 2008, https://www.economist.com/leaders/2008/10/16/capitalism-at-bay.
19. Sorrell, "After a Week of Turmoil."
20. Kagarlitsky, "From Global Crisis to Neo-Imperialism," 267.
21. Toynbee and Walker, *Unjust Rewards*, 10.
22. Gamble, *Spectre at the Feast*, 8.

23. Harman, *Zombie Capitalism*, 332–37; Law and Mooney, "Financialisation and Proletarianisation," 153–55.

24. Kennedy, "Foreword," 10–11.

25. Elliott and Atkinson, *Gods That Failed*, 36.

26. Stewart, "Pay Cuts, Recruit Freezes"; Webb, "Industrial Inaction."

27. Whiting, "Participation," 91–92.

28. At the time of writing, these have taken place in Argentina, Britain, Canada, China, Egypt, France, Ireland, South Korea, Turkey, Ukraine, and the USA. See *Labour Research*, "'What Do We Have to Lose?,'" and Macalister, "Global Trend for Sit-Ins."

29. Doogan, *New Capitalism?*, 191–92, 198; Harman, "Theorizing Neoliberalism," 109–12; Neilson and Rossiter, "Precarity as a Political Concept," 54–55.

30. Dunn, *Global Political Economy*, 241–4.

31. Davis, "Barren Marriage of American Labour," 55–56.

32. Benjamin, "Diary Entries, 1938," 340.

33. Bissett, *Unstated*, 33–34.

INDEX

"Passim" (literally "scattered") indicates intermittent discussion of a topic over a cluster of pages.

ABOUT HAYMARKET BOOKS

Haymarket Books is a radical, independent, nonprofit book publisher based in Chicago. Our mission is to publish books that contribute to struggles for social and economic justice. We strive to make our books a vibrant and organic part of social movements and the education and development of a critical, engaged, and internationalist Left.

We take inspiration and courage from our namesakes, the Haymarket Martyrs, who gave their lives fighting for a better world. Their 1886 struggle for the eight-hour day—which gave us May Day, the international workers' holiday—reminds workers around the world that ordinary people can organize and struggle for their own liberation. These struggles—against oppression, exploitation, environmental devastation, and war—continue today across the globe.

Since our founding in 2001, Haymarket has published more than nine hundred titles. Radically independent, we seek to drive a wedge into the risk-averse world of corporate book publishing. Our authors include Angela Y. Davis, Arundhati Roy, Keeanga-Yamahtta Taylor, Eve L. Ewing, Aja Monet, Mariame Kaba, Naomi Klein, Rebecca Solnit, Olúfẹ́mi O. Táíwò, Mohammed El-Kurd, José Olivarez, Noam Chomsky, Winona LaDuke, Robyn Maynard, Leanne Betasamosake Simpson, Howard Zinn, Mike Davis, Marc Lamont Hill, Dave Zirin, Astra Taylor, and Amy Goodman, among many other leading writers of our time. We are also the trade publishers of the acclaimed Historical Materialism Book Series.

Haymarket also manages a vibrant community organizing and event space in Chicago, Haymarket House, the popular Haymarket Books Live event series and podcast, and the annual Socialism Conference.

ALSO AVAILABLE FROM HAYMARKET BOOKS

ABOUT THE AUTHOR

Neil Davidson (1957-2020) lectured in Sociology at the School of Social and Political Science at the University of Glasgow. He authored *The Origins of Scottish Nationhood, Discovering the Scottish Revolution,* for which he was awarded the Deutscher Memorial Prize, *How Revolutionary Were the Bourgeois Revolutions?* (2012), *Holding Fast to an Image of the Past (2014) and We Cannot Escape History* (2015). Davidson was on the editorial boards of rs21 and the Scottish Left Project website, and was a member of the Radical Independence Campaign.

Printed in the USA
CPSIA information can be obtained
at www.ICGtesting.com
JSHW010933161023
50103JS00003B/3